Get the eBook FREE!
(PDF, ePub, Kindle, and liveBook all included)

We believe that once you buy a book from us, you should be able to read it in any format we have available. To get electronic versions of this book at no additional cost to you, purchase and then register this book at the Manning website.

Go to https://www.manning.com/freebook and follow the instructions to complete your pBook registration.

That's it!
Thanks from Manning!

Distributed Machine Learning Patterns

Distributed Machine Learning Patterns

YUAN TANG

MANNING

SHELTER ISLAND

Manning Publications Co.
20 Baldwin Road
PO Box 761
Shelter Island, NY 11964

Development editor: Patrick Barb and Karen Miller
Technical editor: Gerald Kuch
Review editor: Mihaela Batinić
Production editor: Andy Marinkovich
Copy editor: Alisa Larson
Proofreader: Jason Everett
Technical proofreader: Ninoslav Cerkez
Typesetter: Dennis Dalinnik
Cover designer: Marija Tudor

ISBN: 9781617299025
Printed in the United States of America

brief contents

contents

preface

In recent years, advances in machine learning have made tremendous progress, yet large-scale machine learning remains challenging. Take model training as an example. With the variety of machine learning frameworks such as TensorFlow, PyTorch, and XGBoost, it's not easy to automate the process of training machine learning models on distributed Kubernetes clusters. Different models require different distributed training strategies, such as utilizing parameter servers and collective communication strategies that use the network structure. In a real-world machine learning system, many other essential components, such as data ingestion, model serving, and workflow orchestration, must be designed carefully to make the system scalable, efficient, and portable. Machine learning researchers with little or no DevOps experience cannot easily launch and manage distributed training tasks.

Many books have been written on either machine learning or distributed systems. However, there is currently no book available that talks about the combination of both and bridges the gap between them. This book will introduce many patterns and best practices in large-scale machine learning systems in distributed environments.

This book also includes a hands-on project that builds an end-to-end distributed machine learning system that incorporates a lot of the patterns that we cover in the book. We will use several state-of-art technologies to implement the system, including Kubernetes, Kubeflow, TensorFlow, and Argo. These technologies are popular choices when building a distributed machine learning system from scratch in a cloud-native way, making it very scalable and portable.

I've worked in this area for years, including maintaining some of the open source tools used in this book and leading teams to provide scalable machine learning infrastructure. These patterns and their tradeoffs are always considered when designing systems from scratch or improving existing systems in my daily work. I hope this book will be helpful to you as well!

acknowledgments

First and foremost, I want to thank my wife, Wenxuan. You've always supported me, always patiently listened while I struggled to get this book done, always made me believe I could finish this project, and helped take care of the kids while I was working on the book. Thanks to my three lovely kids, who brought smiles to me whenever I got stuck. I love you all.

Next, I'd like to acknowledge Patrick Barb, my previous development editor, for your patience and guidance over the years. I also thank Michael Stephens for guiding the direction of this book and helping me get through the tough times when I doubted myself. Thanks also to Karen Miller and Malena Selic for providing a smooth transition and helping me move quickly to the production stage. Your commitment to the quality of this book has made it better for everyone who reads it. Thanks as well to all the other folks at Manning who worked with me on the production and promotion of the book. It was truly a team effort.

Thanks also to my technical editor, Gerald Kuch, who brought over 30 years of industry experience from several large companies as well as startups and research labs. Gerald's knowledge and teaching experience covering data structures and algorithms, functional programming, concurrent programming, distributed systems, big data, data engineering, and data science made him an excellent resource for me as the manuscript was developed.

Finally, I'd also like to thank the reviewers who took the time to read my manuscript at various stages during its development and provided invaluable feedback. To Al Krinker, Aldo Salzberg, Alexey Vyskubov, Amaresh Rajasekharan, Bojan Tunguz,

Cass Petrus, Christopher Kottmyer, Chunxu Tang, David Yakobovitch, Deepika Fernandez, Helder C. R. Oliveira, Hongliang Liu, James Lamb, Jiri Pik, Joel Holmes, Joseph Wang, Keith Kim, Lawrence Nderu, Levi McClenny, Mary Anne Thygesen, Matt Welke, Matthew Sarmiento, Michael Aydinbas, Michael Kareev, Mikael Dautrey, Mingjie Tang, Oleksandr Lapshyn, Pablo Roccatagliata, Pierluigi Riti, Prithvi Maddi, Richard Vaughan, Simon Verhoeven, Sruti Shivakumar, Sumit Pal, Vidhya Vinay, Vladimir Pasman, and Wei Yan, your suggestions helped me improve this book.

about this book

Distributed Machine Learning Patterns is filled with practical patterns for running machine learning systems on distributed Kubernetes clusters in the cloud. Each pattern is designed to help solve common challenges faced when building distributed machine learning systems, including supporting distributed model training, handling unexpected failures, and dynamic model serving traffic. Real-world scenarios provide clear examples of how to apply each pattern, alongside the potential tradeoffs for each approach. Once you've mastered these cutting-edge techniques, you'll put them all into practice and finish up by building a comprehensive distributed machine learning system.

Who should read this book?

Distributed Machine Learning Patterns is for data analysts, data scientists, and software engineers familiar with the basics of machine learning algorithms and running machine learning in production. Readers should be familiar with the basics of Bash, Python, and Docker.

How this book is organized: A roadmap

The book has three sections that cover nine chapters.

Part 1 provides some background and concepts around distributed machine learning systems. We will discuss the growing scale of machine learning applications and the complexity of distributed systems and introduce a couple of patterns often seen in both distributed systems and distributed machine learning systems.

Part 2 presents some of the challenges involved in various components of a machine learning system and introduces a few established patterns adopted heavily in industries to address those challenges:

- Chapter 2 introduces the data ingestion patterns, including batching, sharding, and caching, to efficiently process large datasets.
- Chapter 3 includes three patterns that are often seen in distributed model training, which involves parameter servers, and collective communication, as well as elasticity and fault-tolerance.
- Chapter 4 demonstrates how useful replicated services, sharded services, and event-driven processing can be to model serving.
- Chapter 5 describes several workflow patterns, including fan-in and fan-out patterns, synchronous and asynchronous patterns, and step memoization patterns, which will usually be used to create complex and distributed machine learning workflows.
- Chapter 6 ends this part with scheduling and metadata patterns that can be useful for operations.

Part 3 goes deep into an end-to-end machine learning system to apply what we learned previously. Readers will gain hands-on experience implementing many patterns previously learned in this project:

- Chapter 7 goes through the project background and system components.
- Chapter 8 covers the fundamentals of the technologies we will use for our project.
- Chapter 9 ends the book with a complete implementation of an end-to-end machine learning system.

In general, if readers already know what a distributed machine learning system is, Part 1 can be skipped. All chapters in Part 2 can be read independently since each covers a different perspective in distributed machine learning systems. Chapters 7 and 8 are prerequisites for the project we build in chapter 9. Chapter 8 can be skipped if readers are already familiar with the technologies.

About the code

You can get executable snippets of code from the liveBook (online) version of this book at https://livebook.manning.com/book/distributed-machine-learning-patterns. The complete code for the examples in the book is available for download from the Manning website at www.manning.com and from the GitHub repo at https://github .com/terrytangyuan/distributed-ml-patterns. Please submit any issues to the GitHub repo, which will be actively watched and maintained.

liveBook discussion forum

Purchase of *Distributed Machine Learning Patterns* includes free access to liveBook, Manning's online reading platform. Using liveBook's exclusive discussion features, you can attach comments to the book globally or to specific sections or paragraphs. It's a snap to make notes for yourself, ask and answer technical questions, and receive help from the author and other users. To access the forum, go to https://livebook.manning .com/book/distributed-machine-learning-patterns/discussion. You can also learn more about Manning's forums and the rules of conduct at https://livebook.manning.com/ discussion.

Manning's commitment to our readers is to provide a venue where a meaningful dialogue between individual readers and between readers and the author can take place. It is not a commitment to any specific amount of participation on the part of the author, whose contribution to the forum remains voluntary (and unpaid). We suggest you try asking the author some challenging questions lest their interest stray! The forum and the archives of previous discussions will be accessible from the publisher's website for as long as the book is in print.

about the author

YUAN TANG is a founding engineer at Akuity, building an enterprise-ready platform for developers. He has previously led data science and engineering teams at Alibaba and Uptake, focusing on AI infrastructure and AutoML platforms. He's a project lead of Argo and Kubeflow, a maintainer of TensorFlow and XGBoost, and the author of numerous open source projects. In addition, Yuan has authored three machine learning books and several publications. He's a regular speaker at various conferences and a technical advisor, leader, and mentor at various organizations.

about the cover illustration

The figure on the cover of *Distributed Machine Learning Patterns* is "Homme Corfiote," or "Man from Corfu," taken from a collection by Jacques Grasset de Saint-Sauveur, published in 1797. Each illustration is finely drawn and colored by hand.

In those days, it was easy to identify where people lived and what their trade or station in life was just by their dress. Manning celebrates the inventiveness and initiative of the computer business with book covers based on the rich diversity of regional culture centuries ago, brought back to life by pictures from collections such as this one.

Part 1

Basic concepts
and background

This part of the book will provide some background and concepts related to distributed machine learning systems. We will start by discussing the growing scale of machine learning applications (given users' demand for faster responses to meet real-life requirements), machine learning pipelines, and model architectures. Then we will talk about what a distributed system is, describe its complexity, and introduce one concrete example pattern that's often used in distributed systems.

In addition, we will discuss what distributed machine learning systems are, examine similar patterns that are often used in those systems, and talk about some real-life scenarios. At the end of this part, we will take a glance at what we'll be learning in this book.

Introduction to distributed machine learning systems

This chapter covers
- Handling the growing scale in large-scale machine learning applications
- Establishing patterns to build scalable and reliable distributed systems
- Using patterns in distributed systems and building reusable patterns

Machine learning systems are becoming more important nowadays. Recommendation systems learn to generate recommendations of potential interest with the right context according to user feedback and interactions, anomalous event detection systems help monitor assets to prevent downtime due to extreme conditions, and fraud detection systems protect financial institutions from security attacks and malicious fraud behaviors.

There is increasing demand for building large-scale distributed machine learning systems. If a data analyst, data scientist, or software engineer has basic knowledge of and hands-on experience in building machine learning models in Python and wants to take things a step further by learning how to build something more robust, scalable, and reliable, this book is the right one to read. Although experience in production environments or distributed systems is not a requirement, I expect readers in this position to have at least some exposure to machine learning applications running in production and should have written Python and Bash scripts for at least one year.

Being able to handle large-scale problems and take what's developed on your laptop to large distributed clusters is exciting. This book introduces best practices in various patterns that help you speed up the development and deployment of machine learning models, use automations from different tools, and benefit from hardware acceleration. After reading this book, you will be able to choose and apply the correct patterns for building and deploying distributed machine learning systems; use common tooling such as TensorFlow (https://www.tensorflow.org), Kubernetes (https://kubernetes.io), Kubeflow (https://www.kubeflow.org), and Argo Workflows appropriately within a machine learning workflow; and gain practical experience in managing and automating machine learning tasks in Kubernetes. A comprehensive, hands-on project in chapter 9 provides an opportunity to build a real-life distributed machine learning system that uses many of the patterns we learn in the second part of the book. In addition, supplemental exercises at the end of some sections in the following chapters recap what we've learned.

1.1 Large-scale machine learning

The scale of machine learning applications has become unprecedentedly large. Users are demanding faster responses to meet real-life requirements, and machine learning pipelines and model architectures are getting more complex. In this section, we'll talk about the growing scale in more detail and what we can do to address the challenges.

1.1.1 The growing scale

As the demand for machine learning grows, the complexity involved in building machine learning systems is increasing as well. Machine learning researchers and data analysts are no longer satisfied with building simple machine learning models on their laptops on gigabytes of Microsoft Excel sheets. Due to the growing demand and complexity, machine learning systems have to be built with the ability to handle the growing scale, including the increasing volume of historical data; frequent batches of incoming data; complex machine learning architectures; heavy model serving traffic; and complicated end-to-end machine learning pipelines.

Let's consider two scenarios. First, imagine that you have a small machine learning model that has been trained on a small dataset (less than 1 GB). This approach might work well for your analysis at hand because you have a laptop with sufficient computational resources. But you realize that the dataset grows by 1 GB every hour, so the original model is no longer useful and predictive in real life. Suppose that you want to build a time-series model that predicts whether a component of a train will fail in the next hour to prevent failures and downtime. In this case, we have to build a machine learning model that uses the knowledge gained from the original data and the most recent data that arrives every hour to generate more accurate predictions. Unfortunately, your laptop has a fixed amount of computational resources and is no longer sufficient for building a new model that uses the entire dataset.

Second, suppose that you have successfully trained a model and developed a simple web application that uses the trained model to make predictions based on the user's input. The web application may have worked well in the beginning, generating accurate predictions, and the user was quite happy with the results. This user's friends heard about the good experience and decided to try it as well, so they sat in the same room and opened the website. Ironically, they started seeing longer delays when they tried to see the prediction results. The reason for the delays is that the single server used to run the web application can't handle the increasing number of user requests as the application gets more popular. This scenario is a common challenge that many machine learning applications will encounter as they grow from beta products to popular applications. These applications need to be built on scalable machine learning system patterns to handle the growing scale of throughput.

1.1.2 What can we do?

When the dataset is too large to fit in a single machine, as in the first scenario in section 1.1.1, how can we store the large dataset? Perhaps we can store different parts of the dataset on different machines and then train the machine learning model by sequentially looping through the various parts of the dataset on different machines.

If we have a 30 GB dataset like the one in figure 1.1, we can divide it into three partitions of 10 GB data, with each partition sitting on a separate machine that has enough disk storage. Then, we can consume the partitions one by one without having to train the machine learning model by using the entire dataset at the same time.

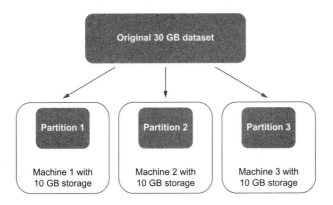

Figure 1.1 An example of dividing a large dataset into three partitions on three separate machines that have sufficient disk storage

Then, we might ask what will happen if looping through different parts of the dataset is quite time-consuming. Assume that the dataset at hand has been divided into three partitions. As illustrated in figure 1.2, first, we initialize the machine learning model on the first machine, and then we train it, using all the data in the first data partition. Next, we transfer the trained model to the second machine, which continues training by using the second data partition. If each partition is large and time-consuming, we'll spend a significant amount of time waiting.

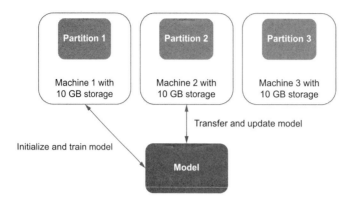

Transfer and update model

Initialize and train model

Figure 1.2 An example of training the model sequentially on each data partition

In this case, we can think about adding workers. Each worker is responsible for consuming each of the data partitions, and all workers train the same model in parallel without waiting for others. This approach is definitely good for speeding up the model training process. But what if some workers finish consuming the data partitions that they are responsible for and want to update the model at the same time? Which of the worker's results (gradients) should we use to update the model first? Then, we must consider the conflicts and tradeoffs between performance and model quality. In figure 1.2, if the data partition that the first worker uses has better quality due to a more rigorous data collection process than the one that the second worker uses, using the first worker's results first would produce a more accurate model. On the other hand, if the second worker has a smaller partition, it could finish training faster, so we could start using that worker's computational resources to train a new data partition. When more workers are added, such as the three workers shown in figure 1.2, the conflicts in completion time for data consumption by different workers become even more obvious.

Similarly, if the application that uses the trained machine learning model to make predictions observes much heavier traffic, can we simply add servers, with each new server handling a certain percentage of the traffic? Unfortunately, the answer is not that simple. This naive solution would need to take other things into consideration, such as deciding the best load balancer strategy and processing duplicate requests in different servers.

We will learn more about handling these types of problems in the second part of the book. For now, the main takeaway is that we have established patterns and best practices to deal with certain situations, and we will use those patterns to make the most of our limited computational resources.

1.2   Distributed systems

A single machine or laptop can't satisfy the requirements for training a large machine learning model with a large amount of data. We need to write programs that can run on multiple machines and be accessed by people all over the world. In this section, we'll talk about what a distributed system is and discuss one concrete example pattern that's often used in distributed systems.

1.2.1   What is a distributed system?

Computer programs have evolved from being able to run on only one machine to working with multiple machines. The increasing demand for computing power and the pursuit of higher efficiency, reliability, and scalability have boosted the advancement of large-scale data centers that consist of hundreds or thousands of computers communicating via the shared network, which have resulted in the development of distributed systems. A *distributed system* is one in which components are located on different networked computers and can communicate with one another to coordinate workloads and work together via message passing.

Figure 1.3 illustrates a small distributed system consisting of two machines communicating with each other via message passing. One machine contains two CPUs, and the other machine contains three CPUs. Obviously, a machine contains computational resources other than the CPUs; we use only CPUs here for illustration purposes. In real-world distributed systems, the number of machines can be extremely large—tens of thousands, depending on the use case. Machines with more computational resources can handle larger workloads and share the results with other machines.

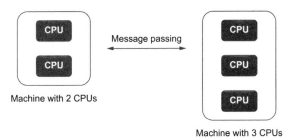

Figure 1.3   An example of a small distributed system consisting of two machines with different amounts of computational resources communicating with each other via message passing

1.2.2   The complexity and patterns

These distributed systems can run on multiple machines and be accessed by users all over the world. They are often complex and need to be designed carefully to be more reliable and scalable. Bad architectural considerations can lead to problems, often on a large scale, and result in unnecessary costs.

Lots of good patterns and reusable components are available for distributed systems. The *work-queue pattern* in a batch processing system, for example, makes sure that each piece of work is independent of the others and can be processed without any interventions within a certain amount of time. In addition, workers can be scaled up and down to ensure that the workload can be handled properly.

Figure 1.4 depicts seven work items, each of which might be an image that needs to be modified to grayscale by the system in the processing queue. Each of the three existing workers takes two to three work items from the processing queue, ensuring that no worker is idle to avoid waste of computational resources and maximizing the performance by processing multiple images at the same time. This performance is possible because each work item is independent of the others.

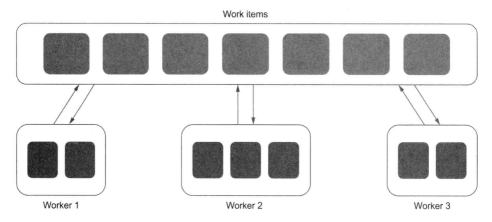

Figure 1.4   An example of a batch processing system using the work-queue pattern to modify images to grayscale

1.3 *Distributed machine learning systems*

Distributed systems are useful not only for general computing tasks but also for machine learning applications. Imagine that we could use multiple machines with large amounts of computational resources in a distributed system to consume parts of the large dataset, store different partitions of a large machine learning model, and so on. Distributed systems can greatly speed up machine learning applications with scalability and reliability in mind. In this section, we'll introduce distributed machine learning systems, present a few patterns that are often used in those systems, and talk about some real-life scenarios.

1.3.1 *What is a distributed machine learning system?*

A *distributed machine learning system* is a distributed system consisting of a pipeline of steps and components that are responsible for different steps in machine learning applications, such as data ingestion, model training, and model serving. It uses patterns and best practices similar to those of a distributed system, as well as patterns designed specifically to benefit machine learning applications. Through careful design, a distributed machine learning system is more scalable and reliable for handling large-scale problems, such as large datasets, large models, heavy model serving traffic, and complicated model selection or architecture optimization.

1.3.2   Are there similar patterns?

To handle the increasing demand for and scale of machine learning systems that will be deployed in real-life applications, we need to design the components in a distributed machine learning pipeline carefully. Design is often nontrivial, but using good patterns and best practices allows us to speed the development and deployment of machine learning models, use automations from different tools, and benefit from hardware accelerations.

There are similar patterns in distributed machine learning systems. As an example, multiple workers can be used to train the machine learning model asynchronously, with each worker being responsible for consuming certain partitions of the dataset. This approach, which is similar to the work-queue pattern used in distributed systems, can speed up the model training process significantly. Figure 1.5 illustrates how we can apply this pattern to distributed machine learning systems by replacing the work items with data partitions. Each worker takes some data partitions from the original data stored in a database and then uses them to train a centralized machine learning model.

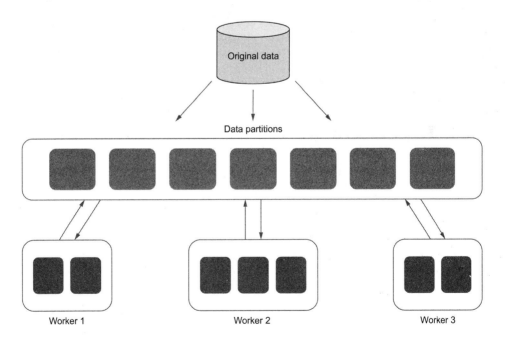

Figure 1.5   An example of applying the work-queue pattern in distributed machine learning systems

Another example pattern commonly used in machine learning systems instead of general distributed systems is the *parameter server pattern* for distributed model training. As shown in figure 1.6, the parameter servers are responsible for storing and updating a particular part of the trained model. Each worker node is responsible for taking a particular part of the dataset that will be used to update a certain part of the model parameters. This pattern is useful when the model is too large to fit in a single server and dedicated parameter servers for storing model partitions without allocating unnecessary computational resources.

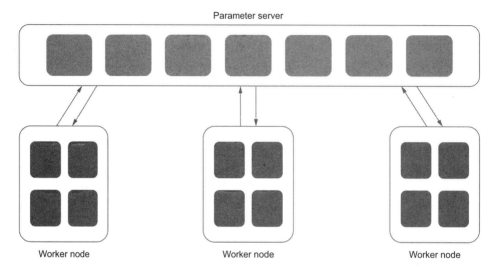

Figure 1.6   An example of applying the parameter server pattern in a distributed machine learning system

Part 2 of this book illustrates patterns like these. For now, keep in mind that some patterns in distributed machine learning systems also appear in general-purpose distributed systems, as well as patterns specially designed to handle machine learning workloads at large scale.

1.3.3   *When should we use a distributed machine learning system?*

If the dataset is too large to fit on our local laptops, as illustrated in figures 1.1 and 1.2, we can use patterns such as data partitioning or introduce additional workers to speed up model training. We should start thinking about designing a distributed machine learning system when any of the following scenarios occurs:

- The model is large, consisting of millions of parameters that a single machine cannot store and that must be partitioned on different machines.
- The machine learning application needs to handle increasing amounts of heavy traffic that a single server can no longer manage.
- The task at hand involves many parts of the model's life cycle, such as data ingestion, model serving, data/model versioning, and performance monitoring.

- We want to use many computing resources for acceleration, such as dozens of servers that have many GPUs each.

If any of these scenarios occur, it's usually a sign that a well-designed distributed machine learning system will be needed in the near future.

1.3.4   When should we not use a distributed machine learning system?

Although a distributed machine learning system is helpful in many situations, it is usually harder to design and requires experience to operate efficiently. Additional overhead and tradeoffs are involved in developing and maintaining such a complicated system. If you encounter any of the following cases, stick with a simple approach that already works well:

- The dataset is small, such as a CSV file smaller than 10 GBs.
- The model is simple and doesn't require heavy computation, such as linear regression.
- Computing resources are limited but sufficient for the tasks at hand.

1.4   What we will learn in this book

In this book, we'll learn to choose and apply the correct patterns for building and deploying distributed machine learning systems to gain practical experience in managing and automating machine learning tasks. We'll use several popular frameworks and cutting-edge technologies to build components of a distributed machine learning workflow, including the following:

- TensorFlow (https://www.tensorflow.org)
- Kubernetes (https://kubernetes.io)
- Kubeflow (https://www.kubeflow.org)
- Docker (https://www.docker.com)
- Argo Workflows (https://argoproj.github.io/workflows/)

A comprehensive hands-on project in the last part of the book consists of an end-to-end distributed machine learning pipeline system. Figure 1.7 is the architecture diagram of the system that we will be building. We will gain hands-on experience implementing many of the patterns covered in the following chapters. Handling large-scale problems and taking what we've developed on our personal laptops to large distributed clusters should be exciting.

We'll be using TensorFlow with Python to build machine learning and deep learning models for various tasks, such as building useful features based on a real-life dataset, training predictive models, and making real-time predictions. We'll also use Kubeflow to run distributed machine learning tasks in a Kubernetes cluster. Furthermore, we will use Argo Workflows to build a machine learning pipeline that consists of many important components of a distributed machine learning system. The basics of these technologies are introduced in chapter 2, and we'll gain hands-on experience

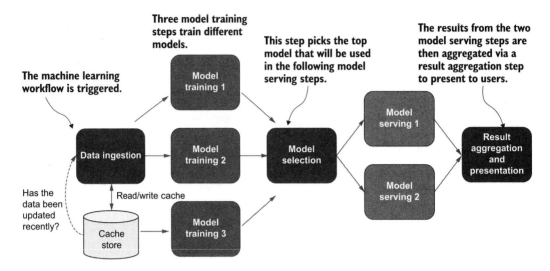

Figure 1.7   An architecture diagram of the end-to-end machine learning system that we will be building in the last part of the book

with them in part 2. Table 1.1 shows the key technologies that will be covered in this book and example uses.

Table 1.1   The technologies covered in this book and their uses

Technology	Use
TensorFlow	Building machine learning and deep learning models
Kubernetes	Managing distributed environments and resources
Kubeflow	Submitting and managing distributed training jobs easily on Kubernetes clusters
Argo Workflows	Defining, orchestrating, and managing workflows
Docker	Building and managing images to be used for starting containerized environments

Before we dive into details in chapter 2, I recommend that readers have basic knowledge of and hands-on experience in building machine learning models in Python. Although experience in production environments or distributed systems is not a requirement, I expect readers in this position to have at least some exposure to machine learning applications running in production and to have written Python and Bash scripts for at least one year. In addition, understanding the basics of Docker and being able to manage images/containers by using the Docker command-line interface is required. Familiarity with basic YAML syntax is helpful but not required; the syntax is intuitive and should be easy to pick up along the way. If most of these topics are new to you, I suggest that you learn more about them from other resources before reading further.

Summary

- Machine learning systems deployed in real-life applications usually need to handle the growing scale of larger datasets and heavier model serving traffic.
- It's nontrivial to design large-scale distributed machine learning systems.
- A distributed machine learning system is usually a pipeline of many components, such as data ingestion, model training, serving, and monitoring.
- Using good patterns to design the components of a machine learning system can speed up the development and deployment of machine learning models, enable the use of automations from different tools, and benefit from hardware acceleration.

Part 2

Patterns of distributed machine learning systems

Now that you know the basic concepts and background of distributed machine learning systems, you should be able to proceed to this part of the book. We will explore some of the challenges involved in various components of a machine learning system and introduce a few established patterns adopted heavily in industries to address those challenges.

Chapter 2 introduces the batching pattern, used to handle and prepare large datasets for model training; the sharding pattern, used to split huge datasets into multiple data shards that spread among multiple worker machines; and the caching pattern, which could greatly speed the data ingestion process when a previously used dataset is re-accessed for model training.

In chapter 3, we will explore the challenges of the distributed model training process. We'll cover the challenges of training large machine learning models that tag main themes in new YouTube videos but cannot fit on a single machine. The chapter also covers how to overcome the difficulty of using the parameter server pattern. In addition, we see how to use the collective communication pattern to speed distributed training for smaller models and avoid unnecessary communication overhead among parameter servers and workers. At the end of this chapter, we talk about some of the vulnerabilities of distributed machine learning systems due to corrupted datasets, unstable networks, and preemptive worker machines, and we see how we can address those issues.

Chapter 4 focuses on the model serving component, which needs to be scalable and reliable to handle the growing number of user requests and the growing size of individual requests. We will go through the tradeoffs of making design decisions to build a distributed model serving system. We will use the replicated services to handle the growing number of model serving requests. We will also learn how to assess model serving systems and determine whether the event-driven design would be beneficial in real-world scenarios.

In chapter 5, we'll see how to build a system that executes complex machine learning workflows to train multiple machine learning models and pick the most performant models to provide good entity tagging results in the model serving system, using the fan-in and fan-out patterns. We'll also incorporate the synchronous and asynchronous patterns to make machine learning workflows more efficient and avoid delays due to the long-running model training steps that block consecutive steps.

Chapter 6, the last chapter in this part of the book, covers some operational efforts and patterns that can greatly accelerate the end-to-end workflow, as well as reduce the maintenance and communication efforts that arise when engineering and data science teams collaborate. We'll introduce a couple of scheduling techniques that prevent resource starvation and deadlocks when many team members work in the same cluster with limited computational resources. We will also discuss the benefits of the metadata pattern, which we could use to gain insights from the individual steps in machine learning workflows and handle failures more appropriately to reduce the negative effect on users.

Data ingestion patterns

2

This chapter covers

- Understanding data ingestion and its responsibilities
- Handling large datasets in memory by consuming smaller datasets in batches (the batching pattern)
- Preprocessing extremely large datasets as smaller chunks on multiple machines (the sharding pattern)
- Fetching and re-accessing the same dataset for multiple training rounds (the caching pattern)

Chapter 1 discussed the growing scale of modern machine learning applications such as larger datasets and heavier traffic for model serving. It also talked about the complexity and challenges of building distributed systems—distributed systems for machine learning applications in particular. We learned that a distributed machine learning system is usually a pipeline of many components, such as data ingestion, model training, serving, and monitoring, and that some established patterns are available for designing each component to handle the scale and complexity of real-world machine learning applications.

All data analysts and scientists should have some level of exposure to data ingestion, either hands-on experience in building a data ingestion component or simply using a dataset from the engineering team or customer. Designing a good data ingestion component is nontrivial and requires understanding the characteristics of the dataset we want to use for building a machine learning model. Fortunately, we can follow established patterns to build that model on a reliable and efficient foundation.

This chapter explores some of the challenges involved in the data ingestion process and introduces a few established patterns adopted heavily in industries. In section 2.3, we will use the batching pattern in cases where we want to handle and prepare large datasets for model training, either when the machine learning framework we are using cannot handle large datasets or requires domain expertise in the underlying implementation of the framework. In section 2.4, we will learn how to apply the sharding pattern to split extremely large datasets into multiple data shards spread among multiple worker machines; then we speed up the training process as we add worker machines that are responsible for model training on each data shard independently. Section 2.5 introduces the caching pattern, which could greatly speed up the data ingestion process when a previously used dataset is re-accessed and processed for multi-epoch model training.

2.1   *What is data ingestion?*

Let's assume that we have a dataset at hand, and we would like to build a machine learning system that builds a machine learning model from it. What is the first thing we should think about? The answer is quite intuitive: first, we should get a better understanding of the dataset. Where did the dataset come from, and how was it collected? Are the source and the size of the dataset changing over time? What are the infrastructure requirements for handling the dataset? We should ask these types of questions first. We should also consider different perspectives that might affect the process of handling the dataset before we start building a distributed machine learning system. We will walk through these questions and considerations in the examples in the remaining sections of this chapter and learn how to address some of the problems we may encounter by using different established patterns.

Data ingestion is the process that monitors the data source, consumes the data all at once (nonstreaming) or in a streaming fashion, and performs preprocessing to prepare for the training process of machine learning models. In short, streaming data ingestion often requires long-running processes to monitor the changes in data sources; nonstreaming data ingestion happens in the form of offline batch jobs that process datasets on demand. Additionally, the data grows over time in streaming data ingestion, whereas the size of the dataset is fixed in nonstreaming data ingestion. Table 2.1 summarizes the differences.

Table 2.1   Comparison of streaming and nonstreaming data ingestion in machine learning applications

	Streaming data ingestion	Nonstreaming data Ingestion
Dataset size	Increases over time	Fixed size
Infrastructure requirements	Long-running processes to monitor the changes in data source	Offline batch jobs to process datasets on demand

The remaining sections of this chapter focus on data ingestion patterns from a nonstreaming perspective, but they can be applied to streaming data ingestion as well.

Data ingestion is the first step and an inevitable step in a machine learning pipeline, as shown in figure 2.1. Without a properly ingested dataset, the rest of the processes in a machine learning pipeline would not be able to proceed.

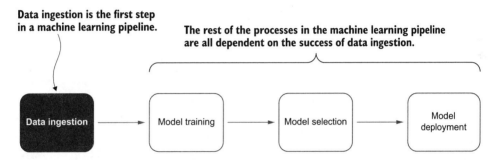

Figure 2.1   A flowchart that represents the machine learning pipeline. Note that data ingestion is the first step in the pipeline.

The next section introduces the Fashion-MNIST dataset, which I use to illustrate the patterns in the remaining sections of this chapter. I focus on building patterns around data ingestion in distributed machine learning applications, which are distinct from data ingestion that happens on local machines or laptops. Data ingestion in distributed machine learning applications is often more complex and requires careful design to handle large-scale datasets or datasets that are growing rapidly.

2.2   *The Fashion-MNIST dataset*

The MNIST dataset by LeCun et al. (http://yann.lecun.com/exdb/mnist/) is one of the most widely used datasets for image classification. It contains 60,000 training images and 10,000 testing images extracted from images of handwritten digits; it is used widely in the machine learning research community as a benchmark dataset to validate state-of-art algorithms and machine learning models. Figure 2.2 shows some example images of handwritten digits, with each row representing images of a particular handwritten digit.

Each row represents images
for a particular handwritten
digit. For example, the first
row represents images of
the digit 0.

Figure 2.2 **A screenshot of some example images for handwritten digits from 0 to 9, with each row representing images of a particular handwritten digit (Source: Josep Steffan, licensed under CC BY-SA 4.0)**

Despite wide adoption in the community, researchers have found this dataset to be unsuitable for distinguishing between stronger models and weaker ones; many simple models nowadays can achieve good classification accuracy over 95%. As a result, the MNIST dataset now serves as more a sanity check than a benchmark.

> **NOTE** The creators of the MNIST dataset kept a list of the machine learning methods tested on the dataset. In the original paper, "Gradient-Based Learning Applied to Document Recognition," published in 1998 on the MNIST dataset (http://yann.lecun.com/exdb/publis/index.html#lecun-98), LeCun et al. stated that they used a support-vector machine model to get an error rate of 0.8%. A similar but extended dataset called EMNIST was published in 2017. EMNIST contains 240,000 training images and 40,000 testing images of handwritten digits and characters.

Instead of using MNIST in several examples throughout this book, I will focus on a quantitatively similar but relatively more complex dataset: the Fashion-MNIST dataset, which was released in 2017 (https://github.com/zalandoresearch/fashion-mnist). Fashion-MNIST is a dataset of Zalando's article images consisting of a training set of 60,000 examples and a test set of 10,000 examples. Each example is a 28 × 28 grayscale image associated with a label from ten classes. The Fashion-MNIST dataset is designed to serve as a direct drop-in replacement for the original MNIST dataset for benchmarking machine learning algorithms. It uses the same image size and structure for training and testing splits.

Figure 2.3 shows the collection of images for all 10 classes (T-shirt/top, trouser, pullover, dress, coat, sandal, shirt, sneaker, bag, and ankle boot) from Fashion-MNIST. Each class takes up three rows of the screenshot.

Figure 2.4 provides a closer look at the first few example images in the training set, together with their corresponding text labels. Next, I discuss the scenario for the case study.

Every three rows represent example images that represent a class. For example, the top three rows are images of T-shirts.

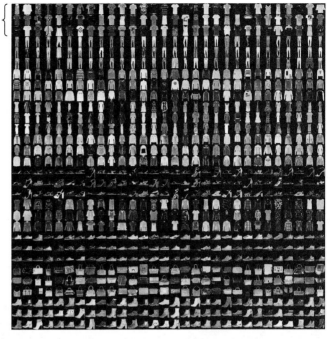

Figure 2.3   A screenshot of the collection of images from Fashion-MNIST dataset for all 10 classes: T-shirt/top, trouser, pullover, dress, coat, sandal, shirt, sneaker, bag, and ankle boot (Source: Zalando SE, licensed under MIT License)

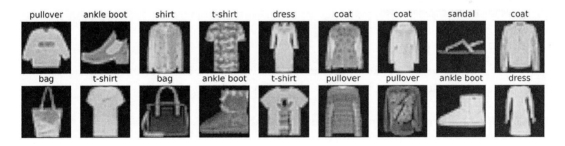

Figure 2.4   The first few example images in the training set (Source: Zalando SE, licensed under MIT License)

Assume that we've downloaded the Fashion-MNIST dataset. The compressed version should only take 30 MB on disk. Even though the dataset is small, it's trivial to load the downloaded dataset into memory at one time by using available implementations. If we're using a machine learning framework like TensorFlow, for example, we can download and load the entire Fashion-MNIST dataset into memory with a couple of lines of Python code, as shown in the following listing.

Listing 2.1 Loading the Fashion-MNIST dataset into memory with TensorFlow

```
> import tensorflow as tf          ◁──┐  Loads the                    Downloads the
>                                       TensorFlow library            Fashion-MNIST
> train, test = tf.keras.datasets.fashion_mnist.load_data()   ◁─┐    dataset and
                                                                    then loads it
32768/29515 [==============================] - 0s 0us/step         into memory
26427392/26421880 [==============================] - 0s 0us/step
8192/5148 [==============================] - 0s 0us/step
4423680/4422102 [==============================] - 0s 0us/step
```

Alternatively, if the dataset is already in memory—in the form of NumPy (https://numpy.org) arrays, for example—we can load the dataset from an in-memory array representation into formats that the machine learning framework accepts, such as `tf.Tensor` objects, which can easily be used for model training later. The following listing shows an example.

Listing 2.2 Loading the Fashion-MNIST dataset from memory into TensorFlow

Normalizes the images

```
> from tensorflow.data import Dataset          Splits the training        Loads in-memory
>                                               dataset object into        array representation
> images, labels = train     ◁─────────┐       images and labels          into a tf.data.Dataset
> images = images/255                                                      object that will make
>                                                                          it easier to use for
> dataset = Dataset.from_tensor_slices((images, labels))   ◁──────         training in TensorFlow
> dataset
<TensorSliceDataset shapes: ((28, 28), ()), types: (tf.float64, tf.uint8)>
```

Inspects the dataset's information,
such as shapes and data types

2.3 Batching pattern

Now that we know what the Fashion-MNIST dataset looks like, let's examine a potential problem we might face in a real-world scenario.

2.3.1 The problem: Performing expensive operations for Fashion MNIST dataset with limited memory

Even though it's easy to load a small dataset like Fashion-MNIST into memory to prepare for model training, in real-world machine learning applications, this process can be challenging. The code snippet in listing 2.1, for example, can be used to load the Fashion-MNIST into memory to prepare for model training in TensorFlow; it embeds the features and labels arrays in our TensorFlow graph as `tf.constant()` operations. This process works well for a small dataset, but it wastes memory because the contents of the NumPy array will be copied multiple times and can run into the 2 GB limit for the `tf.GraphDef` protocol buffer that TensorFlow uses. In real-world applications, the datasets are much larger, especially in distributed machine learning systems in which datasets grow over time.

Figure 2.5 shows a 1.5-GB in-memory NumPy array representation that will be copied two times with a `tf.constant()` operation. This operation would result in an out-of-memory error because the total 3 GB exceeds the maximum size of the `tf.Graph-Def` protocol buffer that TensorFlow uses.

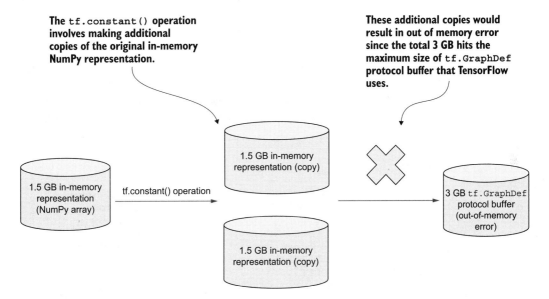

Figure 2.5 An example 1.5-GB in-memory NumPy array representation that hits an out-of-memory error when being converted to a `tf.GraphDef` protocol buffer

Problems like this one happen often in different machine learning or data loading frameworks. Users may not be using the specific framework in an optimal way, or the framework may not be able to handle larger datasets.

In addition, even for small datasets like Fashion-MNIST, we may perform additional computations before feeding the dataset into the model, which is common in tasks that require additional transformations and cleaning. For computer vision tasks, images often need to be resized, normalized, or converted to grayscale, or they may require even more complex mathematical operations, such as convolution operations. These operations may require a lot of additional memory space allocation, but we may not have many computational resources available after we load the entire dataset into memory.

2.3.2 The solution

Consider the first problem mentioned in section 2.2. We'd like to use TensorFlow's `from_tensor_slices()` API to load the Fashion-MNIST dataset from an in-memory

NumPy array representation to a `tf.Dataset` object that TensorFlow's model training program can use. Because the contents of the NumPy array will be copied multiple times, however, we can run into the 2 GB limit for the `tf.GraphDef` protocol buffer. As a result, we cannot load larger datasets that go beyond this limit.

It's not uncommon to see problems like this one for specific frameworks like TensorFlow. In this case, the solution is simple because we are not making the best use of TensorFlow. Other APIs allow us to load large datasets without loading the entire dataset into in-memory representation first.

TensorFlow's I/O library, for example, is a collection of filesystems and file formats that are not available in TensorFlow's built-in support. We can load datasets like MNIST from a URL to access the dataset files that are passed directly to the `tfio.IODataset.from_mnist()` API call, as shown in the following listing. This ability is due to the inherent support that TensorFlow (https://github.com/tensorflow/io) I/O library provides for the HTTP filesystem, eliminating the need to download and save datasets in a local directory.

Listing 2.3 Loading the MNIST dataset with TensorFlow I/O

> **Loads the TensorFlow I/O library**

> **Loads the MNIST dataset from a URL to access dataset files directly without downloading via HTTP filesystem support**

```
> import tensorflow_io as tfio       <─┐  (Loads the TensorFlow I/O library)
>
> d_train = tfio.IODataset.from_mnist(     <─┘
      'http://yann.lecun.com/exdb/mnist/train-images-idx3-ubyte.gz',
      'http://yann.lecun.com/exdb/mnist/train-labels-idx1-ubyte.gz')
```

For larger datasets that might be stored in distributed file systems or databases, some APIs can load them without having to download everything at one time, which could cause memory- or disk-related problems. For demonstration purposes, without going into too many details here, the following listing shows how to load a dataset from a PostgreSQL database (https://www.postgresql.org). (You'll need to set up your own PostgreSQL database and provide the required environment variables to run this example.)

Listing 2.4 Loading a dataset from the PostgreSQL database

Loads Python's built-in OS library for loading environment variables related to the PostgreSQL database

Loads the TensorFlow I/O library

Constructs the endpoint for accessing the PostgreSQL database

```
> import os
> import tensorflow_io as tfio       <─┐  (Loads the TensorFlow I/O library)
>
> endpoint="postgresql://{}:{}@{}?port={}&dbname={}".format(     <─┘
      os.environ['TFIO_DEMO_DATABASE_USER'],
      os.environ['TFIO_DEMO_DATABASE_PASS'],
      os.environ['TFIO_DEMO_DATABASE_HOST'],
```

```
        os.environ['TFIO_DEMO_DATABASE_PORT'],
        os.environ['TFIO_DEMO_DATABASE_NAME'],
    )
>
> dataset = tfio.experimental.IODataset.from_sql(
    query="SELECT co, pt08s1 FROM AirQualityUCI;",
    endpoint=endpoint)
> print(dataset.element_spec)
{
    'co': TensorSpec(shape=(), dtype=tf.float32, name=None),
    'pt08s1': TensorSpec(shape=(), dtype=tf.int32, name=None)
}
```

Selects two columns from the AirQualityUCI table in the database and instantiates a tf.data.Dataset object

Inspects the specification of the dataset, such as the shape and data type of each column

Now let's go back to our scenario. In this case, assume that TensorFlow does not provide APIs like TensorFlow I/O that can deal with large datasets. Given that we don't have too much free memory, we should not load the entire Fashion-MNIST dataset into memory directly. Let's assume that the mathematical operations we would like to perform on the dataset can be performed on subsets of the entire dataset. Then we can divide the dataset into smaller subsets (*mini-batches*), load each mini-batch of example images, perform expensive mathematical operations on each batch, and use only one mini-batch of images in each model training iteration.

If the first mini-batch consists of the 19 example images in figure 2.4, we can perform convolution or other heavy mathematical operations on those images first and then send the transformed images to the machine learning model for model training. We repeat the same process for the remaining mini-batches while continuing model training in the meantime.

Because we've divided the dataset into many small subsets or mini-batches, we avoid potential out-of-memory problems when performing the heavy mathematical operations necessary for achieving an accurate classification model. Then we can handle even larger datasets by reducing the size of the mini-batches. This approach is called *batching*. In data ingestion, batching involves grouping data records from the entire dataset into batches that will be used to train the machine learning model sequentially.

If we have a dataset with 100 records, we can take 50 of the 100 records to form a batch and then train the model using this batch of records. We repeat this batching and model training process for the remaining records. In other words, we make two batches in total; each batch consists of 50 records, and the model we are training consumes the batches one by one. Figure 2.6 illustrates the process of dividing the original dataset into two batches. The first batch gets consumed to train the model at time t0, and the second batch gets consumed at time t1. As a result, we don't have to load the entire dataset into memory at one time; instead, we are consuming the dataset sequentially, batch by batch.

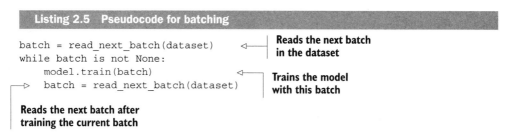

Figure 2.6 The dataset gets divided into two batches. The first batch gets consumed to train the model at time t0, and the second batch gets consumed at time t1.

This *batching pattern* can be summarized as the pseudocode in the following listing, where we continuously try to read the next batch from the dataset and train the model, using the batches until no more are left.

Listing 2.5   Pseudocode for batching

```
batch = read_next_batch(dataset)          ◁——   Reads the next batch
while batch is not None:                          in the dataset
    model.train(batch)                    ◁——   Trains the model
    batch = read_next_batch(dataset)             with this batch
```

Reads the next batch after training the current batch

We can apply the batching pattern when we want to handle and prepare large datasets for model training. When the framework we are using can handle only in-memory datasets, we can process small batches of the entire large datasets to ensure that each batch can be handled within limited memory. In addition, if a dataset is divided into batches, we can perform heavy computations on each batch sequentially without requiring a huge amount of computational resources. We'll apply this pattern in section 9.1.2.

2.3.3   Discussion

Other considerations need to be taken into account when performing batching. This approach is feasible only if the mathematical operations or algorithms we are performing can be done on subsets of the entire dataset in a streaming fashion. If an algorithm requires knowledge of the entire dataset, such as the sum of a particular feature over the entire dataset, batching would no longer be a feasible approach, as it's not possible to obtain this information over a subset of the entire dataset.

In addition, machine learning researchers and practitioners often try different machine learning models on the Fashion-MNIST dataset to get a better-performing, more accurate model. If an algorithm would like to see at least 10 examples for each class to initialize some of its model parameters, for example, batching is not an appropriate approach. There is no guarantee that every mini-batch contains at least 10 examples from each class, especially when batch sizes are small. In an extreme case, the batch size would be 10, and it would be rare to see at least one image from each class in all batches.

Another thing to keep in mind is that the batch size of a machine learning model, especially for deep learning models, depends strongly on allocation of resources, making it particularly difficult to decide in advance in shared-resource environments. Also, the allocation of resources that a machine learning job can use efficiently depends not only on the structure of the model being trained but also on the batch size. This codependency between the resources and the batch size creates a complex web of considerations that a machine learning practitioner must make to configure their job for efficient execution and resource use.

Fortunately, algorithms and frameworks are available that eliminate manual tuning of batch size. AdaptDL (https://github.com/petuum/adaptdl), for example, offers automatic batch-size scaling, enabling efficient distributed training without requiring any effort to tune the batch size manually. It measures the system performance and gradient noise scale during training and adaptively selects the most efficient batch size. Figure 2.7 compares the effects of automatically and manually tuned batch sizes on the overall training time of the ResNet18 model (https://arxiv.org/abs/1512.03385).

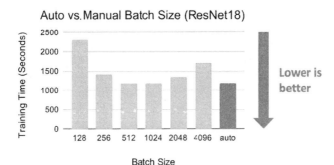

Figure 2.7 A comparison of the effect of automatically and manually tuned batch sizes on the overall training time of the ResNet18 model (Source: Petuum, licensed under Apache License 2.0)

The batching pattern provides a great way to extract subsets of the entire dataset so that we can feed the batches sequentially for model training. For extremely large datasets that may not fit in a single machine, we'll need other techniques. The next section introduces a new pattern in that addresses the challenges.

2.3.4 *Exercises*

1 Are we training the model using the batches in parallel or sequentially?
2 If the machine learning framework we are using does not handle large datasets, can we use the batching pattern?

3 If a machine learning model requires knowing the mean of a feature of the entire dataset, can we still use the batching pattern?

2.4 Sharding pattern: Splitting extremely large datasets among multiple machines

Section 2.3 introduced the Fashion-MNIST dataset, the compressed version of which takes only 30 MB on disk. Even though it is trivial to load the whole dataset into memory at one time, it's challenging to load larger datasets for model training.

The batching pattern covered in section 2.3 addresses the problem by grouping data records from the entire dataset into batches that will be used to train the machine learning model sequentially. We can apply the batching pattern when we want to handle and prepare large datasets for model training, either when the framework we are using cannot handle large datasets or when the underlying implementation of the framework requires domain expertise.

Suppose that we have a much larger dataset at hand. This dataset is about 1,000 times bigger than the Fashion-MNIST dataset. In other words, the compressed version of it takes 30 MB × 1,000 = 30 GB on disk, and it's about 50 GB when it's decompressed. This new dataset has 60,000 × 1,000 = 60,000,000 training examples.

We'll try to use this larger dataset to train our machine learning model to classify images into classes in the expanded Fashion-MNIST dataset (T-shirts, bags, and so on). For now, I won't address the detailed architecture of the machine learning model (chapter 3); instead, I'll focus on its data ingestion component. Assume that we are allowed to use three machines for any potential speed-ups.

Given our experience, because the dataset is large, we could try applying the batching pattern first, dividing the entire dataset into batches small enough to load into memory for model training. Let's assume that our laptop has enough resources to store the entire 50 GB decompressed dataset on disk. We divide the dataset into 10 small batches (5 GB each). With this batching approach, we can handle large datasets as long as our laptop can store the large datasets and divide them into batches.

Next, we start the model training process by using the batches of data. In section 2.3, we trained the model sequentially. In other words, one batch was completely consumed by the machine learning model before the next batch was consumed. In figure 2.8, the second batch is consumed at time t1 by model fitting only after the first batch has been completely consumed by the model at time t0. t0 and t1 represent two consecutive time points in this process.

2.4.1 The problem

Unfortunately, this sequential process of consuming data can be slow. If each 5 GB batch of data takes about 1 hour to complete for the specific model we are training, it would take 10 hours to finish the model training process on the entire dataset. In other words, the batching approach may work well if we have enough time to train the model sequentially, batch by batch. In real-world applications, however, there's always

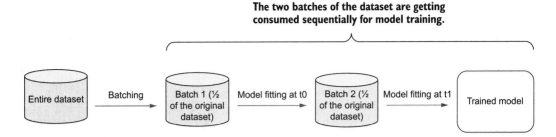

Figure 2.8 The dataset gets divided into two batches. The first batch gets consumed to train the model at time t0, and the second batch gets consumed at time t1.

demand for more efficient model training, which will be affected by the time spent ingesting batches of data.

2.4.2 The solution

Now that we understand the slowness of training the model sequentially by using the batching pattern alone, what can we do to speed up the data ingestion part, which will greatly affect the model training process? The major problem is that we need to train the model sequentially, batch by batch. Can we prepare multiple batches and then send them to the machine learning model for consumption at the same time? Figure 2.9 shows that the dataset gets divided into two batches, with each batch being consumed to train the model at the same time. This approach does not work yet, as we cannot keep the entire dataset (two batches) in memory at the same time, but it is close to the solution.

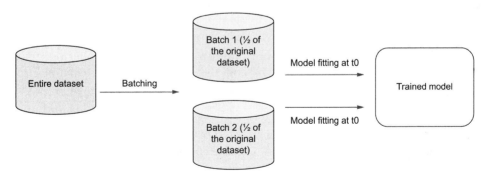

Figure 2.9 The dataset gets divided into two batches; each batch is consumed to train the model at the same time.

Let's assume that we have multiple worker machines, each of which contains a copy of the machine learning model. Each copy can consume one batch of the original dataset; hence, the worker machines can consume multiple batches independently. Figure 2.10 shows an architecture diagram of multiple worker machines; each consumes batches independently to train the copy of the model located on it.

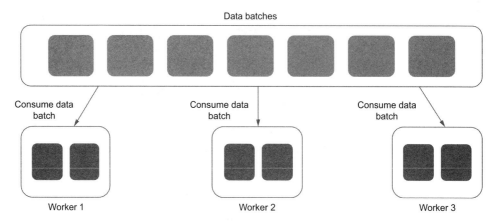

Figure 2.10   An architecture diagram of multiple worker machines. Each worker machine consumes batches independently to train the copy of the model located on it.

You may wonder how multiple model copies would work if they consumed multiple different batches independently and where we would obtain the final machine learning model from these model copies. These are great questions. Rest assured that I will go through how the model training process works in chapter 3. For now, assume that we have patterns that allow multiple worker machines to consume multiple batches of datasets independently. These patterns will greatly speed up the model training process, which was slowed down due to the nature of sequential model training.

> **NOTE**   We will be using a pattern called the *collection communication pattern* in chapter 3 to train models with multiple model copies located on multiple worker machines. The collective communication pattern, for example, will be responsible for communicating updates of gradient calculations among worker machines and keeping the model copies in sync.

How would we produce the batches used by those worker machines? In our scenario, the dataset has 60 million training examples, and three worker machines are available. It's simple to split the dataset into multiple non-overlapping subsets and then send each to the three worker machines, as shown in figure 2.11. The process of breaking large datasets into smaller chunks spread across multiple machines is called *sharding*, and the smaller data chunks are called *data shards*. Figure 2.11 shows the original dataset being sharded into multiple non-overlapping data shards and then consumed by multiple worker machines.

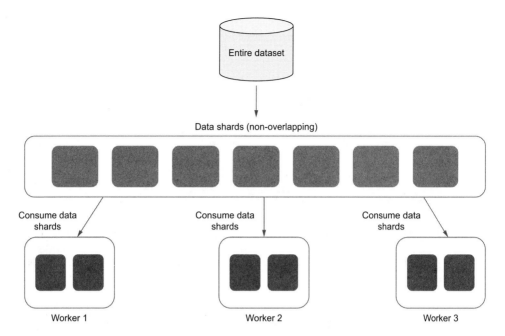

Figure 2.11   An architecture diagram in which the original dataset gets sharded into multiple non-overlapping data shards and then consumed by multiple worker machines

NOTE Although I am introducing sharding here, the concept isn't new; it's often used in distributed databases. Sharding in distributed databases is extremely useful for solving scaling challenges such as providing high availability of the databases, increasing throughput, and reducing query response time.

A shard is essentially a horizontal data partition that contains a subset of the entire dataset, and sharding is also referred to as *horizontal partitioning*. The distinction between horizontal and vertical comes from the traditional tabular view of a database. A database can be split vertically—storing different table columns in a separate database—or horizontally—storing rows of the same table in multiple databases. Figure 2.12 compares vertical partitioning and horizontal partitioning. Note that for vertical partitioning, we split the database into columns. Some of the columns may be empty, which is why we see only three of the five rows in the partition on the right side of the figure.

This *sharding pattern* can be summarized in the pseudocode in listing 2.6, where, first, we create data shards from one of the worker machines (in this case, worker machine with rank 0) and then send it to all other worker machines. Next, on each worker machine, we continuously try to read the next shard locally that will be used to train the model until no more shards are left locally.

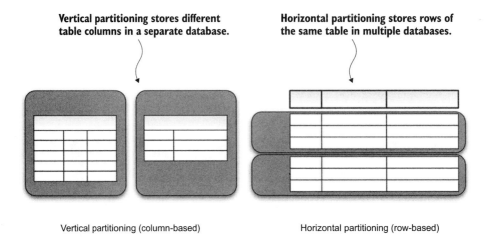

Vertical partitioning stores different table columns in a separate database.

Horizontal partitioning stores rows of the same table in multiple databases.

Vertical partitioning (column-based)

Horizontal partitioning (row-based)

Figure 2.12   Vertical partitioning vs. horizontal partitioning (Source: YugabyteDB, licensed under Apache License 2.0)

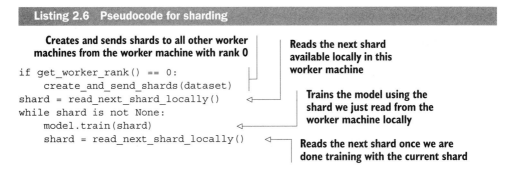

Listing 2.6   Pseudocode for sharding

Creates and sends shards to all other worker machines from the worker machine with rank 0

Reads the next shard available locally in this worker machine

```
if get_worker_rank() == 0:
    create_and_send_shards(dataset)
shard = read_next_shard_locally()
while shard is not None:
    model.train(shard)
    shard = read_next_shard_locally()
```

Trains the model using the shard we just read from the worker machine locally

Reads the next shard once we are done training with the current shard

With the help of the sharding pattern, we can split extremely large datasets into multiple data shards that can be spread among multiple worker machines, and then each of the worker machines is responsible for consuming individual data shards independently. As a result, we have just avoided the slowness of sequential model training due to the batching pattern. Sometimes it's also useful to shard large datasets into subsets of different sizes so that each shard can run different computational workloads depending on the amount of computational resource available in each worker machine. We'll apply this pattern in section 9.1.2.

2.4.3   *Discussion*

We have successfully used the sharding pattern to split an extremely large dataset into multiple data shards that spread among multiple worker machines and then sped up the training process as we add additional worker machines that are responsible for model training on each of the data shards independently. This is great, and with this approach, we can train machine learning models on extremely large datasets.

Now here comes the question: What if the dataset is growing continuously and we need to incorporate the new data that just arrived into the model training process? In this case, we'll have to reshard every once in a while if the dataset has been updated to rebalance each data shard to make sure they are split relatively evenly among the different worker machines.

In section 2.3.2, we simply divided the dataset into two non-overlapping shards, but unfortunately in real-world systems, this manual approach is not ideal and may not work at all. One of the most significant challenges with manual sharding is uneven shard allocation. The disproportionate distribution of data could cause shards to become unbalanced, with some overloaded while others remain relatively empty. This imbalance could cause unexpected hanging of the model training process that involves multiple worker machines, which we'll talk about further in the next chapter. Figure 2.13 is an example where the original dataset gets sharded into multiple imbalanced data shards and then consumed by multiple worker machines.

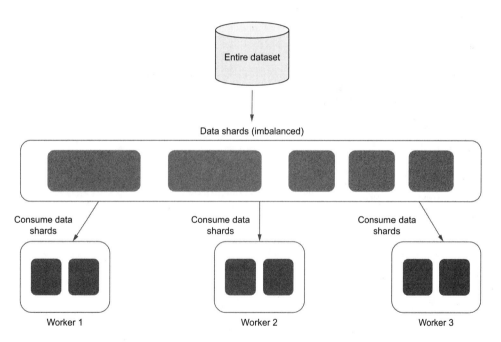

Figure 2.13 The original dataset gets sharded into multiple imbalanced data shards and then consumed by multiple worker machines.

It's best to avoid having too much data in one individual shard, which could lead to slowdowns and machine crashes. This problem could also happen when we force the dataset to be spread across too few shards. This approach is acceptable in development and testing environments but not ideal in production.

In addition, when manual sharding is used every time we see an update in the growing dataset, the operational process is nontrivial. Now we will have to perform backups for multiple worker machines, and we must carefully coordinate data migration and schema changes to ensure that all shards have the same schema copy.

To address that problem, we can apply autosharding based on algorithms instead of manually sharding datasets. Hash sharding, shown in figure 2.14, takes the key value of a data shard, which generates a hash value. Then the generated hash value is used to determine where a subset of the dataset should be located. With a uniform hashing algorithm, the hash function can distribute data evenly across different machines, reducing the problems mentioned earlier. In addition, data with shard keys that are close to one another are unlikely to be placed in the same shard.

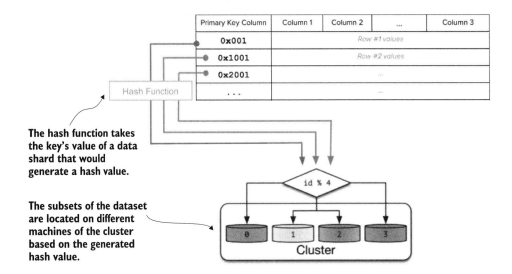

Figure 2.14 A diagram of hash sharding. A hash value is generated to determine where a subset of the dataset should be located. (Source: YugabyteDB, licensed under Apache License 2.0)

The sharding pattern works by splitting extremely large datasets into multiple data shards spread among multiple worker machines; then each of the worker machines is responsible for consuming individual data shards independently. With this approach, we can avoid the slowness of sequential model training due to the batching pattern. Both the batching and sharding patterns work well for the model training process; eventually, the dataset will be iterated thoroughly. Some machine learning algorithms, however, require multiple scans of the dataset, which means that we might perform batching and sharding twice. The next section introduces a pattern to speed up this process.

2.4.4 Exercises

1 Does the sharding pattern introduced in this section use horizontal partitioning or vertical partitioning?
2 Where does the model read each shard from?
3 Is there any alternative to manual sharding?

2.5 Caching pattern

Let's recap the patterns we've learned so far. In section 2.3, we successfully used the batching pattern to handle and prepare large datasets for model training when the machine learning framework could not handle large datasets or the underlying implementation of the framework required domain expertise. With the help of batching, we can process large datasets and perform expensive operations under limited memory. In section 2.4, we applied the sharding pattern to split large datasets into multiple data shards spread among multiple worker machines. We speed up the training process as we add more worker machines that are responsible for model training on each data shard independently. Both of these patterns are great approaches that allow us to train machine learning models on large datasets that won't fit on a single machine or that slows down the model training process.

One fact that I haven't mentioned is that modern machine learning algorithms, such as tree-based algorithms and deep learning algorithms, often require training for multiple epochs. Each *epoch* is a full pass-through of all the data we are training on, when every sample has been seen once. A single epoch refers to the single time the model sees all examples in the dataset. A single epoch in the Fashion-MNIST dataset means that the model we are training has processed and consumed all the 60,000 examples once. Figure 2.15 shows model training for multiple epochs.

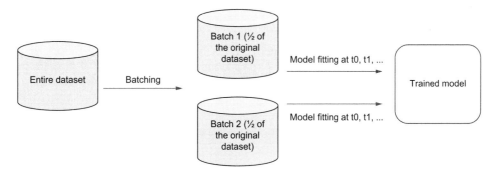

Figure 2.15 **A diagram of model training for multiple epochs at time t0, t1, and so on**

Training these types of machine learning algorithms usually involves optimizing a large set of parameters that are heavily interdependent. In fact, it can require a lot of labeled training examples to get the model close to the optimal solution. This problem is exacerbated by the stochastic nature of batch gradient descent in deep learning algorithms, in which the underlying optimization algorithm is data-hungry.

Unfortunately, the types of multidimensional data that these algorithms require, such as the data in the Fashion-MNIST dataset, may be expensive to label and take up large amounts of storage space. As a result, even though we need to feed the model lots of data, the number of samples available is generally much smaller than the number of samples that the optimization algorithm needs to reach a good-enough solution. There may be enough information in these training samples, but the gradient descent algorithm takes time to extract it.

Fortunately, we can compensate for the limited number of samples by making multiple passes over the data. This approach gives the algorithm time to converge without requiring an impractical amount of data. In other words, we can train a good-enough model that consumes the training dataset for multiple epochs.

2.5.1 The problem: Re-accessing previously used data for efficient multi-epoch model training

Now that we know that we can train a machine learning model for multiple epochs on the training dataset, let's assume that we want to do this on the Fashion-MNIST dataset. If training one epoch on the entire training dataset takes 3 hours, we need to double the amount of time spent on model training if we want to train two epochs, as shown in figure 2.16. In real-world machine learning systems, an even larger number of epochs is often required, so this approach is not efficient.

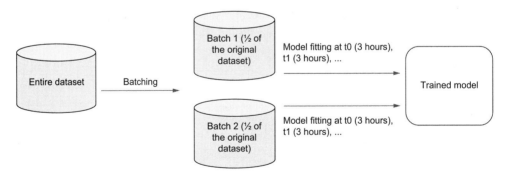

Figure 2.16   A diagram of model training for multiple epochs at time t0, t1, and so on. We spent 3 hours on each epoch.

2.5.2 The solution

Given the unreasonable amount of time needed to train a machine learning model for multiple epochs, is there anything we can do to speed up the process? There isn't anything we can do to improve the process for the first epoch because that epoch is the first time that the machine learning model sees the entire set of training datasets.

What about the second epoch? Can we make use of the fact that the model has already seen the entire training dataset once?

Assume that the laptop we are using to train the model has sufficient computational resources, such as memory and disk space. As soon as the machine learning model consumes each training example from the entire dataset, we can hold off recycling, instead keeping the consumed training examples in memory. In other words, we are storing a *cache* of the training examples in the form of in-memory representation, which could provide speed-ups when we access it again in the following training epochs.

In figure 2.17, after we finish fitting the model for the first epoch, we store a cache for both of the batches that we used for the first epoch of model training. Then we can start training the model for the second epoch by feeding the stored in-memory cache to the model directly without having to read from the data source again for future epochs.

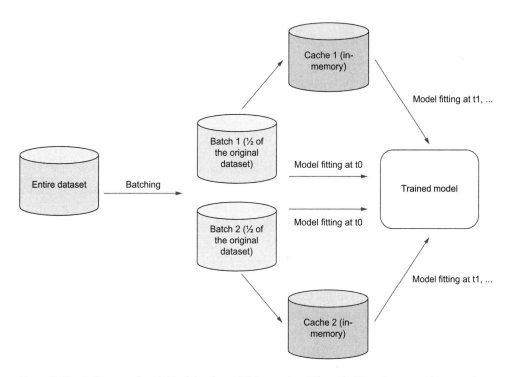

Figure 2.17 A diagram of model training for multiple epochs at time t0, t1, and so on, using a cache instead of reading from the data source again

This *caching pattern* can be summarized as the pseudocode in the following listing. We read the next batch to train the model and then append this batch to the initialized cache during the first epoch. For the remaining epochs, we read batches from the cache and then use those batches for model training.

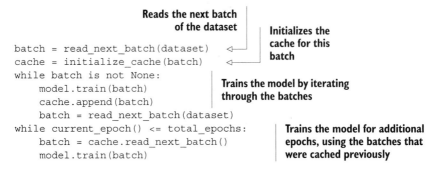

Listing 2.7   Pseudocode for caching

Reads the next batch of the dataset

Initializes the cache for this batch

```
batch = read_next_batch(dataset)
cache = initialize_cache(batch)
while batch is not None:
    model.train(batch)
    cache.append(batch)
    batch = read_next_batch(dataset)
while current_epoch() <= total_epochs:
    batch = cache.read_next_batch()
    model.train(batch)
```

Trains the model by iterating through the batches

Trains the model for additional epochs, using the batches that were cached previously

If we have performed expensive preprocessing steps on the original dataset, we could cache the processed dataset instead of the original dataset and avoid wasting time by processing the dataset again. The pseudocode is shown in the following listing.

Listing 2.8   Pseudocode for caching with preprocessing

```
batch = read_next_batch(dataset)
cache = initialize_cache(preprocess(batch))
while batch is not None:
    batch = preprocess(batch)
    model.train(batch)
    cache.append(batch)
    batch = read_next_batch(dataset)
while current_epoch() <= total_epochs:
    processed_batch = cache.read_next_batch()
    model.train(processed_batch)
```

Initializes the cache with the preprocessed batch

Retrieves the processed batch from the cache and uses it for model training

Note that listing 2.8 is similar to listing 2.7. Two slight differences are that we initialize the cache with the preprocessed batch instead of the raw batch, as in listing 2.7, and we read the processed batch from the batch directly without having to preprocess the batch again before model training.

With the help of the caching pattern, we can greatly speed up re-access to the dataset for a model training process that involves training on the same dataset for multiple epochs. Caching can also be useful for recovering from any failures quickly; a machine learning system can easily re-access the cached dataset and continue the rest of the processes in the pipeline. We'll apply this pattern in section 9.1.1.

2.5.3   *Discussion*

We have successfully used the caching pattern to store the cache in memory on each worker machine, speeding up the process of accessing previously used data for multiple epochs of model training. What if a failure happens on the worker machine? If the training process gets killed due to an out-of-memory error, for example, we would lose all the previously stored cache in memory.

To avoid losing the previously stored cache, we can write the cache to disk instead of storing it in memory and persist it as long as the model training process still needs it. This way, we can easily recover the training process by using a previously stored cache of training data on disk. Chapter 3 discusses in depth how to recover the training process or make the training process more tolerant of failure.

Storing the cache on disk is a good solution. One thing to note, however, that reading from or writing to memory is about six times faster when we are doing sequential access but about 100,000 times faster when we are doing random access rather than accessing from disk. Random-access memory (RAM) takes nanoseconds, whereas hard drive access speed is measured in milliseconds. In other words, there's a tradeoff between storing a cache in memory and storing it on a disk due to the difference in access speedspeed. Figure 2.18 provides a diagram of model training with an on-disk cache.

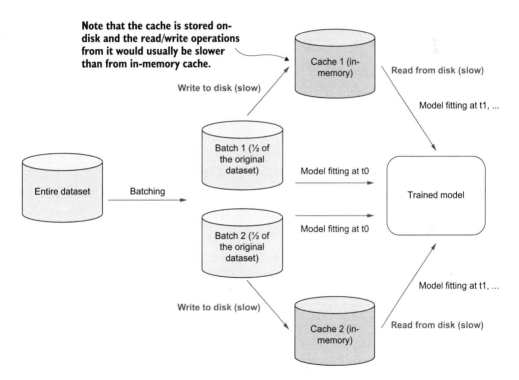

Figure 2.18   A diagram of model training for multiple epochs at time t0, t1, and so on with an on-disk cache

Generally speaking, storing a cache on disk is preferable if we want to build a more reliable and fault-tolerant system; storing a cache in memory is preferable when we want to have more efficient model training and data ingestion processes. An on-disk cache can be extremely useful when the machine learning system requires reading from remote databases, whereas reading from memory cache is much faster than reading from remote databases, especially when the network connection isn't fast and stable enough.

What if the dataset gets updated and accumulated over time, as in section 2.3.3, where the data shard on each worker machine needs to be redistributed and balanced? In this case, we should take the freshness of the cache into account and update it on a schedule based on the specific application.

2.5.4 Exercises

1 Is caching useful for model training that requires training on the same dataset or on a different dataset for multiple epochs?
2 What should we store in the cache if the dataset needs to be preprocessed?
3 Is an on-disk cache faster to access than an in-memory cache?

2.6 Answers to exercises

Section 2.3.4

1 Sequentially
2 Yes. That's one of the main use cases of batching.
3 No

Section 2.4.4

1 Horizontal partitioning
2 Locally on each worker machine
3 Automatic sharding, such as hash sharding

Section 2.5.4

1 Same dataset
2 We should store the preprocessed batches in the cache to avoid wasting time on preprocessing again in the following epochs.
3 No. Generally, an in-memory cache is faster to access.

Summary

- Data ingestion is usually the beginning process of a machine learning system, responsible for monitoring any incoming data and performing necessary processing steps to prepare for model training.
- The batching pattern helps handle large datasets in memory by consuming datasets in small batches.
- The sharding pattern prepares extremely large datasets as smaller chunks that are located on different machines.
- The caching pattern makes data fetching for multiple training rounds more efficient by caching previously accessed data that can be reused for the additional rounds of model training on the same dataset.

Distributed
training patterns

The previous chapter introduced a couple of practical patterns that can be incorporated into the data ingestion process, which is usually the beginning process in a distributed machine learning system that's responsible for monitoring any incoming data and performing necessary preprocessing steps to prepare model training.

Distributed training, the next step after the data ingestion process, is what distinguishes distributed machine learning systems from other distributed systems. It's the most critical part of a distributed machine learning system.

The system design needs to be scalable and reliable to handle datasets and models of different sizes and various levels of complexity. Some large and complex models cannot fit in a single machine, and some medium-size models that are small enough to fit in single machines struggle to improve the computational performance of distributed training.

It's also essential to know what to do when we see performance bottlenecks and unexpected failures. Parts of the dataset may be corrupted or cannot be used to train the model successfully, or the distributed cluster that the distributed training depends on may experience an unstable or even disconnected network due to weather conditions or human error.

In this chapter, I'll explore some of the challenges involved in the distributed training process and introduce a few established patterns adopted heavily in industries. Section 3.2 discusses challenges in training large machine learning models that tag main themes in new YouTube videos but cannot fit in a single machine; it also shows how to overcome the difficulty using the parameter server pattern. Section 3.3 shows how to use the collective communication pattern to speed up distributed training for smaller models and avoid unnecessary communication overhead among parameter servers and workers. The last section discusses some of the vulnerabilities of distributed machine learning systems due to corrupted datasets, unstable networks, and preemptive worker machines, as well as ways to address those problems.

3.1   *What is distributed training?*

Distributed training is the process of taking the data that has already been processed by data ingestion (discussed in chapter 2), initializing the machine learning model, and then training the model with the processed data in a distributed environment such as multiple nodes. It's easy to get this process confused with the traditional training process of machine learning models, which takes place in a single-node environment where the datasets and the machine learning model objects are on the same machine, such as a laptop. By contrast, distributed model training usually happens in a cluster of machines that could work concurrently to greatly speed up the training process.

In addition, the dataset is often located on the local disk of a single laptop or machine in traditional model training, whereas in distributed model training, a remote distributed database is used to store the dataset, or the dataset has to be partitioned on disks of multiple machines. If the model is not small enough to fit on a single machine, it's not possible to train the model in a traditional way with a single machine. From a network infrastructure perspective, an InfiniBand (https://wiki .archlinux.org/title/InfiniBand) or remote direct memory access (RDMA; https:// www.geeksforgeeks.org/remote-direct-memory-access-rdma/) network is often preferred for distributed training instead of a single local host. Table 3.1 provides a comparison of these training methods.

Table 3.1 Comparison of traditional (nondistributed) training and distributed training for machine learning models

	Traditional model training	Distributed model training
Computational resources	Laptop or single remote server	Cluster of machines
Dataset location	Local disk on a single laptop or machine	Remote distributed database or partitions on disks of multiple machines
Network infrastructure	Local hosts	InfiniBand or RDMA
Model size	Small enough to fit on a single machine	Medium to large

InfiniBand and RDMA

InfiniBand is a computer networking communications standard used in high-performance computing. It features high throughput and low latency for data interconnecting both among and within computers or storage systems, which is often required for distributed training.

RDMA provides direct access from the memory of multiple machines without involving any machine's operating system. This standard permits high-throughput, low-latency networking—especially useful in the distributed training process, in which communications among machines are frequent.

3.2 Parameter server pattern: Tagging entities in 8 million YouTube videos

Suppose that we have a dataset called YouTube-8M (http://research.google.com/youtube8m; figure 3.1) that consists of millions of YouTube video IDs, with high-quality machine-generated annotations from a diverse vocabulary of more than 3,800 visual entities (such as Food, Car, and Music). We'd like to train a machine learning model to tag the main themes of YouTube videos that the model hasn't seen.

This dataset consists of both coarse and fine-grained entities. *Coarse entities* are the ones nondomain experts can recognize after studying some existing examples, and *fine-grained entities* can be identified by domain experts who know how to differentiate among extremely similar entities. These entities have been semiautomatically curated and manually verified by three raters to be visually recognizable. Each entity has at least 200 corresponding video examples, with an average 3,552 training videos. When the raters identify the entities in the videos, they are given a guideline to assess how specific and visually recognizable each entity is, using a discrete scale from 1 to 5, where 1 represents an entity that a layperson can easily identify (figure 3.2).

In the online dataset explorer provided by YouTube-8M (http://research.google.com/youtube8m/explore.html), the list of entities appears on the left side, and

Figure 3.1   The website that hosts the YouTube-8M dataset, featuring millions of YouTube videos from a diverse vocabulary of more than 3,800 visual entities (Source: Sudheendra Vijayanarasimhan et al. Licensed under Nonexclusive License 1.0)

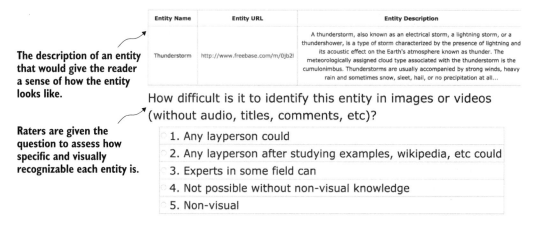

Figure 3.2   A screenshot of a question and guideline displayed to human raters for identifying the entities in the YouTube videos to assess how visually recognizable each entity is (Source: Sudheendra Vijayanarasimhan et al. Licensed under Nonexclusive License 1.0)

the number of videos that belong to each entity appears next to the entity name (figure 3.3).

Note that in the dataset explorer, the entities are ordered by the number of videos in each entity. In figure 3.3, the three most popular entities are Games, Video game,

Different entities are listed here and they are ordered by the number of videos in each entity. For example, the entity Games is the most popular entity in this dataset.

Figure 3.3   A screenshot of the dataset explorer provided by the YouTube-8M website, ordering the entities by number of videos (Source: Sudheendra Vijayanarasimhan et al. Licensed under Nonexclusive License 1.0)

and Vehicle, respectively, ranging from 415,890 to 788,288 training examples. The least popular entities (not shown in the figure) are Cylinder and Mortar, with 123 and 127 training videos, respectively.

3.2.1   The problem

With this dataset, we'd like to train a machine learning model to tag the main themes of new YouTube videos that the model hasn't seen. This task may be trivial for a simpler dataset and machine learning model, but that's certainly not the case for the YouTube-8M dataset. This dataset comes with precomputed audiovisual features from billions of frames and audio segments, so we don't have to calculate and obtain them on our own—tasks that often take a long time and require a large amount of computational resources.

Even though it is possible to train a strong baseline model on this dataset in less than a day on a single GPU, the dataset's scale and diversity can enable deep exploration of complex audiovisual models that can take weeks to train. Is there any solution for training this potentially large model efficiently?

3.2.2   The solution

First, let's take a look at some of the entities using the data explorer on the YouTube-8M website and see whether any relationships exist among the entities. Are these entities unrelated, for example, or do they have some level of overlap in content? After some exploration, we will make necessary adjustments to the model to take those relationships into account.

Figure 3.4 shows a list of YouTube videos that belong to the Pet entity. In the third video of the first row, a child is playing with a dog.

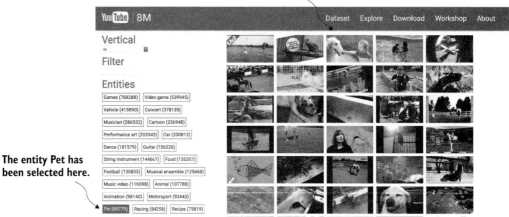

Figure 3.4   Example videos that belong to the Pet entity (Source: Sudheendra Vijayanarasimhan et al. Licensed under Nonexclusive License 1.0)

Let's a look a similar entity. Figure 3.5 shows a list of YouTube videos that belong to the Animal entity, in which we can see animals such as fish, horses, and pandas. Interestingly, a cat is getting cleaned by a vacuum in the third video of the fifth row. One

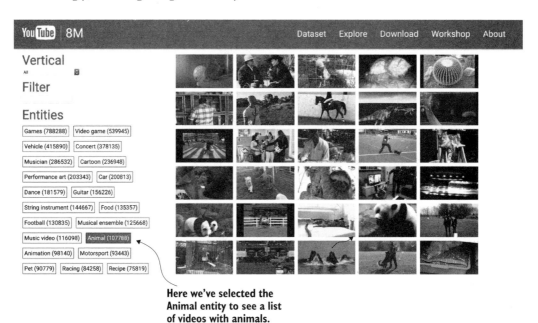

Figure 3.5   Example videos that belong to the Animal entity (Source: Sudheendra Vijayanarasimhan et al. Licensed under Nonexclusive License 1.0)

might guess that this video is in the Pet entity as well because a cat can be a pet if it's adopted by human beings.

If we'd like to build machine learning models for this dataset, we may need to do some additional feature engineering before fitting the model directly to the dataset. We might combine the audiovisual features of these two entities (Animal and Pet) into a derived feature because they provide similar information and overlap, which can boost the model's performance depending on the specific machine learning model we selected. If we continue exploring the combinations of the existing audiovisual features in the entities or perform a huge number of feature engineering steps, we may no longer be able to train a machine learning model on this dataset in less than a day on a single GPU.

If we are using a deep learning model instead of a traditional machine learning model that requires a lot of feature engineering and exploration of the dataset, the model itself learns the underlying relationships among features, such as audiovisual features of similar entities. Each neural network layer in the model architecture consists of vectors of weights and biases representing a trained neural network layer that gets updated over training iterations as the model gathers more knowledge from the dataset.

If we use only 10 of the 3,862 entities, we could build a LeNet model (figure 3.6) that classifies new YouTube videos into 1 of the 10 selected entities. At a high level, LeNet consists of a convolutional encoder consisting of two convolutional layers and a dense block consisting of three fully connected layers. For simplicity, we assume that each individual frame from the videos is a 28 × 28 image and that it will be processed by various convolution and pooling layers that learn the underlying feature mapping between the audiovisual features and the entities.

> ### Brief history of LeNet
>
> LeNet (https://en.wikipedia.org/wiki/LeNet) is one of the first published convolutional neural networks (CNNs; https://en.wikipedia.org/wiki/Convolutional_neural_network) to capture wide attention for its performance on computer vision tasks. It was introduced by Yann LeCun, a researcher at AT&T Bell Labs, to recognize handwritten digits in images. In 1989, LeCun published the first study that successfully trained CNNs via backpropagation after a decade of research and development.
>
> At that time, LeNet achieved outstanding results matching the performance of support vector machines, the dominant approach in supervised machine learning algorithms.

In fact, those learned feature maps contain parameters that are related to the model. These parameters are numeric vectors that are used as weights and biases for this layer of model representation. For each training iteration, the model takes every frame in the YouTube videos as features, calculates the loss, and then updates those model parameters to optimize the model's objective so that the relationships between features and the entities can be modeled more closely.

**The original image is processed by various convolution and
pooling layers that learns the underlying feature mapping.**

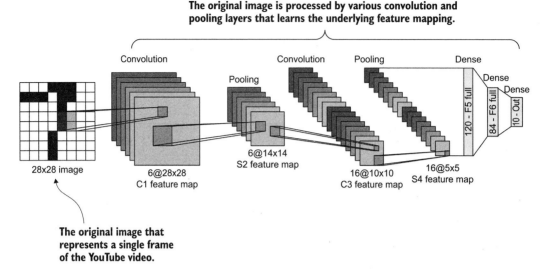

28x28 image

6@28x28
C1 feature map

6@14x14
S2 feature map

16@10x10
C3 feature map

16@5x5
S4 feature map

Convolution

Pooling

Convolution

Pooling

Dense

Dense

Dense

120 - F5 full

84 - F6 full

10 - Out

**The original image that
represents a single frame
of the YouTube video.**

**Figure 3.6   LeNet model architecture that could be used to classify new YouTube videos in 1 of 10 selected
entities. (Source: Aston Zhang et al. Licensed under Creative Commons Attribution-ShareAlike 4.0 International
Public License)**

Unfortunately, this training process is slow, as it involves updating all the parameters
in different layers. We have two potential solutions to speed up the training process.

Let's take a look at the first approach. We want to make an assumption here, and
we'll remove it later when we discuss a better approach. Let's assume that the model is
not too large and we can fit the entire model using existing resources without any possibility of out-of-memory or disk errors.

In this case, we can use one dedicated server to store all the LeNet model parameters and use multiple worker machines to split the computational workloads. Figure 3.7
shows an architecture diagram.

Each worker node takes a particular part of the dataset to calculate the gradients
and then sends the results to the dedicated server to update the LeNet model parameters. Because the worker nodes use isolated computational resources, they can perform the heavy computations asynchronously without having to communicate.
Therefore, we've achieved around a triple speedup simply by introducing additional
worker nodes if costs such as message passing among nodes are neglected.

This dedicated single server responsible for storing and updating the model
parameters is called a *parameter server*. We've designed a more efficient distributed
machine learning training system by incorporating the *parameter server pattern*.

Next comes the real-world challenge. Deep learning models often get complex;
additional layers with custom structures can be added on top of a baseline model.
Those complex models usually take up a lot of disk space due to the large number of
model parameters in those additional layers. A lot of computational resources are

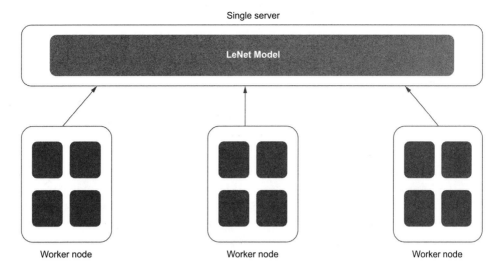

Figure 3.7   A machine learning training component with a single parameter server

required to meet the memory footprint requirement for successful training. What if the model is large, and we cannot fit all of its parameters on a single parameter server?

A second solution could address the challenges in this situation. We can introduce additional parameter servers, each responsible for storing and updating a particular *model partition*. Each worker node is responsible for taking a particular part of the dataset to update the model parameters in a model partition.

Figure 3.8 shows an architecture diagram of this pattern using multiple parameter servers. This diagram is different from figure 3.7, in which a single server stores all the

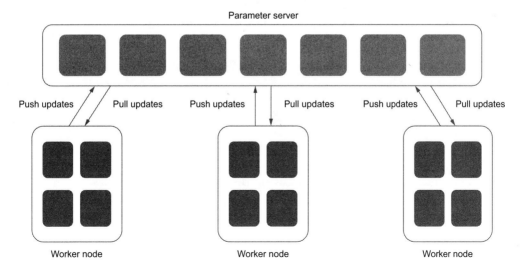

Figure 3.8   A machine learning training component with multiple parameter servers

LeNet model parameters and use worker machines split the computational workloads. Each worker node takes a subset of the dataset, performs the calculations required in each neural network layer, and then sends the calculated gradients to update one model partition that's stored in one of the parameter servers. Note that because all workers perform calculations in an asynchronous fashion, the model partitions that each worker node uses to calculate the gradients may not be up to date. To guarantee that the model partitions each worker node is using or each parameter server is storing are the most recent ones, we constantly have to pull and push updates of the model among the worker nodes.

With the help of parameter servers, we could effectively resolve the challenges of building a machine learning model to tag the main themes of new YouTube videos that the model hasn't seen. Figure 3.9 shows a list of YouTube videos that are not used for model training, tagged with the Aircraft theme by the trained machine learning model. Even when the model is too large to fit on a single machine, we could train the model efficiently. Note that although the parameter server pattern would be useful in this scenario, it is specially designed to train models with a lot of parameters.

Figure 3.9   A list of new YouTube videos not used for model training, tagged with the Aircraft theme (Source: Sudheendra Vijayanarasimhan et al. Licensed under Nonexclusive License 1.0)

3.2.3   *Discussion*

The previous section introduced the parameter server pattern and showed how it can be used to address potential challenges in the YouTube-8M video identification application. Even though the parameter server pattern is useful when the model is too large to fit on a single machine and even though the patterns seem like a straightforward approach to the challenge, in real-world applications, we still have to make decisions to make the distributed training system efficient.

Machine learning researchers and DevOps engineers often struggle to figure out a good ratio between the number of parameter servers and the number of workers for different machine learning applications. There are nontrivial communication costs to send the calculated gradients from workers to parameter servers, as well as costs for pulling and pushing the updates of the most recent model partitions. If we find that the model is getting larger and adds too many parameter servers to the system, the system will end up spending a lot of time communicating among nodes and a small amount of time making the computations among neural network layers.

Section 3.3 discusses these practical challenges in more detail. The section introduces a pattern that addresses these challenges so that engineers no longer need to spend time tuning the performance of workers and parameter servers for different types of models.

3.2.4 Exercises

1 If we'd like to train a model with multiple CPUs or GPUs on a single laptop, is this process considered distributed training?

2 What's the result of increasing the number of workers or parameter servers?

3 What types of computational resources (such as CPUs, GPUs, memory, or disk) should we allocate to parameter servers, and how much of those types of resources should we allocate?

3.3 Collective communication pattern

Section 3.2.2 introduced the parameter server pattern, which comes in handy when the model is too large to fit in a single machine, such as the one we would have to build to tag entities in 8 million YouTube videos. Although we could use parameter servers to handle extremely large and complex models with a large number of parameters, it's nontrivial to incorporate the pattern into the design of an efficient distributed training system.

Section 3.2.3 stated that DevOps engineers, who support the distributed machine learning infrastructure for data scientists or analysts, often have a hard time figuring out a good ratio between the number of parameter servers and the number of workers for different machine learning applications. Suppose that there are three parameter servers and three workers in the model training component of our machine learning system, as shown in figure 3.10. All three workers perform intensive computations asynchronously and then send the calculated gradients to the parameter servers to update different partitions of the model's parameters.

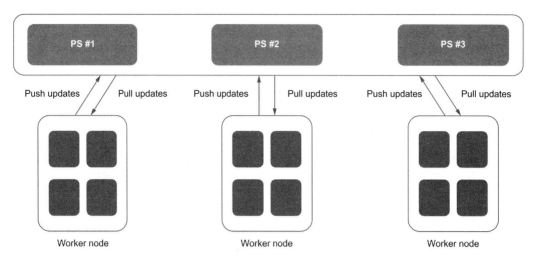

Figure 3.10 **A distributed model training component that consists of three parameter servers and three worker nodes**

In reality, worker nodes and parameter servers do not provide one-on-one mapping, particularly if the number of worker nodes is different from the number of parameter servers. In other words, multiple workers may send updates to the same subset of parameter servers. Now suppose that two workers have finished calculating the gradients at the same time, and they both want to update the model parameters stored on the same parameter server (figure 3.11).

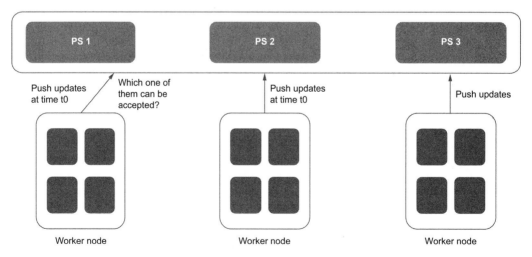

Figure 3.11 **Two of the worker nodes have finished calculating gradients and want to push updates to the first parameter server at the same time.**

As a result, the two workers are *blocking* each other from sending the gradients to the parameter server. In other words, the gradients from both worker nodes cannot be accepted by the same parameter server simultaneously.

3.3.1 *The problem: Improving performance when parameter servers become a bottleneck*

In this case, only two workers are blocking each other when sending gradients to the same parameter server, which makes it hard to gather the calculated gradients on time and which requires a strategy to resolve the blocking problem. Unfortunately, in real-world distributed training systems that incorporate parameter servers, multiple workers may be sending the gradients at the same time; thus, we must resolve many communications blocks.

When the ratio between the number of workers and the number of parameter servers is not optimal, for example, many workers are sending gradients to the same parameter server at the same time. The problem gets even worse, and eventually, the blocking of communications among different workers or parameter servers becomes a bottleneck. Is there a way to prevent this problem?

3.3.2 *The solution*

In this situation, the two workers need to figure out an approach to continue. They have to reconcile, decide which worker will take the next step first, and then take turns sending the calculated gradients to that particular parameter server. In addition, when one worker finishes sending gradients to update the model parameters on that parameter server, the parameter server starts sending the updated model partition back to that worker. Thus, the worker has the most up-to-date model to be fine-tuned as it's fed incoming data. If, at the same time, another worker is also sending calculated gradients to that parameter server, as shown in figure 3.12, another blocking communication occurs, and the workers need to reconcile again.

This time, unfortunately, the reconciliation may not be easy to resolve, as the worker that is trying to send the calculated gradients may not have used the latest model when calculating the gradients. This situation may be fine when the differences among model versions are small, but eventually, it may cause a huge difference in the statistical performance of the trained model.

If each parameter server stores different model partitions unevenly—perhaps the first parameter server stores two-thirds of the model parameters, as shown in figure 3.13—calculated gradients using this outdated model partition will have a huge effect on the final trained model. In such cases, we may want to drop the calculated gradients and let the other worker send the updated gradients to the parameter servers.

Now another challenge arises. What if the dropped gradients that we consider to be outdated were calculated from a larger portion of the entire training data, and it could take a long time to recalculate them using the latest model partition

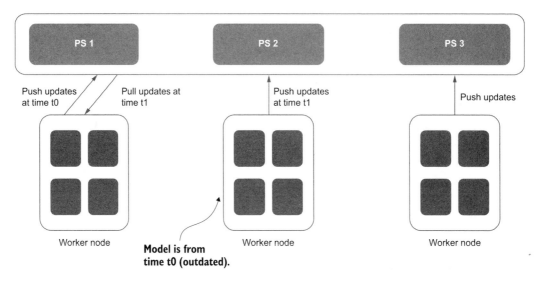

Figure 3.12   One worker is pulling updates while another worker is pushing updates to the same parameter server.

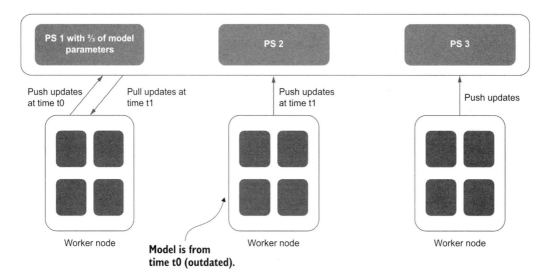

Figure 3.13   An example of imbalanced model partitions in which the first parameter server contains two-thirds of the entire set of model parameters.

(figure 3.14)? In this case, we probably want to keep those gradients so we don't waste too much time recalculating them.

In real-world distributed machine learning systems with parameter servers, we may encounter many challenges and problems that cannot be resolved completely. When

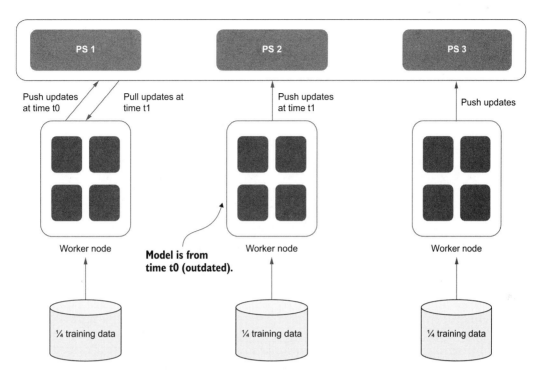

Figure 3.14 The second worker is trying to push gradients calculated from half of the training data.

those situations happen, we have to consider reconciliation and tradeoff approaches. As the numbers of workers and parameter servers increase, the cost of reconciliation and communication required to pull and push model parameters among workers and parameter servers becomes nontrivial. The system will end up spending a lot of time communicating between nodes and a small amount of making computations among neural network layers.

Even though we may have a lot of experience with the tradeoffs and performance differences involved in applying different ratios and computational resources for parameter servers and workers to our system, it still seems counterintuitive and time-consuming to tune toward a perfect system. In some circumstances, some of the workers or parameters fail during training, or the network becomes unstable, causing problems when nodes are communicating with push and pull updates. In other words, the parameter server pattern may not be suitable for a particular use case due to our lack of expertise or available time to work with the underlying distributed infrastructure.

Is there any alternative to this problem? The parameter server pattern may be one of the few good options for large models, but for simplicity and demonstration purposes, let's assume that the model size does not change. The whole model is small enough to fit on a single machine. In other words, each machine has enough disk space to store the model.

With that assumption in mind, what would be an alternative to parameter servers if we want only to improve the performance of distributed training? Without parameter servers, we have only worker nodes, each of which node stores a copy of the entire set of model parameters, as shown in figure 3.15.

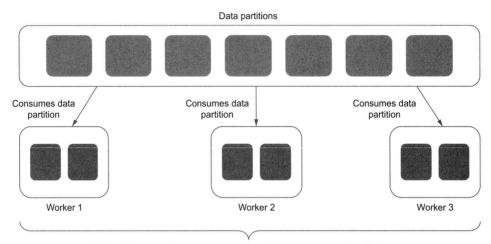

Data partitions

Consumes data partition   Consumes data partition   Consumes data partition

Worker 1   Worker 2   Worker 3

Each of these workers contains a copy of the entire set of model parameters and consumes partitions of data to calculate the gradients.

Figure 3.15 A distributed model training component with only worker nodes. Every worker stores a copy of the entire set of model parameters and consumes partitions of data to calculate the gradients.

How do we perform model training in this case? Recall that every worker consumes some portions of data and calculates the gradients required to update the model parameters stored locally on this worker node. When all the worker nodes have successfully completed their calculations of gradients, we need to aggregate all the gradients and make sure that every worker's entire set of model parameters is updated based on the aggregated gradients. In other words, each worker should store a copy of the same updated model. How do we aggregate all the gradients?

We are already familiar with the process for sending gradients from one node to another, such as sending the calculated gradients from a worker node to a parameter server to update the model parameters in a particular model partition. In general, that process is called *point-to-point communication* (figure 3.16). No other process is involved.

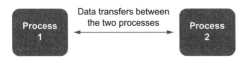

Data transfers between the two processes

Process 1   Process 2

Figure 3.16 An example of point-to-point communication with data being transferred between two processes. Note that no other process is involved.

In this situation, point-to-point communication is somewhat inefficient. Only worker nodes are involved, and we need to perform some kind of aggregation on the results from all workers. Fortunately, we can use another type of communication. *Collective communication* allows communication patterns across all processes in a *group*, which is composed of a subset of all processes. Figure 3.17 illustrates collective communication between one process and a group that consists of three other processes. In this case, each worker node carries the gradients and wants to send them to a group, including the rest of the worker nodes, so that all worker nodes will obtain the results from every worker.

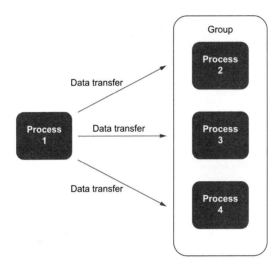

Figure 3.17 An example of collective communication between one process and a group that consists of three other processes

For our machine learning models, we usually perform some kind of aggregate operation on all the received gradients before sending the aggregated result to all the workers. This type of aggregation is called a *reduce function*, which involves making a set of numbers into a smaller set of numbers. Examples of reduce functions are finding the sum, maximum, minimum, or average of the set of numbers—in our case, the gradients we received from all the workers.

Figure 3.18 illustrates a reduce operation. Vectors v0, v1, and v2 in each of the processes in the process group are merged with the first process via a reduce operation.

When the gradients are reduced in a distributed fashion, we send the reduced gradients to all the workers so that they are on the same page and can update the model parameters in the same way, ensuring that they have exactly the same models. This kind of operation is called a *broadcast* operation and is often used to perform collective communications. Figure 3.19 illustrates a broadcast operation that sends a value to every process in the process group.

The combination of reduce and broadcast operations here is called *allreduce*, which reduces the results based on a specified reduce function and then distributes

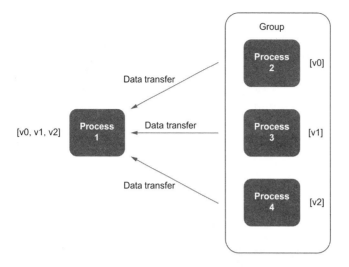

Figure 3.18   An example of a reduce operation with the sum as the reduce function

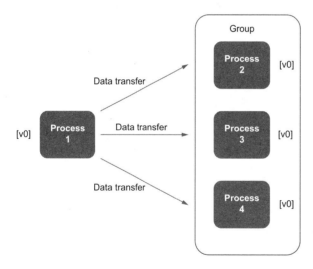

Figure 3.19   An example of a broadcast operation that sends a value to every process in the process group

the reduced results to all processes—in our case, to all the workers so that the model stored on each worker is exactly the same and is up to date (figure 3.20). When we finish a round of an allreduce operation, we start the next round by feeding new data to the updated model, calculating gradients, and performing the allreduce operation again to gather all gradients from workers to update the model.

Let's take a break to see what we've accomplished. We've successfully used the collective communication pattern, which takes advantage of the underlying network infrastructure, to perform allreduce operations for communicating gradients among multiple workers and allows us to train a medium-sized machine learning model in a distributed fashion. As a result, we no longer need parameter servers; thus, there is no

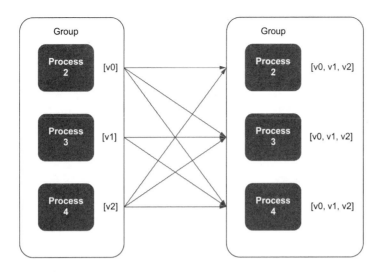

Figure 3.20 An example of an allreduce operation that reduces the results on each process in the group and then sends the result to every process in the group

communication overhead between parameter servers and workers. The collective communication pattern is useful in machine learning systems and also in distributed and parallel computing systems, where concurrency is applied to computations and communication primitives such as broadcast and reduce are critical for communicating among different nodes. We'll apply this pattern in section 9.2.2.

3.3.3 Discussion

The collective communication pattern is a great alternative to parameter servers when the machine learning model we are building is not too large. As a result, there is no communication overhead among parameter servers and workers, and it's no longer necessary to spend a lot of effort on tuning the ratio between the number of workers and parameter servers. In other words, we can easily add workers to speed up the model training process without worrying about performance regression.

One potential problem is worth mentioning, though. After we incorporate the collective communication pattern by applying the allreduce operation, each worker will need to communicate with all its peer workers, which may slow down the entire training process if the number of workers becomes large. Actually, collective communications rely on communication over the network infrastructure, and we still haven't fully used all the benefits of that yet in the allreduce operation.

Fortunately, we could use better collective communication algorithms to update the model more efficiently. One example is the *ring-allreduce* algorithm. The process is similar to that of the allreduce operation, but the data is transferred in ringlike fashion without the reduce operation. Each N worker needs to communicate with only two of its peer workers $2 * (N - 1)$ times to update all the model parameters completely. In other words, this algorithm is bandwidth-optimal; if the aggregated gradients are large enough, it will optimally use the underlying network infrastructure.

Both the parameter server pattern and the collective communication pattern make distributed training scalable and efficient. In practice, however, any of the workers or parameter servers may not start due to a lack of resources and may fail in the middle of distributed training. Section 3.4 introduces patterns that will help in those situations and make the entire distributed training process more reliable.

3.3.4 *Exercises*

1 Do blocking communications happen only among the workers?
2 Do workers update the model parameters stored on them asynchronously or synchronously?
3 Can you represent an allreduce operation with a composition of other collective communication operations?

3.4 *Elasticity and fault-tolerance pattern*

Both the parameter server pattern and the collective communication pattern enable us to scale up the distributed model training process. Parameter servers can be useful for handling large models that don't fit on a single machine; a large model can be partitioned and stored on multiple parameter servers, while individual workers can perform heavy computations and update each individual partition of model parameters asynchronously. When we observe too much communication overhead when using parameter servers, however, we can use the collective communication pattern to speed up the training process for medium-size models.

Let's assume that our distributed training component is well designed; can train machine learning models efficiently; and can handle the requirements of different types of models, using patterns such as parameter server and collective communication. One thing worth mentioning is that distributed model training is a long-running task, usually persisting for hours, days, or even weeks. Like all other types of software and systems, this long-running task is vulnerable to unexpected intervention. Because model training is a long-running process, it may be affected by internal or external intervention at any minute. Following are some examples of interventions that often occur in a distributed model training system:

- Parts of the dataset are corrupted or cannot be used to train the model successfully.
- The distributed cluster that the distributed training model depends on may experience an unstable or disconnected network due to weather conditions or human error.
- Some of the parameter servers or worker nodes are preempted; the computational resources they rely on are rescheduled for tasks and nodes that have higher priority.

3.4.1   The problem: Handling unexpected failures when training with limited computational resources

When unexpected interventions happen, if no actions are taken to address them, problems start to accumulate. In the first example in the preceding section, all workers use the same logic to consume the data to fit the model; when they see corrupted data that the training code is not able to handle, all of them fail eventually. In the second example, when the network becomes unstable, communications among parameter servers and workers will hang until the network recovers. In the third example, when the parameter servers or worker nodes are preempted, the entire training process is forced to stop, leading to unrecoverable failure. What should we do to help the distributed training system recover in those situations? Do we have a way to prevent unexpected failures?

3.4.2   The solution

Let's take a look at the first situation. Assume that the training process encounters a batch of data that's corrupted. In figure 3.21, some of the videos in the YouTube-8M dataset were accidentally modified by third-party video editing software after they were downloaded from the original source. The first worker node is trying to read

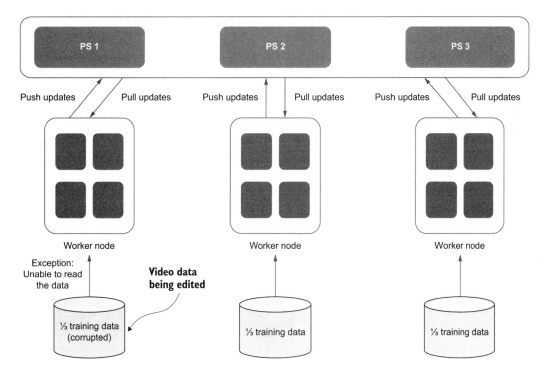

Figure 3.21   A worker encounters new batches of training data that's being edited and cannot be consumed successfully.

those portions of the data to feed the model. The machine learning model object that was initialized earlier cannot be fed with the edited and incompatible video data.

When this situation happens, the training process encounters an unexpected failure: the existing code does not contain the logic to handle an edited or corrupted dataset. In other words, we need to modify the distributed model training logic to handle this situation and then retrain the model from scratch.

Let's start the distributed training process again and see whether everything works well. We can skip the batches of data that we found to be corrupted and continue to train the machine learning model with the next batches of the remaining data.

Unfortunately, after the model has been trained for hours with half of the data, we realize that the new batches of data are being consumed much more slowly than before. After some digging and communicating with the DevOps team, we found that the network has become extremely unstable due to an incoming storm at one of our data centers—the second scenario mentioned earlier. If our dataset is residing on a remote machine instead of having been downloaded to a local machine, as shown in figure 3.22, the training process would be stuck waiting for a successful connection with the remote database. While waiting, we should *checkpoint* (store) the current trained model parameters and pause the training process. Then we can easily resume the training process when the network becomes stable again.

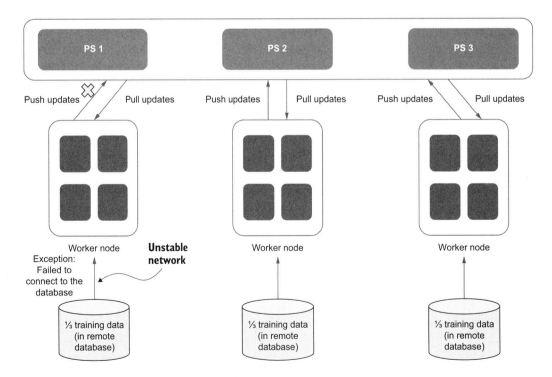

Figure 3.22 A worker encounters an unstable network while fetching data from a remote database.

Did the unstable network have other effects? We neglected one fact: we also rely on the network for communication between worker and parameter server nodes to send the calculated gradients and update the model parameters. Recall that if the collective communication pattern is incorporated, the training process is synchronous. In other words, one worker's communication blocks other workers' communications; we would need to obtain all gradients from all workers to aggregate the results to update the model parameters. If at least one worker becomes slow in communicating, the cascading effect eventually leads to a stuck training process.

In figure 3.23, three worker processes in the same process group are performing an allreduce operation. Two of the communications become slow due to the unstable network that the underlying distributed cluster is experiencing. As a result, two of the processes that depend on the slow communications do not receive some values (denoted by question marks) on time, and the entire allreduce operation is stuck until everything is received.

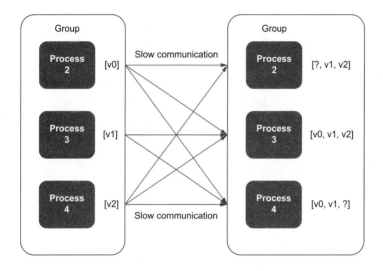

Figure 3.23 An allreduce process with slow communications due to the unstable network that blocks the entire training process

Can we do anything to continue training without being affected by the degrading network performance of individual nodes? In this case, first, we can abandon the two worker processes that are experiencing slow network connection; then we can abandon the current allreduce operation. Given the nature of the collective communication pattern, the remaining workers still have exactly the same copy of the model, so we can continue the training process by reconstructing a new worker process group that consists of the remaining workers and then performing the allreduce operation again.

The approach could also deal with situations in which some worker nodes are preempted, with their computational resources rescheduled to higher-priority tasks and nodes. When those workers get preempted, we reconstruct the worker process group and then perform the allreduce operation. This approach allows us to avoid wasting resources to train the model from scratch when unexpected failures happen. Instead, we can pick up the training process from where it paused and use the existing workers to which we've already allocated computational resources. If we have additional resources, we can easily add workers and then reconstruct the worker process groups to train more efficiently. In other words, we can easily scale the distributed training system up and down so that the entire system is elastic in terms of available resources. Many other distributed systems apply the same idea to make sure that the systems in place are reliable and scalable.

3.4.3 Discussion

We've successfully continued and recovered the distributed training process without wasting the resources we used to calculate the gradients from each worker. What if our distributed training uses parameter servers instead of collective communications with only workers?

Recall that when parameter servers are used, each parameter server stores a model partition that contains a subset of the complete set of model parameters. If we need to abandon any of the workers or parameter servers, such as when some communications failed or got stuck due to an unstable network on one parameter server or when the workers got preempted, we need to checkpoint the model partition in the failed nodes and then repartition the model partitions to the parameter servers that are still alive.

In reality, many challenges are still involved. How do we checkpoint the model partitions, and where do we save them? How often should we checkpoint them to make sure that they are as recent as possible?

3.4.4 Exercises

1 What is the most important thing to save in a checkpoint in case any failures happen in the future?
2 When we abandon the workers that are stuck or unable to recover without having time to make model checkpoints, where should we obtain the latest model, assuming that we are using the collective communication pattern?

3.5 Answers to exercises

Section 3.2.4

1 No, because the training happens on a single laptop.
2 The system will end up spending a lot of time communicating between nodes and a small amount of time making the computations among neural network layers.
3 We need more disk space for parameter servers to store large model partitions and less CPUs/GPUs/memory on them because parameter servers do not perform heavy computations.

Section 3.3.4

1 No. They also appear between workers and parameter servers.
2 Asynchronously
3 You use a reduce operation and then a broadcast operation.

Section 3.4.4

1 The most recent model parameters
2 Under the collective communication pattern, the remaining workers still have the same copy of the model, which we can use to continue training.

Summary

- Distributed model training is different from the traditional model training process, given the size and location of the dataset, the size of the model, the computational resources, and the underlying network infrastructure.
- We can use parameter servers to build large and complex models, storing partitions of the model parameters on each server.
- If communications between workers and parameter servers develop a bottleneck, we can switch to the collective communication pattern to improve distributed model training performance for small or medium-sized models.
- Unexpected failures happen during distributed model training, and we can take various approaches to avoid wasting computational resources.

Model serving patterns

This chapter covers

- Using model serving to generate predictions or make inferences on new data with previously trained machine learning models
- Handling model serving requests and achieving horizontal scaling with replicated model serving services
- Processing large model serving requests using the sharded services pattern
- Assessing model serving systems and event-driven design

In the previous chapter, we explored some of the challenges involved in the distributed training component, and I introduced a couple of practical patterns that can be incorporated into this component. Distributed training is the most critical part of a distributed machine learning system. For example, we've seen challenges when training very large machine learning models that tag main themes in new YouTube videos but cannot fit in a single machine. We looked at how we can overcome the difficulty of using the parameter server pattern. We also learned how to use the collective communication pattern to speed up distributed training for smaller models and avoid unnecessary communication overhead between parameter servers and workers. Last but not least, we talked about some of the vulnerabilities often seen in distributed machine learning systems due to corrupted datasets, unstable networks, and preempted worker machines and how we can address those problems.

Model serving is the next step after we have successfully trained a machine learning model. It is one of the essential steps in a distributed machine learning system. The model serving component needs to be scalable and reliable to handle the growing number of user requests and the growing size of individual requests. It's also essential to know what tradeoffs we may see when making different design decisions to build a distributed model serving system.

In this chapter, we'll explore some of the challenges involved in distributed model serving systems, and I'll introduce a few established patterns adopted heavily in industry. For example, we'll see challenges when handling the increasing number of model serving requests and how we can overcome these challenges to achieve horizontal scaling with the help of replicated services. We'll also discuss how the sharded services pattern can help the system process large model serving requests. In addition, we'll learn how to assess model serving systems and determine whether event-driven design would be beneficial in real-world scenarios.

4.1 What is model serving?

Model serving is the process of loading a previously trained machine learning model to generate predictions or make inferences on new input data. It's the step after we've successfully trained a machine learning model. Figure 4.1 shows where model serving fits in the machine learning pipeline.

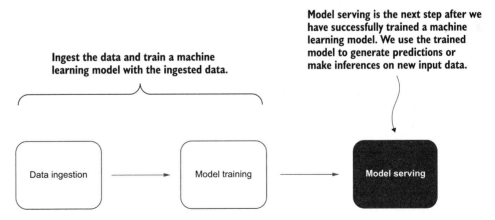

Figure 4.1 A diagram showing where model serving fits in the machine learning pipeline

Note that model serving is a general concept that appears in distributed and traditional machine learning applications. In traditional machine learning applications, model serving is usually a single program that runs on a local desktop or machine and generates predictions on new datasets that are not used for model training. Both the dataset and the machine learning model used should be small enough to fit on a single machine for traditional model serving, and they are stored in the local disk of a single machine.

In contrast, distributed model serving usually happens in a cluster of machines. Both the dataset and the trained machine learning model used for model serving can be very large and must be stored in a remote distributed database or partitioned on disks of multiple machines. The differences between traditional model serving and distributed model serving systems is summarized in table 4.1.

Table 4.1   Comparison between traditional model serving and distributed model serving systems

	Traditional model serving	**Distributed model serving**
Computational resources	Personal laptop or single remote server	Cluster of machines
Dataset location	Local disk on a single laptop or machine	Remote distributed database or partitioned on disks of multiple machines
Size of model and dataset	Small enough to fit on a single machine	Medium to large

It's nontrivial to build and manage a distributed model serving system that's scalable, reliable, and efficient for different use cases. We will examine a couple of use cases as well as some established patterns that may address different challenges.

4.2   *Replicated services pattern: Handling the growing number of serving requests*

As you may recall, in the previous chapter, we built a machine learning model to tag the main themes of new videos that the model hasn't seen before using the YouTube-8M dataset (http://research.google.com/youtube8m/), which consists of millions of YouTube video IDs, with high-quality machine-generated annotations from a diverse vocabulary of 3,800+ visual entities such as Food, Car, Music, etc. A screenshot of what the videos in the YouTube-8M dataset look like is shown in Figure 4.2.

Now we would like to build a model serving system that allows users to upload new videos. Then, the system would load the previously trained machine learning model to tag entities/themes that appear in the uploaded videos. Note that the model serving system is stateless, so users' requests won't affect the model serving results.

The system basically takes the videos uploaded by users and sends requests to the model server. The model server then retrieves the previously trained entity-tagging machine learning model from the model storage to process the videos and eventually generate possible entities that appear in the videos. A high-level overview of the system is shown in figure 4.3.

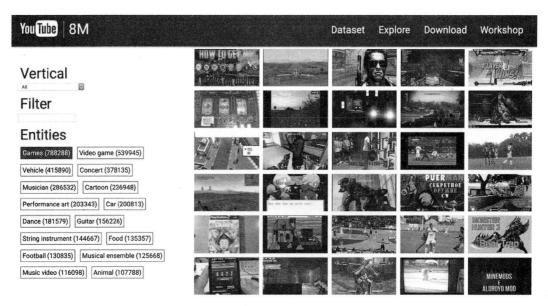

Figure 4.2 A screenshot of what the videos in the YouTube-8M dataset look like. (Source: Sudheendra Vijayanarasimhan et al. Licensed under Nonexclusive License 1.0)

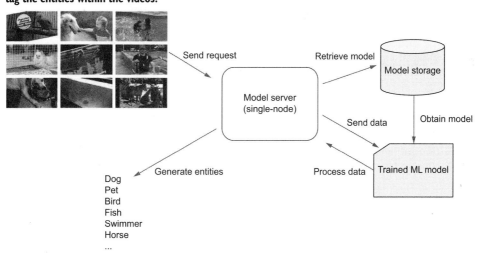

Figure 4.3 A high-level architecture diagram of the single-node model serving system

Note that this initial version of the model server only runs on a single machine and responds to model serving requests from users on a first-come, first-served basis, as shown in figure 4.4. This approach may work well if only very few users are testing the system. However, as the number of users or model serving requests increases, users will experience huge delays while waiting for the system to finish processing any previous requests. In the real world, this bad user experience would immediately lose our users' interest in engaging with this system.

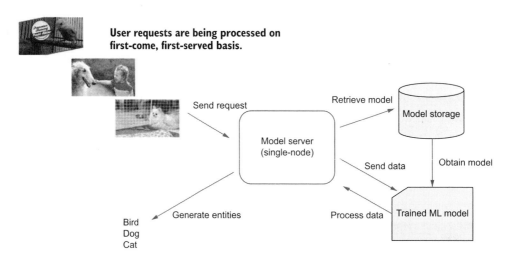

Figure 4.4 The model server only runs on a single machine and responds to model serving requests from users on a first-come, first-served basis.

4.2.1 The problem

The system takes the videos uploaded by users and then sends the requests to the model server. These model serving requests are queued and must wait to be processed by the model server.

Unfortunately, due to the nature of the single-node model server, it can only effectively serve a limited number of model serving requests on a first-come, first-served basis. As the number of requests grows in the real world, the user experience worsens when users must wait a long time to receive the model serving result. All requests are waiting to be processed by the model serving system, but the computational resources are bound to this single node. Is there a better way to handle model serving requests than sequentially?

4.2.2 The solution

One fact we've neglected is that the existing model server is stateless, meaning that the model serving results for each request aren't affected by other requests, and the machine learning model can only process a single request. In other words, the model server doesn't require a saved state to operate correctly.

Since the model server is stateless, we can add more server instances to help handle additional user requests without the requests interfering with each other, as shown in figure 4.5. These additional model server instances are exact copies of the original

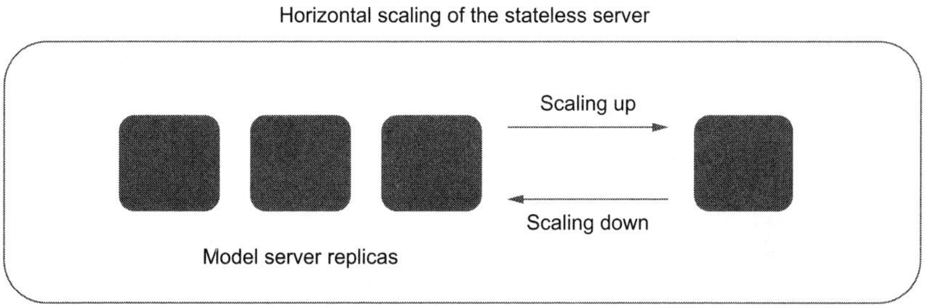

Horizontal scaling of the stateless server

Figure 4.5 Additional server instances help handle additional user requests without the requests interfering with each other.

model server but with different server addresses, and each handles different model serving requests. In other words, they are *replicated services* for model serving or, in short, *model server replicas.*

Adding additional resources into our system with more machines is called *horizontal scaling*. Horizontal scaling systems handle more and more users or traffic by adding more replicas. The opposite of horizontal scaling is *vertical scaling*, which is usually implemented by adding computational resources to existing machines.

> ### An analogy: Horizontal scaling vs. vertical scaling
> You can think of vertical scaling like retiring your sports car and buying a race car when you need more horsepower. While a race car is fast and looks amazing, it's also expensive and not very practical, and at the end of the day, they can only take you so far before running out of gas. In addition, there's only one seat, and the car must be driven on a flat surface. It is really only suitable for racing.
>
> Horizontal scaling gets you that added horsepower—not by favoring sports cars over race cars, but by adding another vehicle to the mix. In fact, you can think of horizontal scaling like several vehicles that could fit a lot of passengers at once. Maybe none of these machines is a race car, but none of them need to be—across the fleet, you have all the horsepower you need.

Let's return to our original model serving system, which takes the videos uploaded by users and sends requests to the model server. Unlike our previous design of the model serving system, the system now has multiple model server replicas to process the model serving requests asynchronously. Each model server replica takes a single request, retrieves the previously trained entity-tagging machine learning model from model storage, and then processes the videos in the request to tag possible entities in the videos.

As a result, we've successfully scaled up our model server by adding model server replicas to the existing model serving system. The new architecture is shown in figure 4.6. The model server replicas are capable of handling many requests at a time since each replica can process individual model serving requests independently.

Users upload videos and then submit requests to model serving system to tag the entities within the videos.

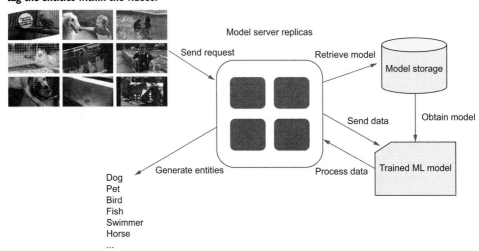

Figure 4.6   The system architecture after we've scaled up our model server by adding model server replicas to the system

In the new architecture, multiple model serving requests from users are sent to the model server replicas at the same time. However, we haven't discussed how they are being distributed and processed. For example, which request is being processed by which model server replica? In other words, we haven't yet defined a clear mapping relationship between the requests and the model server replicas.

To do that, we can add another layer—namely, a *load balancer*, which handles the distribution of model serving requests among the replicas. For example, the load balancer takes multiple model serving requests from our users and then distributes the requests evenly to each of the model server replicas, which then are responsible for processing individual requests, including model retrieval and inference on the new data in the request. Figure 4.7 illustrates this process.

The load balancer uses different algorithms to decide which request goes to which model server replica. Example algorithms for load balancing include round robin, the least connection method, hashing, etc.

The replicated services pattern provides a great way to scale our model serving system horizontally. It can also be generalized for any systems that serve a large amount of traffic. Whenever a single instance cannot handle the traffic, introducing this pattern ensures that all traffic can be handled equivalently and efficiently. We'll apply this pattern in section 9.3.2.

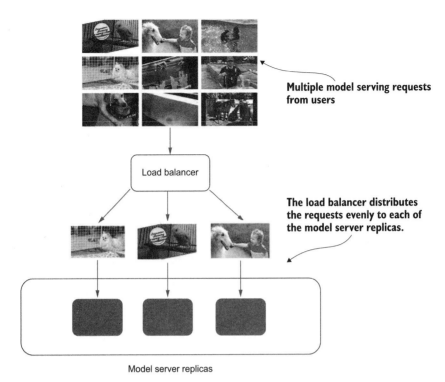

Figure 4.7 A diagram showing how a loader balancer is used to distribute the requests evenly across model server replicas

Round robin for load balancing

Round robin is a simple technique in which the load balancer forwards each request to a different server replica based on a rotating list.

Even though it's easy to implement a load balancer with the round-robin algorithm, the load is already on a load balancer server, and it might be dangerous if the load balancer server itself receives a lot of requests that require expensive processing. It may become overloaded past the point it can effectively do its job.

4.2.3 Discussion

Now that we have load-balanced model server replicas in place, we should be able to support the growing number of user requests, and the entire model serving system achieves horizontal scaling. Not only can we handle model serving requests in a scalable way, but the overall model serving system also becomes *highly available* (https://mng.bz/EQBd). High availability is a characteristic of a system that maintains an agreed-on level of operational performance, usually uptime, for a longer-than-normal period. It's often expressed as a percentage of uptime in a given year.

For example, some organizations may require services to reach a highly available service-level agreement, which means the service is up and running 99.9% of the time (known as three-nines availability). In other words, the service can only get 1.4 minutes of downtime per day (24 hours × 60 minutes × 0.1%). With the help of replicated model services, if any of the model server replicas crashes or gets preempted on a spot instance, the remaining model server replicas are still available and ready to process any incoming model serving requests from users, which provides a good user experience and makes the system reliable.

In addition, since our model server replicas will need to retrieve previously trained machine learning models from a remote model storage, they need to be *ready* in addition to being *alive*. It's important to build and deploy *readiness probes* to inform the load balancer that the replicas are all successfully established connections to the remote model storage and are ready to serve model serving requests from users. A readiness probe helps the system determine whether a particular replica is ready to serve. With readiness probes, users do not experience unexpected behaviors when the system is not ready due to internal system problems.

The replicated services pattern addresses our horizontal scalability problem that prevents our model serving system from supporting a large number of model serving requests. However, in real-world model serving systems, not only the number of serving requests increases but also the size of each request, which can get extremely large if the data or the payload is large. In that case, replicated services may not be able to handle the large requests. We will talk about that scenario and introduce a pattern that would alleviate the problem in the next section.

4.2.4   Exercises

1   Are replicated model servers stateless or stateful?
2   What happens when we don't have a load balancer as part of the model serving system?
3   Can we achieve three-nines service-level agreements with only one model server instance?

4.3   *Sharded services pattern*

The replicated services pattern efficiently resolves our horizontal scalability problem so that our model serving system can support a growing number of user requests. We achieve the additional benefit of high availability with the help of model server replicas and a load balancer.

> **NOTE** Each model server replica has a limited and pre-allocated amount of computational resources. More important, the amount of computational resources for each replica must be identical for the load balancer to distribute requests correctly and evenly.

Next, let's imagine that a user wants to upload a high-resolution YouTube video that needs to be tagged with an entity using the model server application. Even though the high-resolution video is too large, it may be uploaded successfully to the model server replica if it has sufficient disk storage. However, we could not process the request in any of the individual model server replicas themselves since processing this single large request would require a larger memory allocated in the model server replica. This need for a large amount of memory is often due to the complexity of the trained machine learning model, as it may contain a lot of expensive matrix computations or mathematical operations, as we've seen in the previous chapter.

For instance, a user uploads a high-resolution video to the model serving system through a large request. One of the model server replicas takes this request and successfully retrieves the previously trained machine learning model. Unfortunately, the model then fails to process the large data in the request since the model server replica that's responsible for processing this request does not have sufficient memory. Eventually, we may notify the user of this failure after they have waited a long time, which results in a bad user experience. A diagram for this situation is shown in figure 4.8.

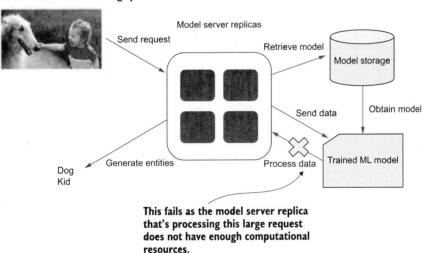

Figure 4.8 A diagram showing that model fails to process the large data in the request since the model server replica responsible for processing this request does not have sufficient memory

4.3.1 The problem: Processing large model serving requests with high-resolution videos

The requests the system is serving are large since the videos users upload are high resolution. In cases where the previously trained machine learning model may contain expensive mathematical operations, these large video requests cannot be successfully processed and served by individual model server replicas with a limited amount of memory. How do we design the model serving system to handle large requests of high-resolution videos successfully?

4.3.2   *The solution*

Given our requirement for the computational resources on each model server replica, can we scale vertically by increasing each replica's computational resources so it can handle large requests like high-resolution videos? Since we are vertically scaling all the replicas by the same amount, we will not affect our load balancer's work.

Unfortunately, we cannot simply scale the model server replicas vertically since we don't know how many such large requests there are. Imagine only a couple of users have high-resolution videos needing to be processed (e.g., professional photographers who have high-end cameras that capture high-resolution videos), and the remaining vast majority of the users only upload videos from their smartphones with much smaller resolutions. As a result, most of the added computational resources on the model server replicas are idling, which results in very low resource utilization. We will examine the resource utilization perspective in the next section, but for now, we know that this approach is not practical.

Remember we introduced the parameter server pattern in chapter 3, which allows us to partition a very large model? Figure 4.9 is the diagram we discussed in chapter 3 that shows distributed model training with multiple parameter servers; the large model has been partitioned, and each partition is located on different parameter servers. Each worker node takes a subset of the dataset, performs calculations required in each neural network layer, and then sends the calculated gradients to update one model partition stored in one of the parameter servers.

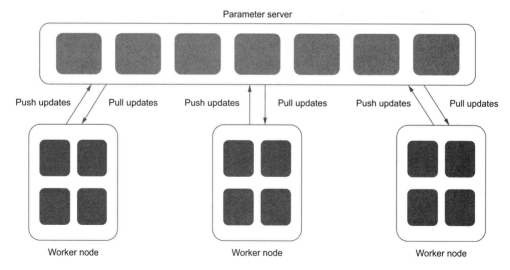

Figure 4.9   Distributed model training with multiple parameter servers where the large model has been sharded and each partition is located on different parameter servers

To deal with our problem of large model serving requests, we can borrow the same idea and apply it to our particular scenario.

We first divide the original high-resolution video into multiple separate videos, and then each video is processed by multiple *model server shards* independently. The model server shards are partitions from a single model server instance, and each is responsible for processing a subset of a large request.

The diagram in figure 4.10 is an example architecture of the *sharded services pattern*. In the diagram, a high-resolution video that contains a dog and a kid gets divided into two separate videos where each of the videos represents a subset of the original large request. One of the separated videos contains the part where the dog appears, and the other video contains the part where the kid appears. These two separated videos become two separate requests and are processed by different model server shards independently.

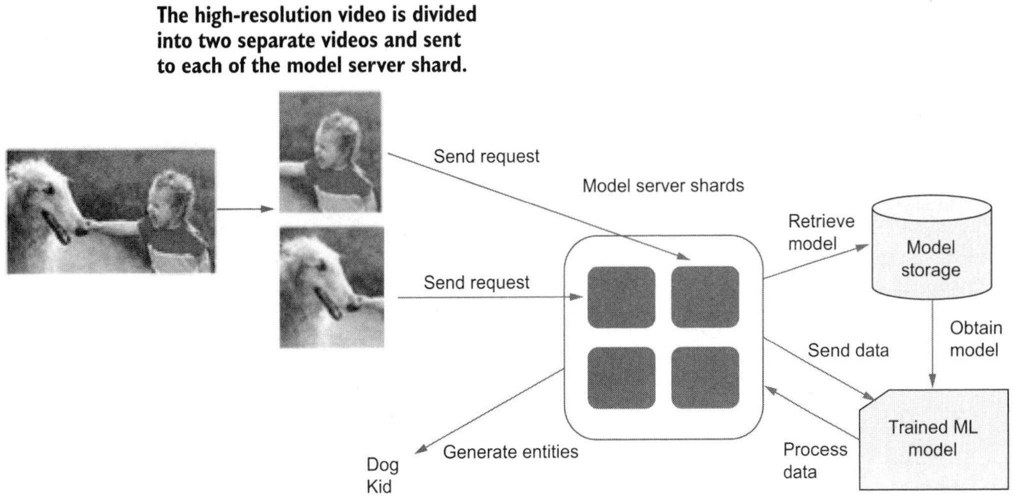

Figure 4.10   An example architecture of the sharded services pattern where a high-resolution video gets divided into two separate videos. Each video represents a subset of the original large request and is processed by different model server shard independently.

After the model server shards receive the sub-requests where each contains part of the original large model serving request, each model server shard then retrieves the previously trained entity-tagging machine learning model from model storage and then processes the videos in the request to tag possible entities that appear in the videos, similar to the previous model serving system we've designed. Once all the sub-requests have been processed by each of the model server shards, we merge the model inference result from two sub-requests—namely, the two entities, dog and kid—to obtain a result for the original large model serving request with the high-resolution video.

How do we distribute the two sub-requests to different model server shards? Similar to the algorithms we use to implement the load balancer, we can use a *sharding function*, which is very similar to a hashing function, to determine which shard in the list of model server shards should be responsible for processing each sub-request.

Usually, the sharding function is defined using a hashing function and the modulo (%) operator. For example, `hash(request) % 10` would return 10 shards even when the outputs of the hash function are significantly larger than the number of shards in a sharded service.

Characteristics of hashing functions for sharding

The hashing function that defines the sharding function transforms an arbitrary object into an integer representing a particular shard index. It has two important characteristics:

1 The output from hashing is always the same for a given input.
2 The distribution of outputs is always uniform within the output space.

These characteristics are important and can ensure that a particular request will always be processed by the same shard server and that the requests are evenly distributed among the shards.

The sharded services pattern solves the problem we encounter when building model serving systems at scale and provides a great way to handle large model serving requests. It's similar to the data-sharding pattern we introduced in chapter 2: instead of applying sharding to datasets, we apply sharding to model serving requests. When a distributed system has limited computational resources for a single machine, we can apply this pattern to offload the computational burden to multiple machines.

4.3.3 *Discussion*

The sharded services pattern helps handle large requests and efficiently distributes the workload of processing large model serving requests to multiple model server shards. It's generally useful when considering any sort of service where the data exceeds what can fit on a single machine.

However, unlike the replicated services pattern we discussed in the previous section, which is useful when building stateless services, the sharded services pattern is generally used for building stateful services. In our case, we need to maintain the state or the results from serving the sub-requests from the original large request using sharded services and then merge the results into the final response so it includes all entities from the original high-resolution video.

In some cases, this approach may not work well because it depends on how we divide the original large request into smaller requests. For example, if the original video has been divided into more than two sub-requests, some may not be meaningful since they don't contain any complete entities that are recognizable by the machine learning model we've trained. For situations like that, we need additional handling and cleaning of the merged result to remove meaningless entities that are not useful to our application.

Both the replicated services pattern and sharded services pattern are valuable when building a model serving system at scale to handle a great number of large model serving requests. However, to incorporate them into the model serving system, we need to know the required computational resources at hand, which may not be available if the traffic is rather dynamic. In the next section, I will introduce another pattern focusing on model serving systems that can handle dynamic traffic.

4.3.4 Exercises

1 Would vertical scaling be helpful when handling large requests?
2 Are the model server shards stateful or stateless?

4.4 The event-driven processing pattern

The replicated services pattern we examined in section 4.2 helps handle a large number of model serving requests, and the sharded services pattern in section 4.3 can be used to process very large requests that may not fit in a single model server instance. While these patterns address the challenges of building model serving systems at scale, they are more suitable when the system knows how much computational resources, model server replicas, or model server shards to allocate before the system starts taking user requests. However, for cases in which we do not know how much model serving traffic the system will be receiving, it's hard to allocate and use resources efficiently.

Now imagine that we work for a company that provides holiday and event planning services to subscribed customers. We'd like to provide a new service that will use a trained machine learning model to predict hotel prices per night for the hotels located in resort areas, given a range of dates and a specific location where our customers would like to spend their holidays.

To provide that service, we can design a machine learning model serving system. This model serving system provides a user interface where users can enter the range of dates and locations they are interested in staying for holidays. Once the requests are sent to the model server, the previously trained machine learning model will be retrieved from the distributed database and process the data in the requests (dates and locations). Eventually, the model server will return the predicted hotel prices for each location within the given date range. The complete process is shown in figure 4.11.

After we test this model serving system for one year on selected customers, we will have collected sufficient data to plot the model serving traffic over time. As it turns out, people prefer to book their holidays at the last moment, so traffic increases abruptly shortly before holidays and then decreases again after the holiday periods. The problem with this traffic pattern is that it introduces a very low resource utilization rate.

In our current architecture of model serving system, the underlying computational resources allocated to the model remain unchanged at all times. This strategy seems far

Users enter date range and location and then submit requests to the serving system.

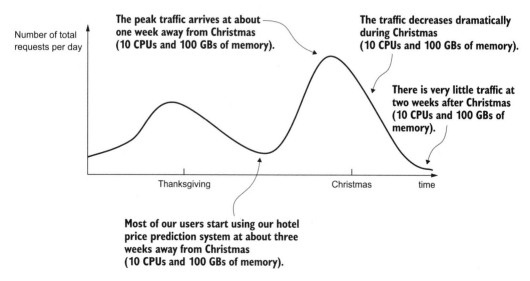

From: 2022-11-25

To: 2022-12-25

City: San Francisco

Send request

Model server instances

Retrieve model

Distributed database

Send data

Obtain model

Generate price predictions

Process data

Trained ML model

Hotel name	Price/night
Hotel 1	$75.00
Hotel 2	$80.00

Figure 4.11   A diagram of the model serving system to predict hotel prices

from optimal: during periods of low traffic, most of our resources are idling and thus wasted, whereas during periods of high traffic, our system struggles to respond in a timely fashion, and more resources than normal are required to operate. In other words, the system has to deal with either high or low traffic with the same amount of computational resources (e.g., 10 CPUs and 100 GB of memory), as shown in figure 4.12.

Number of total requests per day

The peak traffic arrives at about one week away from Christmas (10 CPUs and 100 GBs of memory).

The traffic decreases dramatically during Christmas (10 CPUs and 100 GBs of memory).

There is very little traffic at two weeks after Christmas (10 CPUs and 100 GBs of memory).

Thanksgiving

Christmas

time

Most of our users start using our hotel price prediction system at about three weeks away from Christmas (10 CPUs and 100 GBs of memory).

Figure 4.12   The traffic changes of the model serving system over time with an equal amount of computational resources allocated all the time.

Since we know, more or less, when those holiday periods are, why don't we plan accordingly? Unfortunately, some events make it hard to predict surges in traffic. For example, a huge international conference may be planned near one of the resorts, as shown in figure 4.13. This unexpected event, which happens before Christmas, has suddenly added traffic at that particular time window (solid line). Not knowing about the conferences, we would miss a window that should be taken into account when allocating computational resources. Specifically, in our scenario, two CPUs and 20 GB of memory, although optimized for our use case, no longer is sufficient to handle all resources within this time window. The user experience would be very bad. Imagine all the conference attendants sitting in front of their laptops, waiting a long time to book a hotel room.

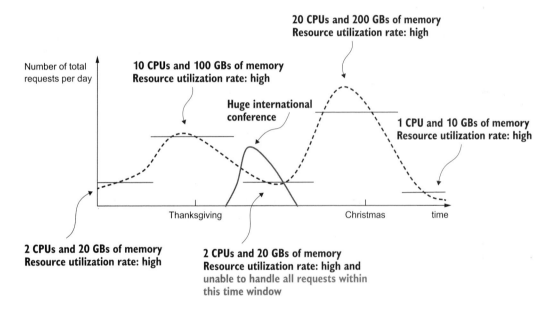

Figure 4.13 The traffic of our model serving system over time with an optimal amount of computational resources allocated for different time windows. In addition, an unexpected event happened before Christmas that suddenly added traffic during that particular time window (solid line).

In other words, this naive solution is still not very practical and effective since it's non-trivial to figure out the time windows to allocate different amounts of resources and how much additional resources are needed for each time window. Can we come up with any better approach?

In our scenario, we are dealing with a dynamic number of model serving requests that varies over time and is highly correlated to times around holidays. What if we can guarantee we have enough resources and forget about our goal of increasing the resource utilization rate for now? If the computational resources are guaranteed to be more than sufficient at all times, we can make sure that the model serving system can handle heavy traffic during holiday seasons.

4.4.1 The problem: Responding to model serving requests based on events

The naive approach, which is to estimate and allocate computational resources accordingly before identifying any possible time windows in which the system might experience a high volume of traffic, is not feasible. It's not easy to determine the exact dates of the high-traffic time windows and the exact amount of computational resources needed during each.

Simply increasing the computational resources to an amount sufficient at all times also is not practical, as the resource utilization rate we were concerned about earlier remains low. For example, if nearly no user requests are made during a particular time period, the computational resources we have allocated are, unfortunately, mostly idling and thus wasted. Is there another approach that allocates and uses computational resources more wisely?

4.4.2 The solution

The solution to our problem is maintaining a pool of computational resources (e.g., CPUs, memory, disk, etc.) allocated not only to this particular model serving system but also to model serving of other applications or other components of the distributed machine learning pipeline.

Figure 4.14 is an example architecture diagram where a shared resource pool is used by different systems—for example, data ingestion, model training, model selection, model deployment, and model serving—at the same time. This shared resource pool gives us enough resources to handle peak traffic for the model serving system by pre-allocating resources required during historical peak traffic and autoscaling when the limit is reached. Therefore, we only use resources when needed and only the specific amount of resources required for each particular model serving request.

For our discussions, I only focus on the model serving system in the diagram, and details for other systems are neglected here. In addition, here I assume that the model training component only utilizes similar types of resources, such as CPUs. If the model training component requires GPUs or a mix of CPUs/GPUs, it may be better to use a separate resource pool, depending on specific use cases.

When the users of our hotel price prediction application enter into the UI the range of dates and locations that they are interested in staying for holidays, the model serving requests are sent to the model serving system. Upon receiving each request, the system notifies the shared resource pool that certain amounts of computational resources are being used by the system.

For example, figure 4.15 shows the traffic of our model serving system over time with an unexpected bump. The unexpected bump is due to a new very large international conference that happens before Christmas. This event suddenly adds traffic,

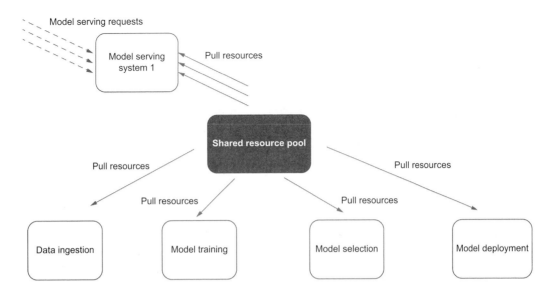

Figure 4.14   An architecture diagram in which a shared resource pool is being used by different components—for example, data ingestion, model training, model selection, and model deployment—and two different model serving systems at the same time. The arrows with solid lines indicate resources, and the arrows with dashed lines indicate requests.

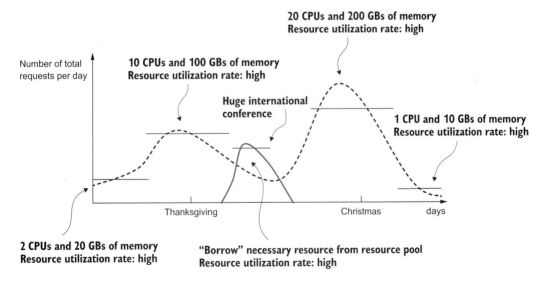

Figure 4.15   The traffic of our model serving system over time. An unexpected bump happened before Christmas that suddenly added traffic. The jump in requests is handled successfully by the model serving system by borrowing the necessary amount of resources from the shared resource pool. The resource utilization rate remains high during this unexpected event.

but the model serving system successfully handles the surge in traffic by borrowing a necessary amount of resources from the shared resource pool. With the help of the shared resource pool, the resource utilization rate remains high during this unexpected event. The shared resource pool monitors the current amount of available resources and autoscales when needed.

This approach, in which the system listens to the user requests and only responds and utilizes the computational resources when the user request is being made, is called *event-driven processing*.

Event-driven processing vs. long-running serving systems

Event-driven processing is different from the model serving systems that we've looked at in previous sections (e.g., systems using replicated services [section 4.2] and sharded services patterns [section 4.3]), where the servers that handle user requests are always up and running. Those long-running serving systems work well for many applications that are under heavy load, keep a large amount of data in memory, or require some sort of background processing.

However, for applications that handle very few requests during nonpeak periods or respond to specific events, such as our hotel price prediction system, the event-driven processing pattern is more suitable. This event-driven processing pattern has flourished in recent years as cloud providers have developed *function-as-a-service* products.

In our scenario, each model serving request made from our hotel price prediction system represents an *event*. Our serving system listens for this type of event, utilizes necessary resources from the shared resource pool, and retrieves and loads the trained machine learning model from the distributed database to estimate the hotel prices for the specified time/location query. Figure 4.16 is a diagram of this event-driven model serving system.

Using this event-driven processing pattern for our serving system, we can make sure that our system is using only the resources necessary to process every request without concerning ourselves with resource utilization and idling. As a result, the system has sufficient resources to deal with peak traffic and return the predicted prices without users experiencing noticeable delays or lags when using the system.

Even though we now have a shared pool of sufficient computational resources where we can borrow computational resources from the shared resource pool to handle user requests on demand, we should also build a mechanism in our model serving system to defend *denial-of-service attacks*. Denial-of-service attacks interrupt an authorized user's access to a computer network, typically caused with malicious intent and often seen in model serving systems. These attacks can cause unexpected use of computational resources from the shared resource pool, which may eventually lead to resource scarcity for other services that rely on the shared resource pool.

Denial-of-service attacks may happen in various cases. For example, they may come from users who accidentally send a huge amount of model serving requests in a very

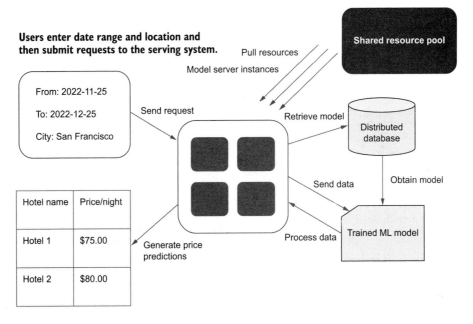

Figure 4.16   A diagram of the event-driven model serving system to predict hotel prices

short period of time. Developers may have misconfigured a client that uses our model serving APIs, so it sends requests constantly or accidentally kicks off an unexpected load/stress test in a production environment.

To deal with these situations, which often happen in real-world applications, it makes sense to introduce a defense mechanism for denial-of-service attacks. One approach to avoid these attacks is via *rate limiting*, which adds the model serving requests to a queue and limits the rate the system is processing the requests in the queue.

Figure 4.17 is a flowchart showing four model serving requests sent to the model serving system. However, only two are under the current rate limit, which allows a maximum of two concurrent model serving requests. In this case, the rate-limiting queue for model serving requests first checks whether the requests received are under the current rate limit. Once the system has finished processing those two requests, it will proceed to the remaining two requests in the queue.

If we are deploying and exposing an API for a model serving service to our users, it's also generally a best practice to have a relatively small rate limit (e.g., only one request is allowed within 1 hour) for users with anonymous access and then ask users to log in to obtain a higher rate limit. This system would allow the model serving system to better control and monitor the users' behavior and traffic so that we can take necessary actions to address any potential problems or denial-of-service attacks. For example, requiring a login provides auditing to find out which users/events are responsible for the unexpectedly large number of model serving requests.

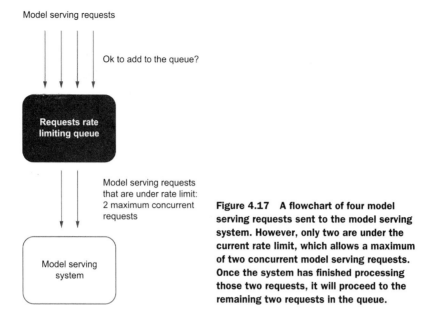

Figure 4.17   A flowchart of four model serving requests sent to the model serving system. However, only two are under the current rate limit, which allows a maximum of two concurrent model serving requests. Once the system has finished processing those two requests, it will proceed to the remaining two requests in the queue.

Figure 4.18 demonstrates the previously described strategy. In the diagram, the flow-chart on the left side is the same as figure 4.17 where four total model serving requests from unauthenticated users are sent to the model serving system. However,

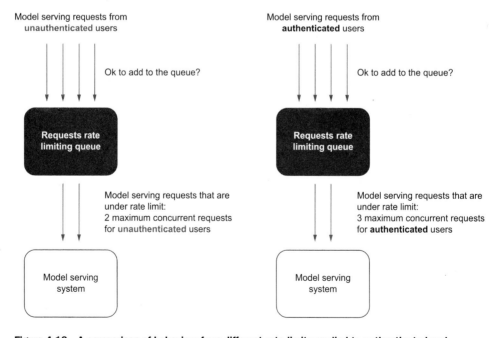

Figure 4.18   A comparison of behaviors from different rate limits applied to authenticated and unauthenticated users

only two can be served by the system due to the current rate limit, which allows a maximum of two concurrent model serving requests for unauthenticated users. Conversely, the model serving requests in the flowchart on the right side all come from authenticated users. Thus, three requests can be processed by the model serving system since the limit of maximum concurrent requests for authenticated users is three.

Rate limits differ depending on whether the user is authenticated. Rate limits thus effectively control the traffic of the model serving system and prevent malicious denial-of-service attacks, which could cause unexpected use of computational resources from the shared resource pool and eventually lead to resource scarcity of other services that rely on it.

4.4.3 Discussion

Even though we've seen how the event-driven processing pattern benefits our particular serving system, we should not attempt to use this pattern as a universal solution. The use of many tools and patterns can help you develop a distributed system to meet unique real-world requirements.

For machine learning applications with consistent traffic—for example, model predictions calculated regularly based on a schedule—an event-driven processing approach is unnecessary as the system already knows when to process the requests, and there will be too much overhead trying to monitor this regular traffic. In addition, applications that can tolerate less-accurate predictions can work well without being driven by events; they can also recalculate and provide good-enough predictions to a particular granularity level, such as per day or per week.

Event-driven processing is more suitable for applications with different traffic patterns that are complicated for the system to prepare beforehand necessary computational resources. With event-driven processing, the model serving system only requests a necessary amount of computational resources on demand. The applications can also provide more accurate and real-time predictions since they obtain the predictions right after the users send requests instead of relying on precalculated prediction results based on a schedule.

From developers' perspective, one benefit of the event-driven processing pattern is that it's very intuitive. For example, it greatly simplifies the process of deploying code to running services since there is no end artifact to create or push beyond the source code itself. The event-driven processing pattern makes it simple to deploy code from our laptops or web browser to run code in the cloud.

In our scenario, we only need to deploy the trained machine learning model that may be used as a *function* to be triggered based on user requests. Once deployed, this model serving function is then managed and scaled automatically without the need to allocate resources manually by developers. In other words, as more traffic is loaded onto the service, more instances of the model serving function are created to handle the increase in traffic using the shared resource pool. If the model serving function fails due to machine failures, it will be restarted automatically on other machines in the shared resource pool.

Given the nature of the event-driven processing pattern, each function that's used to process the model serving requests needs to be *stateless* and independent from other model serving requests. Each function instance cannot have local memory, which requires all states to be stored in a storage service. For example, if our machine learning models depend heavily on the results from previous predictions (e.g., a time-series model), in this case, the event-driven processing pattern may not be suitable.

4.4.4   Exercises

1 Suppose we allocate the same amount of computational resources over the lifetime of the model serving system for hotel price prediction. What would the resource utilization rate look like over time?
2 Are the replicated services or sharded services long-running systems?
3 Is event-driven processing stateless or stateful?

4.5   Answers to exercises

Section 4.2

1 Stateless
2 The model server replicas would not know which requests from users to process, and there will be potential conflicts or duplicate work when multiple model server replicas try to process the same requests.
3 Yes, only if the single server has no more than 1.4 minutes of downtime per day

Section 4.3

1 Yes, it helps, but it would decrease the overall resource utilization.
2 Stateful

Section 4.4

1 It varies over time depending on the traffic.
2 Yes. Servers are required to keep them running to accept user requests, and computational resources need to be allocated and occupied all the time.
3 Stateless

Summary

- Model serving is the process of loading a previously trained machine learning model, generating predictions, or making inferences on new input data.
- Replicated services help handle the growing number of model serving requests and achieve horizontal scaling with the help of replicated services.

- The sharded services pattern allows the system to handle large requests and efficiently distributes the workload of processing large model serving requests to multiple model server shards.
- With the event-driven processing pattern, we can ensure that our system only uses the resources necessary to process every request without worrying about resource utilization and idling.

Workflow patterns

This chapter covers

- Using workflows to connect machine learning system components
- Composing complex but maintainable structures within machine learning workflows with the fan-in and fan-out patterns
- Accelerating machine learning workloads with concurrent steps using synchronous and asynchronous patterns
- Improving performance with the step memoization pattern

Model serving is a critical step after successfully training a machine learning model. It is the final artifact produced by the entire machine learning workflow, and the results from model serving are presented to users directly. Previously, we explored some of the challenges involved in distributed model serving systems—for example, how to handle the growing number of model serving requests and the increased size of those requests—and investigated a few established patterns heavily adopted in industry. We learned how to achieve horizontal scaling with the help of replicated services to address these challenges and how the sharded services pattern can help

90

the system process large model serving requests. Finally, we learned how to assess model serving systems and determine whether an event-driven design would be beneficial in real-world scenarios.

Workflow is an essential component in machine learning systems as it connects all other components in the system. A machine learning workflow can be as easy as chaining data ingestion, model training, and model serving. However, it can be very complex to handle real-world scenarios requiring additional steps and performance optimizations as part of the entire workflow. It's essential to know what tradeoffs we may see when making design decisions to meet different business and performance requirements.

In this chapter, we'll explore some of the challenges involved when building machine learning workflows in practice. Each of these established patterns can be reused to build simple to complex machine learning workflows that are efficient and scalable. For example, we'll see how to build a system to execute complex machine learning workflows to train multiple machine learning models. We will use the fan-in and fan-out patterns to select the most performant models that provide good entity-tagging results in the model serving system. We'll also incorporate synchronous and asynchronous patterns to make machine learning workflows more efficient and avoid delays due to the long-running model training steps that block other consecutive steps.

5.1   What is workflow?

Workflow is the process of connecting multiple components or steps in an end-to-end machine learning system. A workflow consists of arbitrary combinations of the components commonly seen in real-world machine learning applications, such as data ingestion, distributed model training, and model serving, as discussed in the previous chapters.

Figure 5.1 shows a simple machine learning workflow. This workflow connects multiple components or steps in an end-to-end machine learning system that includes the following steps:

1 Data ingestion—Consumes the Youtube-8M videos dataset
2 Model training—Trains an entity-tagging model
3 Model serving—Tags entities in unseen videos

NOTE   A machine learning workflow is often referred to as a *machine learning pipeline*. I use these two terms interchangeably. Although I use different terms to refer to different technologies, there is no difference between the two terms in this book.

Since a machine learning workflow may consist of any combination of the components, we often see machine learning workflows in different forms in different situations. Unlike the straightforward workflow shown in figure 5.1, figure 5.2 illustrates a more complicated workflow where two separate model training steps are launched

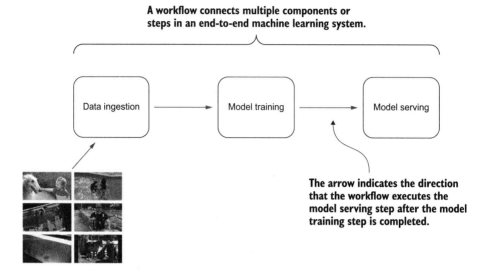

Figure 5.1   A diagram showing a simple machine learning workflow, including data ingestion, model training, and model serving. The arrows indicate directions. For example, the arrow on the right-hand side denotes the order of the step execution (e.g., the workflow executes the model serving step after the model training step is completed).

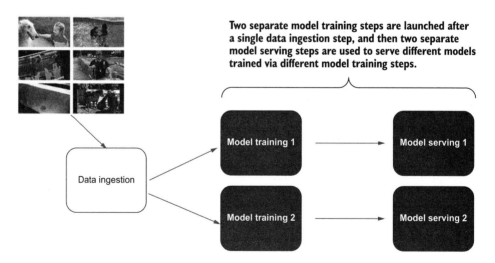

Figure 5.2   A more complicated workflow, where two separate model training steps are launched after a single data ingestion step, and then two separate model serving steps are used to serve different models trained via different model training steps

after a single data ingestion step, and then two separate model serving steps are used to serve different models trained via different model training steps.

Figures 5.1 and 5.2 are just some common examples. In practice, the complexity of machine learning workflows varies, which increases the difficulty of building and maintaining scalable machine learning systems.

We will discuss some of the more complex machine learning workflows in this chapter, but to start, I'll introduce and distinguish the differences between the following two concepts: *sequential workflow* and *directed acyclic graph (DAG)*.

A *sequential workflow* represents a series of steps performed one after another until the last step in the series is complete. The exact order of execution varies, but steps will always be sequential. Figure 5.3 is an example sequential workflow with three steps executed sequentially.

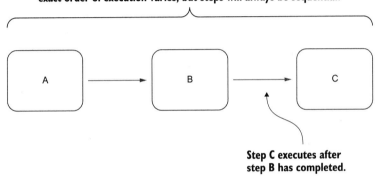

Figure 5.3   An example sequential workflow with three steps that execute in the following order: A, B, and C.

A workflow can be seen as a DAG if it only consists of steps directed from one step to another but never form a closed loop.

For example, the workflow in figure 5.3 is a valid DAG since the three steps are directed from step A to step B and then from step B to step C—the loop is not closed. Another example workflow, shown in figure 5.4, however, is not a valid DAG since there's an additional step D that connects from step C and points to step A, which forms a closed loop.

If step D does not point back to step A, as shown in figure 5.5, where the arrow is crossed out, this workflow becomes a valid DAG. The loop is no longer closed, and thus it becomes a simple sequential workflow, similar to figure 5.3.

In real-world machine learning applications, workflows necessary to meet the requirements of different use cases (e.g., batch retraining of the models, hyperparameter tuning experiments, etc.) can get really complicated. We will go through some more complex workflows and abstract the structural patterns that can be reused to compose workflows for various scenarios.

A workflow where there's an additional step D that connects
from step C and points to step A. These connections form a
closed loop and thus the entire workflow is not a valid DAG.

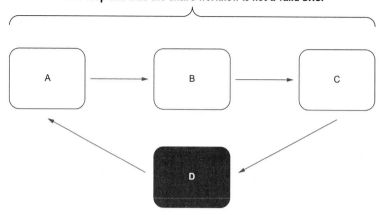

Figure 5.4   An example workflow where step D connects from step C and points
to step A. These connections form a closed loop and thus the entire workflow is
not a valid DAG.

This workflow becomes a valid DAG since the closed loop
no longer exists, and this becomes a simple sequential
workflow similar to what we've seen previously.

The closed loop no longer
exists since this arrow
is crossed out.

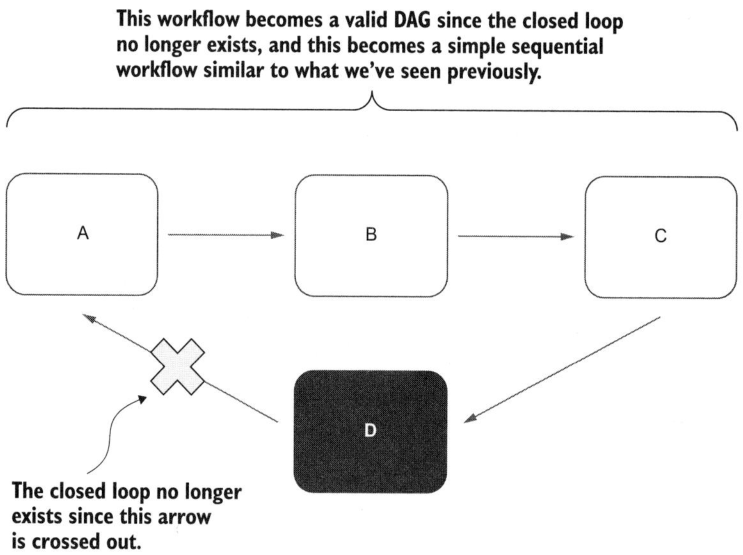

Figure 5.5   An example workflow where the last step D does not point back to
step A. This workflow is not a valid DAG since the closed loop no longer exists.
Instead, it is a simple sequential workflow similar to figure 5.3.

5.2 Fan-in and fan-out patterns: Composing complex machine learning workflows

In chapter 3, we built a machine learning model to tag the main themes of new videos that the model hadn't seen before using the YouTube-8M dataset. The YouTube-8M dataset consists of millions of YouTube video IDs, with high-quality machine-generated annotations from a diverse vocabulary of 3,800+ visual entities such as Food, Car, Music, etc. In chapter 4, we also discussed patterns that are helpful to build scalable model serving systems where users can upload new videos, and then the system loads the previously trained machine learning model to tag entities/themes that appear in the uploaded videos. In real-world applications, we often want to chain these steps together and package them in a way that can be easily reused and distributed.

For example, what if the original YouTube-8M dataset has been updated, and we'd like to train a new model from scratch using the same model architecture? In this case, it's pretty easy to containerize each of these components and chain them together in a machine learning workflow that can be reused by re-executing the end-to-end workflow when the data gets updated. As shown in figure 5.6, new videos are regularly being added to the original YouTube-8M dataset, and the workflow is executed every time the dataset is updated. The next model training step trains the entity-tagging model using the most recent dataset. Then, the last model serving step uses the trained model to tag entities in unseen videos.

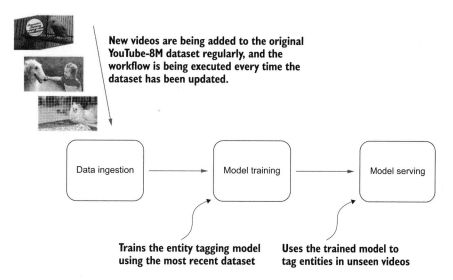

Figure 5.6 New videos are regularly added to the original YouTube-8M dataset, and the workflow is executed every time the dataset is updated.

Now, let's take a look at a more complex real-world scenario. Let's assume we know the implementation details for model training of any machine learning model architecture.

We want to build a machine learning system to train different models. We then want to use the top two models to generate predictions so that the entire system is less likely to miss any entities in the videos since the two models may capture information from different perspectives.

5.2.1   *The problem*

We want to build a machine learning workflow that would train different models after the system has ingested data from the data source. Then, we want to select the top two models and use the knowledge from both to provide model serving that generates predictions for users.

Building a workflow that includes the end-to-end normal process of a machine learning system with only data ingestion, model training, and model serving, where each component only appears once as an individual step in the workflow, is pretty straightforward. However, in our particular scenario, the workflow is much more complex as we need to include multiple model training steps as well as multiple model serving steps. How do we formalize and generalize the structure of this complex workflow so that it can be easily packaged, reused, and distributed?

5.2.2   *The solution*

Let's start with the most basic machine learning workflow that includes only data ingestion, model training, and model serving, where each of these components only appears once as an individual step in the workflow. We will build our system based on this workflow to serve as our baseline, as shown in figure 5.7.

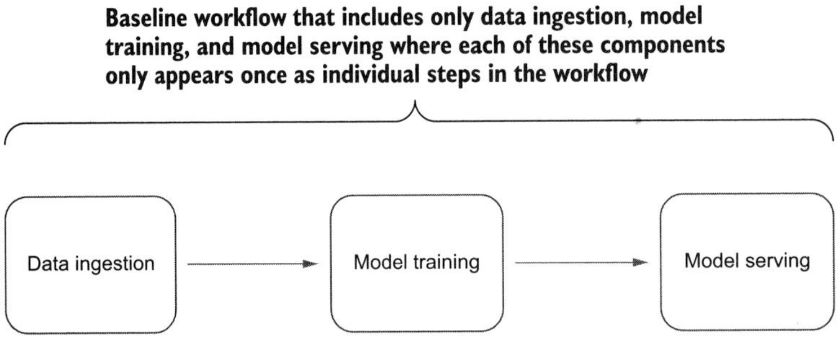

Baseline workflow that includes only data ingestion, model training, and model serving where each of these components only appears once as individual steps in the workflow

Data ingestion → Model training → Model serving

Figure 5.7   A baseline workflow including only data ingestion, model training, and model serving, where each of these components only appears once as an individual step in the workflow

Our goal is to represent the machine learning workflow that builds and selects the top two best-performing models that will be used for model serving to give better inference results. Let's take a moment to understand why this approach might be used in practice. For example, figure 5.8 shows two models: the first model has knowledge of four entities, and the second model has knowledge of three entities. Thus, each can tag the entities it knows from the videos. We can use both models to tag entities at the same time and then aggregate their results. The aggregated result is obviously more knowledgeable and is able to cover more entities. In other words, two models can be more effective and produce more comprehensive entity-tagging results.

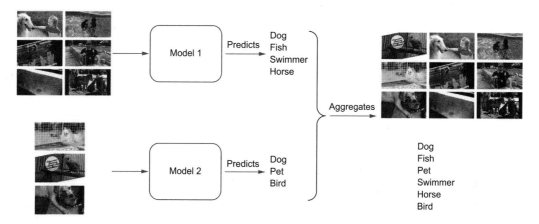

Figure 5.8 A diagram of models where the first model has knowledge of four entities and the second model has knowledge of three entities. Thus, each can tag the entities it knows from the videos. We can use both models to tag entities at the same time and then aggregate their results. The aggregated result covers more entities than each individual model.

Now that we understand the motivation behind building this complex workflow, let's look at an overview of the entire end-to-end workflow process. We want to build a machine learning workflow that performs the following functions sequentially:

1 Ingests data from the same data source
2 Trains multiple different models, either different sets of hyperparameters of the same model architecture or various model architectures
3 Picks the two top-performing models to be used for model serving for each of the trained models
4 Aggregates the models' results of the two model serving systems to present to users

Let's first add some placeholders to the baseline workflow for multiple model training steps after data ingestion. We can then add multiple model serving steps once the multiple model training steps finish. A diagram of the enhanced baseline workflow is shown in figure 5.9.

The key difference from what we've dealt with before in the baseline is the presence of multiple model training and model serving components. The steps do not have direct, one-to-one relationships. For example, each model training step may be connected to a single model serving step or not connected to any steps at all.

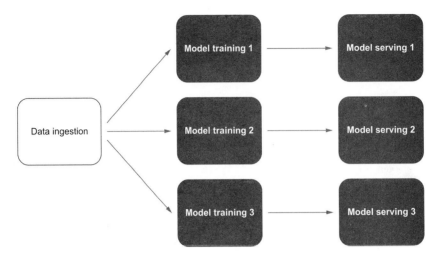

Figure 5.9   A diagram of the enhanced baseline workflow where multiple model training steps occur after data ingestion, followed by multiple model serving steps

Figure 5.10 shows that the models trained from the first two model training steps out-perform the model trained from the third model training step. Thus, only the first two model training steps are connected to the model serving steps.

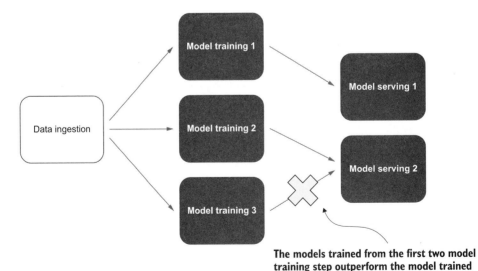

The models trained from the first two model training step outperform the model trained from the third model training step. Thus, only the first two model training steps are connected to model serving steps.

Figure 5.10   The models trained from the first two model training steps outperform the model trained from the third model training step. Thus, only the first two model training steps are connected to the model serving steps.

We can compose this workflow as follows. On successful data ingestion, multiple model training steps are connected to the data ingestion step so that they can use the shared data that's ingested and cleaned from the original data source. Next, a single step is connected to the model training steps to select the top two performing models. It produces two model serving steps that use the selected models to handle model serving requests from users. A final step at the end of this machine learning workflow is connected to the two model serving steps to aggregate the model inference results that will be presented to the users.

A diagram of the complete workflow is shown in figure 5.11. This workflow trains different models via three model training steps resulting in varying accuracy when tagging entities. A model selection step picks the top two models with at least 90% accuracy trained from the first two model training steps that will be used in the following two separate model serving steps. The results from the two model serving steps are then aggregated to present to users via a result aggregation step.

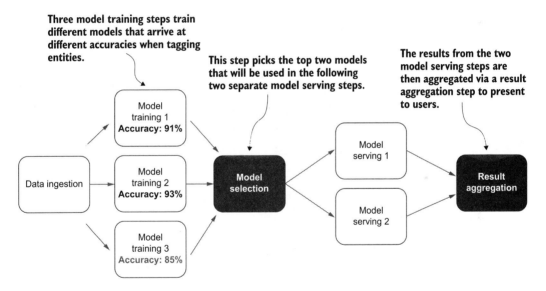

Figure 5.11   A machine learning workflow that trains different models that result in varying accuracy when tagging entities and then selects the top two models with at least 90% accuracy to be used for model serving. The results from the two model serving steps are then aggregated to present to users.

We can abstract out two patterns from this complex workflow. The first one we observe is the *fan-out* pattern. Fan-out describes the process of starting multiple separate steps to handle input from the workflow. In our workflow, the fan-out pattern appears when multiple separate model training steps connect to the data ingestion step, as shown in figure 5.12.

There's also the *fan-in* pattern in our workflow, where we have one single aggregation step that combines the results from the two model serving steps, as shown in

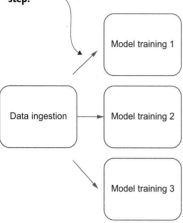

Fanning out to three separate model training steps from one data ingestion step.

Model training 1

Data ingestion

Model training 2

Model training 3

Figure 5.12 A diagram of the fan-out pattern that appears when multiple separate model training steps are connected to the data ingestion step

figure 5.13. Fan-in describes the process of combining results from multiple steps into one step.

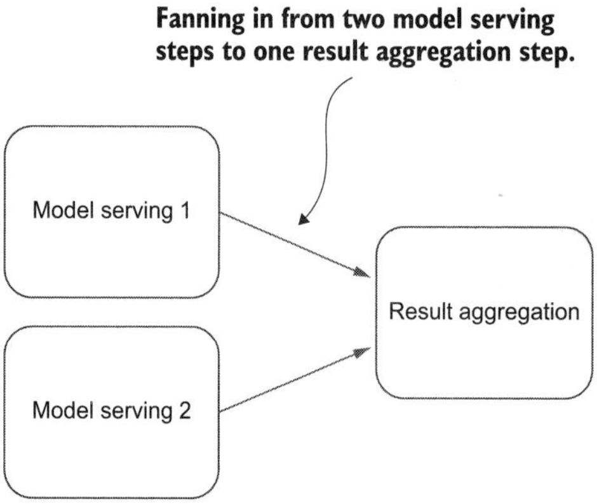

Fanning in from two model serving steps to one result aggregation step.

Model serving 1

Model serving 2

Result aggregation

Figure 5.13 A diagram of the fan-in pattern, where we have one single aggregation step that combines the results from the two model serving steps

Formalizing these patterns would help us build and organize more complex workflows by using different patterns for workflows based on real-world requirements.

We have successfully built the system as a complex workflow that trains different models and then uses the top two models to generate predictions so that the entire system is less likely to miss any entities in the videos. These patterns are powerful when constructing complex workflows to meet real-world requirements. We can construct various workflows, from a single data processing step to multiple model training steps to train different models with the same dataset. We can also start more than one model serving step from each of these model training steps if the predictions from different models are useful in real-world applications. We'll apply this pattern in section 9.4.1.

5.2.3   Discussion

By using the fan-in and fan-out patterns in the system, the system is now able to execute complex workflows that train multiple machine learning models and pick the most performant ones to provide good entity-tagging results in the model serving system.

These patterns are great abstractions that can be incorporated into very complex workflows to meet the increasing demand for complex distributed machine learning workflows in the real world. But what kind of workflows are suitable for the fan-in and fan-out patterns? In general, if both of the following applies, we can consider incorporating these patterns:

- The multiple steps that we are fanning-in or fanning-out are independent of each other.
- It takes a long time for these steps to run sequentially.

The multiple steps need to be order-independent because we don't know the order in which concurrent copies of those steps will run or the order in which they will return. For example, if the workflow also contains a step that trains an ensemble of other models (also known as *ensemble learning*; http://mng.bz/N2vn) to provide a better-aggregated model, this ensemble model depends on the completion of other model training steps. Consequently, we cannot use the fan-in pattern because the ensemble model training step will need to wait for other model training to complete before it can start running, which would require some extra waiting and delay the entire workflow.

> **Ensemble models**
>
> An ensemble model uses multiple machine learning models to obtain better predictive performance than could be obtained from any of the constituent models alone. It often consists of a number of alternative models that can learn the relationships in the dataset from different perspectives.
>
> Ensemble models tend to yield better results when diversity among the constituent models is significant. Therefore, many ensemble approaches try to increase the diversity of the models they combine.

The fan-in and fan-out patterns can create very complex workflows that meet most of the requirements of machine learning systems. However, to achieve good performance on those complex workflows, we need to determine which parts of the workflows to run first and which parts of the workflows can be executed in parallel. As a result of the optimization, data science teams would spend less time waiting for workflows to complete, thus reducing infrastructure costs. I will introduce some patterns to help us organize the steps in the workflow from a computational perspective in the next section.

5.2.4   *Exercises*

1   If the steps are not independent of each other, can we use the fan-in or fan-out patterns?

2   What's the main problem when trying to build ensemble models with the fan-in pattern?

5.3   Synchronous and asynchronous patterns: Accelerating workflows with concurrency

Each model training step in the system takes a long time to complete; however, their durations may vary across different model architectures or model parameters. Imagine an extreme case where one of the model training steps takes two weeks to complete since it is training a complex machine learning model that requires a huge amount of computational resources. All other model training steps only take one week to complete. Many of the steps, such as model selection and model serving, in the machine learning workflow we built earlier that uses the fan-in and fan-out patterns will have to wait an additional week until this long-running model training step is completed. A diagram that illustrates the duration differences among the three model training steps is shown in figure 5.14.

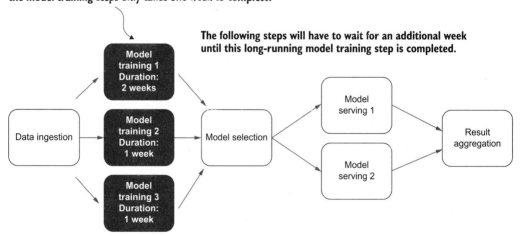

Figure 5.14   A workflow that illustrates the duration differences for the three model training steps

In this case, since the model selection step and the steps following it require all model training steps to finish, the model training step that takes two weeks to complete will slow down the workflow by an entire week. We would rather use that additional week to re-execute all the model training steps that take one week to complete instead of wasting time waiting for one step!

5.3.1 The problem

We want to build a machine learning workflow that trains different models and then selects the top two models to use for model serving, which generates predictions based on the knowledge of both models. Due to varying completion times for each model training step in the existing machine learning workflow, the start of the following steps, such as the model selection step and the model serving, depends on the completion of the previous steps.

However, a problem occurs when at least one of the model training steps takes much longer to complete than the remaining steps because the model selection step that follows can only start after this long model training step has completed. As a result, the entire workflow is delayed by this particularly long-running step. Is there a way to accelerate this workflow so it will not be affected by the duration of individual steps?

5.3.2 The solution

We want to build the same machine learning workflow as we did previously, which would train different models after the system has ingested data from the data source, select the top two models, and then use these two models to provide model serving to generate predictions using knowledge from both models.

However, this time we noticed a performance bottleneck because the start of each following step, such as model selection and model serving, depends on the completion of its previous steps. In our case, we have one long-running model training step that must complete before we can proceed to the next step.

What if we can exclude the long-running model training step completely? Once we do that, the rest of the model training steps will have consistent completion times. Thus, the remaining steps in the workflow can be executed without waiting for a particular step that's still running. A diagram of the updated workflow is shown in figure 5.15.

This naive approach may resolve our problem of extra waiting time for long-running steps. However, our original goal was to use this type of complex workflow to experiment with different machine learning model architectures and different sets of hyperparameters of those models to select the best-performing models to use for model serving. If we simply exclude the long-running model training step, we are essentially throwing away the opportunity to experiment with advanced models that may better capture the entities in the videos.

Is there a better way to speed up the workflow so that it will not be affected by the duration of this individual step? Let's focus on the model training steps that only take one week to complete. What can we do when those short-running model training steps are complete?

After the long-running model training step is excluded, the rest
of the model training steps will have consistent completion time.
Thus, the remaining steps in the workflow can be executed without
having to wait for any particular step that's still running.

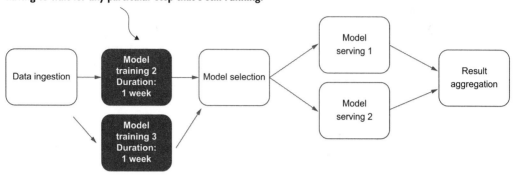

Figure 5.15   The new workflow after the long-running model training step has been removed

When a model training step finishes, we have successfully obtained a trained machine learning model. In fact, we can use this trained model in our model serving system without waiting for the rest of the model training steps to complete. As a result, the users can see the results of tagged entities from their model serving requests that contain videos as soon as we have trained one model from one of the steps in the workflow. A diagram of this workflow is shown in figure 5.16.

After a second model training step finishes, we can then pass the two trained models directly to model serving. The aggregated inference results are presented to

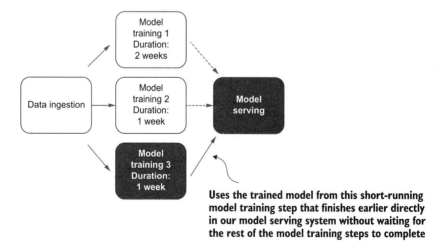

Uses the trained model from this short-running
model training step that finishes earlier directly
in our model serving system without waiting for
the rest of the model training steps to complete

Figure 5.16   A workflow where the trained model from a short-running model training step is applied directly to our model serving system without waiting for the remaining model training steps to complete

users instead of the results from only the model we obtained initially, as shown in figure 5.17.

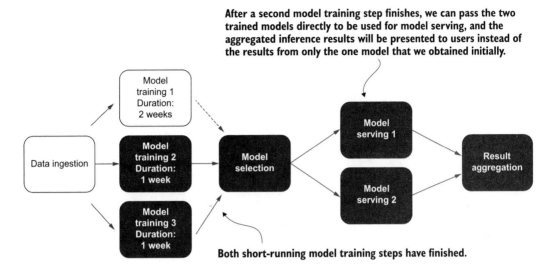

Figure 5.17   After a second model training step finishes, we pass the two trained models directly to model serving. The aggregated inference results are presented to users instead of only the results from the model that we obtained initially.

Note that while we can continue to use the trained models for model selection and model serving, the long-running model training step is still running. In other words, the steps are executed *asynchronously*—they don't depend on each other's completion. The workflow starts executing the next step before the previous step finishes.

Sequential steps are performed one at a time, and only when one has completed does the following step become unblocked. In other words, you must wait for a step to finish to move to the next one. For example, the data ingestion step must be completed before we start any of the model training steps.

Contrary to asynchronous steps, synchronous steps can start running at the same time once dependencies are met. For example, the model training steps can run concurrently, as soon as the previous data ingestion step has finished. A different model training step does not have to wait for another to start. The synchronous pattern is typically useful when you have multiple similar workloads that can run concurrently and finish near the same time.

By incorporating these patterns, the entire workflow will no longer be blocked by the long-running model training step. Instead, it can continue using the already-trained models from the short-running model training steps in the model serving system, which can start handling users' model serving requests.

The synchronous and asynchronous patterns are also extremely useful in other distributed systems to optimize system performance and maximize the use of existing computational resources—especially when the amount of computational resources for heavy workloads is limited. We'll apply this pattern in section 9.4.1.

5.3.3   *Discussion*

By mixing synchronous and asynchronous patterns, we can create more efficient machine learning workflows and avoid any delays due to steps that prevent others from executing, such as a long-running model training step. However, the models trained from the short-running model training steps may not be very accurate. That is, the models with simpler architectures may not discover as many entities in the videos as the more complex model of the long-running model training step (figure 5.18).

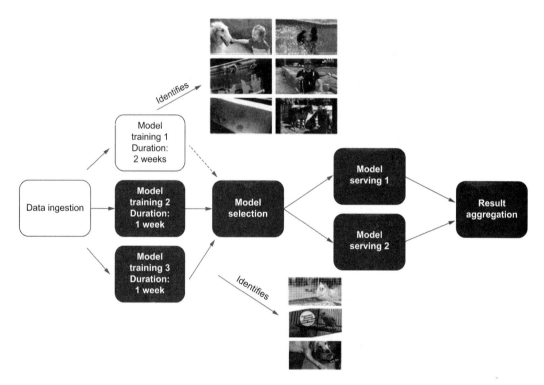

Figure 5.18   A model trained from two finished short-running model training steps with very simple models that serve as a baseline. They can only identify a small number of entities, whereas the model trained from the most time-consuming step can identify many more entities.

As a result, we should keep in mind that the models we get early on may not be the best and may only be able to tag a small number of entities, which may not be satisfactory to our users.

When we deploy this end-to-end workflow to real-world applications, we need to consider whether users seeing inference results faster or seeing better results is more important. If the goal is to allow users to see the inference results as soon as a new model is available, they may not see the results they were expecting. However, if users can tolerate a certain period of delay, it's better to wait for more model training steps to finish. Then, we can be selective about the models we've trained and pick the best-performing models that provide very good entity-tagging results. Whether a delay is acceptable is subject to the requirements of real-world applications.

By using synchronous and asynchronous patterns, we can organize the steps in machine learning workflows from structural and computational perspectives. As a result, data science teams can spend less time waiting for workflows to complete to maximize performance, thus reducing infrastructure costs and idling computational resources. In the next section, we'll introduce another pattern used very often in real-world systems that can save more computational resources and make workflows run even faster.

5.3.4 Exercises

1 What causes each step of the model training steps to start?
2 Are the steps blocking each other if they are running asynchronously?
3 What do we need to consider when deciding whether we want to use any available trained model as early as possible?

5.4 Step memoization pattern: Skipping redundant workloads via memoized steps

With the fan-in and fan-out patterns in the workflow, the system can execute complex workflows that train multiple machine learning models and pick the most performant models to provide good entity-tagging results in the model serving system. The workflows we've seen in this chapter contain only a single data ingestion step. In other words, the data ingestion step in the workflows always executes first before the remaining steps, such as model training and model serving, can begin to process.

Unfortunately, in real-world machine learning applications, the dataset does not always remain unchanged. Now, imagine that new YouTube videos are becoming available and are being added to the YouTube-8M dataset every week. Following our existing workflow architecture, if we would like to retrain the model so that it accounts for the additional videos that arrive on a regular basis, we need to run the entire workflow regularly from scratch—from the data ingestion step to the model serving step—as shown in figure 5.19.

Say the dataset does not change, but we want to experiment with new model architectures or new sets of hyperparameters, which is very common for machine learning practitioners (figure 5.20). For example, we may change the model architecture from simple linear models to more complex models such as tree-based models or convolutional neural networks. We can also stick with the particular model architecture we've used and only change the set of model hyperparameters, such as the number of layers and hidden units in each of those layers for neural network models or the maximum depth of each tree for tree-based models. For cases like these, we

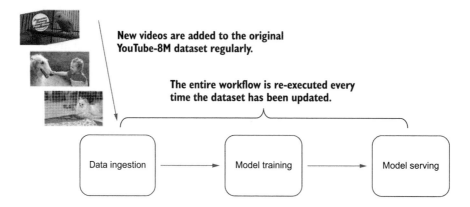

Figure 5.19   A diagram of the entire workflow that is re-executed every time the dataset is updated

still need to run the end-to-end workflow, which includes the data ingestion step to re-ingest the data from the original data source from scratch. Performing data ingestion again is very time-consuming.

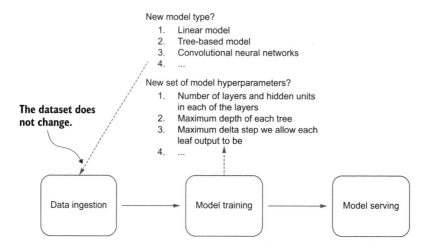

Figure 5.20   A diagram where the entire workflow is re-executed every time we experiment with a new model type or hyperparameter even though the dataset has not changed

5.4.1   *The problem*

Machine learning workflows usually start with a data ingestion step. If the dataset is being updated regularly, we may want to rerun the entire workflow to train a fresh machine learning model that takes the new data into account. To do so, we need to execute the data ingestion step every time. Alternatively, if the dataset is not updated, but we want to experiment with new models, we still need to execute the entire workflow, including the data ingestion step. However, the data ingestion step can take a long time to complete depending on the size of the dataset. Is there a way to make this workflow more efficient?

5.4.2 *The solution*

Given how time-consuming data ingestion steps usually are, we probably don't want to re-execute it to retrain or update our entity tagging models every time the workflow runs. Let's first think about the root cause of this problem. The dataset of YouTube videos is being updated regularly, and the new data is persisted to the data source on a regular basis (e.g., once a month).

We have two use cases in which we need to re-execute the entire machine learning workflow:

- After the dataset has been updated, rerun the workflow to train a new model that uses the updated dataset.
- We want to experiment with a new model architecture using that dataset that's already ingested, which may not have been updated yet.

The fundamental problem is the time-consuming data ingestion step. With the current workflow architecture, the data ingestion step will need to be executed regardless of whether the dataset has been updated.

Ideally, if the new data has not been updated, we don't want to re-ingest the data that's already collected. In other words, we would like to execute the data ingestion step only when we know that the dataset has been updated, as shown in figure 5.21.

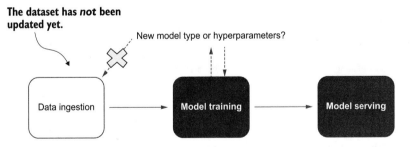

Figure 5.21 A diagram where the data ingestion step is skipped when the dataset has not been updated

Now the challenge comes down to determining whether the dataset has been updated. Once we have a way to identify that, we can conditionally reconstruct the machine learning workflow and control whether we want to include a data ingestion step to be re-executed (figure 5.21).

One way to identify whether the dataset has been updated is through the use of cache. Since our dataset is being updated regularly on a fixed schedule (e.g., once a month), we can create a *time-based cache* that stores the location of the ingested and cleaned dataset (assuming the dataset is located in a remote database) and the time-stamp of its last updated time. The data ingestion step in the workflow will then be constructed and executed dynamically based on whether the last updated timestamp is within a particular window. For example, if the time window is set to two weeks, we consider the ingested data as fresh if it has been updated within the past two weeks. The data ingestion step will be skipped, and the following model training steps will use the already-ingested dataset from the location that's stored in the cache.

Figure 5.22 illustrates the case where a workflow has been triggered, and we check whether the data has been updated within the last two weeks by accessing the cache. If the data is fresh, we skip the execution of the unnecessary data ingestion step and execute the model training step directly.

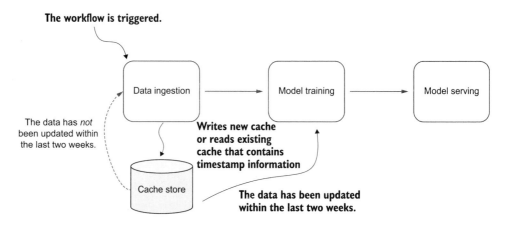

Figure 5.22   The workflow has been triggered, and we check whether the data has been updated within the last two weeks by accessing the cache. If the data is fresh, we skip the execution of the unnecessary data ingestion step and execute the model training step directly.

The time window can be used to control how old a cache can be before we consider the dataset fresh enough to be used directly for model training instead of re-ingesting the data again from scratch.

Alternatively, we can store some of the important metadata about the data source in the cache, such as the number of records in the original data source currently available. This type of cache is called *content-based cache* since it stores information extracted from a particular step, such as the input and output information. With this type of cache, we can identify whether the data source has significant changes (e.g., the number of original records has doubled in the data source). If there's a significant change, it's usually a signal to re-execute the data ingestion step since the current dataset is very old and outdated. A workflow that illustrates this approach is shown in figure 5.23.

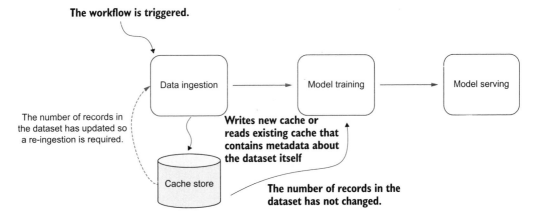

Figure 5.23   The workflow has been triggered, and we check whether the metadata collected from the dataset, such as the number of records in the dataset, has changed significantly. If it's not significant, we then skip the execution of the unnecessary data ingestion step and execute the model training step directly.

This pattern, which uses the cache to determine whether a step should be executed or skipped, is called *step memoization*. With the help of step memoization, a workflow can identify the steps with redundant workloads that can be skipped without being re-executed and thus greatly accelerate the execution of the end-to-end workflow. We'll apply this pattern in section 9.4.2.

5.4.3   Discussion

In real-world machine learning applications, many workloads besides data ingestion are computationally heavy and time-consuming. For example, the model training step uses a lot of computational resources to achieve high-performance model training and can sometimes take weeks to complete. If we are only experimenting with other components that do not require updating the trained model, it might make sense to avoid re-executing the expensive model training step. The step memoization pattern comes in handy when deciding whether you can skip heavy and redundant steps.

If we are creating content-based caches, the decision about the type of information to extract and store in the cache may not be trivial. For example, if we are trying to cache the results from a model training step, we may want to consider using the trained model artifact that includes information such as the type of machine learning model and the set of hyperparameters of the model. When the workflow is executed again, it will decide whether to re-execute the model training step based on whether we are trying the same model. Alternatively, we may store information like the performance statistics (e.g., accuracy, mean-squared error, etc.) to identify whether it's beyond a threshold and worth training a more performant model.

Furthermore, when applying the step memoization pattern in practice, be aware that it requires a certain level of maintenance efforts to manage the life cycle of the created cache. For example, if 1,000 machine learning workflows run every day with an average of 100 steps for each workflow being memoized, 100,000 caches will be created every day. Depending on the type of information they store, these caches require a certain amount of space that can accumulate rather quickly.

To apply this pattern at scale, a garbage collection mechanism must be in place to delete unnecessary caches automatically to prevent the accumulation of caches from taking up a huge amount of disk space. For example, one simple strategy is to record the timestamp when the cache is last hit and used by a step in a workflow and then scan the existing caches periodically to clean up those that are not used or hit after a long time.

5.4.4 Exercises

1 What type of steps can most benefit from step memoization?
2 How do we tell whether a step's execution can be skipped if its workflow has been triggered to run again?
3 What do we need to manage and maintain once we've used the pattern to apply the pattern at scale?

5.5   Answers to exercises

Section 5.2

1 No, because we have no guarantee in what order concurrent copies of those steps will run
2 Training an ensemble model depends on completing other model training steps for the sub-models. We cannot use the fan-in pattern because the ensemble model training step will need to wait for other model training to complete before it can start running, which would require some extra waiting and delay the entire workflow.

Section 5.3

1 Due to the variation in completion times for each model training step in the existing machine learning workflow, the start of each following step, such as model selection and model serving, depends on the completion of the previous step.
2 No, asynchronous steps won't block each other.
3 We need to consider whether we want to use any available trained model as early as possible from the user's perspective. We should think about whether it's more important for users to see inference results faster or see better results. If the goal is to allow users to see the inference results as soon as a new model is

available, those results may not be good enough or what users are expecting. Alternatively, if certain delays are acceptable to users, waiting for more model training steps to finish is preferable. You can then be selective about the trained models and pick the best-performing models that will provide very good entity-tagging results.

Section 5.4

1 Steps that are time-consuming or require a huge amount of computational resources

2 We can use the information stored in the cache, such as when the cache is initially created or metadata collected from the step, to decide whether we should skip the execution of a particular step.

3 We need to set up a garbage collection mechanism to recycle and delete the created caches automatically.

Summary

- Workflow is an essential component in machine learning systems as it connects all other components in a machine learning system. A machine learning workflow can be as easy as chaining data ingestion, model training, and model serving.
- The fan-in and fan-out patterns can be incorporated into complex workflows to make them maintainable and composable.
- The synchronous and asynchronous patterns accelerate the machine learning workloads with the help of concurrency.
- The step memoization pattern improves the performance of workflows by skipping duplicate workloads.

Operation patterns

This chapter covers

- Recognizing areas of improvement in machine learning systems, such as job scheduling and metadata
- Preventing resource starvation and avoiding deadlocks using scheduling techniques, such as fair-share scheduling, priority scheduling, and gang scheduling
- Handling failures more effectively to reduce any negative effect on users via the metadata pattern

In chapter 5, we focused on machine learning workflows and the challenges of building them in practice. Workflow is an essential component in machine learning systems as it connects all components in the system. A machine learning workflow can be as easy as chaining data ingestion, model training, and model serving. It can also be very complex when handling real-world scenarios, requiring additional steps and performance optimizations to be part of the entire workflow.

Knowing the tradeoffs we may encounter when making design decisions to meet specific business and performance requirements is essential. I previously introduced a few established patterns commonly adopted in industry. Each pattern can be reused to build simple to complex machine learning workflows that are efficient and scalable. For example, we learned how to use the fan-in and fan-out patterns to build a system to execute complex machine learning workflows (section 5.2). This system can train multiple machine learning models and pick the most performant ones to provide good entity-tagging results. We also used synchronous and asynchronous patterns to make machine learning workflows more efficient and avoid delays due to the long-running model training steps that block other steps (section 5.3).

Since real-world distributed machine learning workflows can be extremely complex, as seen in chapter 5, a huge amount of *operational* work is involved to help maintain and manage the various components of the systems, such as improvements to system efficiency, observability, monitoring, deployment, etc. These operational work efforts usually require a lot of communication and collaboration between the DevOps and data science teams. For instance, the DevOps team may not have enough domain knowledge in machine learning algorithms used by the data science team to debug any encountered problems or optimize the underlying infrastructure to accelerate the machine learning workflows. For a data science team, the type of computational workload varies, depending on the team structure and the way team members collaborate. As a result, there's no universal way for the DevOps team to handle the requests of different workloads from the data science team.

Fortunately, operational efforts and patterns can be used to greatly accelerate the end-to-end workflow. They can also reduce maintenance and communication efforts when engineering teams are collaborating with teams of data scientists or machine learning practitioners before the systems become production ready.

In this chapter, we'll explore some of the challenges involved when performing operations on machine learning systems in practice and introduce a few commonly used patterns. For example, we'll use scheduling techniques to prevent resource starvation and avoid deadlocks when many team members are working collaboratively in the same cluster with limited computational resources. We will also discuss the benefits of the metadata pattern, which can provide insights into the individual steps in machine learning workflows and help us handle failures more appropriately to reduce any negative effects on users.

6.1   What are operations in machine learning systems?

In this chapter, I will focus on operational techniques and patterns that are commonly seen in more than one component or step in a machine learning workflow, instead of patterns that are specific to each individual component. For example, the workflow shown in figure 6.1 includes three failed steps in the multiple model training steps that occur after data ingestion and in the multiple model serving steps that occur after the multiple model training steps. Unfortunately, each step is like a black box, and we don't know many details about any of them yet. At this point, we only know whether they fail and whether the failures have affected the following steps. As a result, they are really hard to debug.

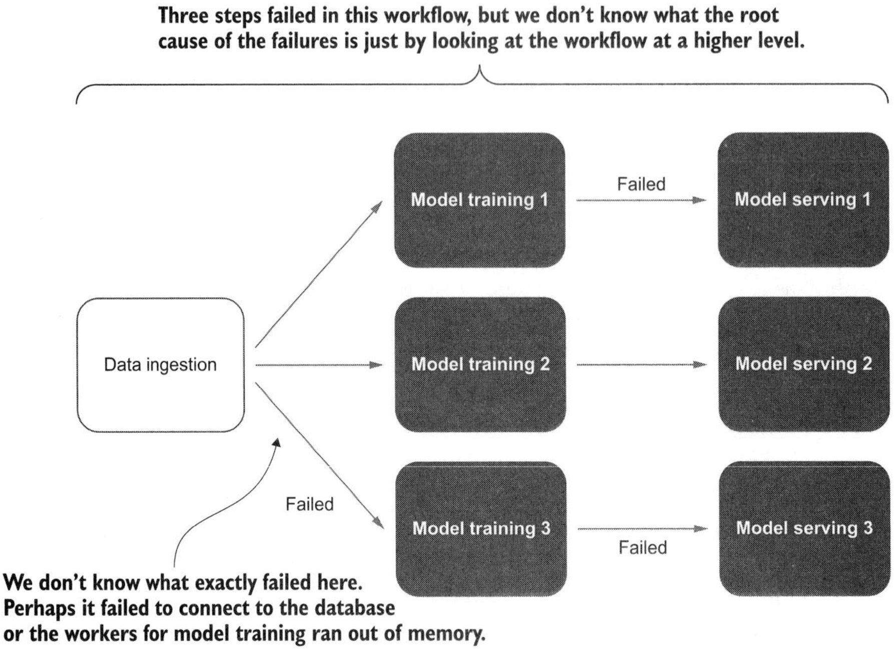

Three steps failed in this workflow, but we don't know what the root cause of the failures is just by looking at the workflow at a higher level.

We don't know what exactly failed here.
Perhaps it failed to connect to the database
or the workers for model training ran out of memory.

Figure 6.1   An example workflow where multiple model training steps occur after data ingestion and multiple model serving steps occur after the multiple model training steps. Note the three failed steps.

The operation patterns I introduce in this chapter can increase the visibility of the entire workflow to help us understand the root cause of the failures and give us some ideas on how to handle the failures properly. In addition, the increased observability may help us develop improvements in system efficiency that are beneficial to future executions of similar workflows.

What about MLOps?

We often hear about *MLOps* nowadays, which is a term derived from machine learning and operations. It usually means a collection of practices for managing machine learning lifecycles in production, including practices from machine learning and DevOps, to efficiently and reliably deploy and manage machine learning models in production.

MLOps usually require communication and collaboration between DevOps and data science teams. It focuses on improving the quality of production machine learning and embracing automation while maintaining business requirements. The scope of MLOps can be extremely large and varies depending on the context.

Given how large the scope of MLOps can be, depending on the context, I will only focus on a selected set of mature patterns at the time of writing. You can expect some updates to any future versions of this chapter as this field evolves.

6.2   Scheduling patterns: Assigning resources effectively in a shared cluster

Let's assume we have successfully set up the distributed infrastructure for users to submit distributed model training jobs that are scheduled to run on multiple CPUs by a default *scheduler*. A scheduler is responsible for assigning computational resources to perform tasks requested by the system. It is designed to keep computational resources busy and allow multiple users to collaborate with shared resources more easily. Multiple users are trying to build models using the shared computational resources in the cluster for different scenarios. For example, one user is working on a fraud detection model that tries to identify fraudulent financial behaviors such as international money laundering. Another user is working on a condition monitoring model that can generate a health score to represent the current condition for industrial assets such as components on trains, airplanes, wind turbines, etc.

Our beginning infrastructure only provides a simple scheduler, which schedules jobs on a first-come, first-served basis, as shown in figure 6.2. For example, the third job is scheduled after the second job has been scheduled, and each job's computational resources are allocated on scheduling.

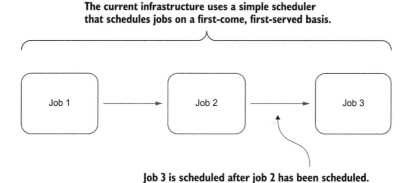

Figure 6.2   A diagram of an infrastructure that only provides a simple scheduler, which schedules jobs on a first-come, first-served basis

In other words, the users who schedule jobs later must wait for all previously submitted jobs to finish before their model training jobs can start executing. Unfortunately, in the real world, users often want to submit multiple model training jobs to experiment with different sets of models or hyperparameters. These multiple models block other users' model training jobs from executing since those previously submitted experiments are already utilizing all the available computational resources.

In this case, users must compete for resources (e.g., waking up in the middle of the night to submit model training jobs when fewer users are using the system). As a result, collaboration among team members may not be pleasant. Some jobs include training very large machine learning models, which usually consume a lot of computational resources and thus increase the time other users have to wait for their jobs to execute.

In addition, if we only schedule some of the requested workers for a distributed model training job, the model training cannot execute until all of the requested workers are ready; the nature of the distribution strategy is distributed training with the collective communication pattern. If necessary computational resources are lacking, the job will never start, and the already-allocated computational resources for the existing workers will be wasted.

6.2.1   *The problem*

We have set up a distributed infrastructure for users to submit distributed model training jobs scheduled to run by a default scheduler responsible for assigning computational resources to perform various tasks requested by the users. However, the default scheduler only provides a simple scheduler that schedules jobs on a first-come, first-served basis. As a result, when multiple users attempt to use this cluster, they often need to wait a long time for available computational resources—that is, until the previously submitted jobs are completed. In addition, distributed model training jobs cannot begin to execute until all of the requested workers are ready due to the nature of the distributed training strategy, such as a collective communication strategy. Are there any alternatives to the existing default scheduler so we could assign the computational resources more effectively in a shared cluster?

6.2.2   *The solution*

In our scenario, the problem starts to occur when multiple users are trying to use the system to submit distributed model training jobs at the same time. Since the jobs are being executed on a first-come, first-served basis, the waiting times for jobs submitted later are long, even when those jobs are submitted by multiple users.

It's easy to identify different users, so an intuitive solution would be to limit how much of the total computational resources each user is allotted. For example, say there are four users (A, B, C, and D). Once user A submits a job that uses 25% of the total available CPU cycles (https://techterms.com/definition/clockcycle), they cannot submit another job until those allocated resources are released and ready to be allocated to new jobs. Other users could submit jobs independent of how much resources user A is using. For example, if user B starts two processes that use the same amount of resources, those processes will be attributed 12.5% of the total CPU cycles each, giving user B 25% of total resources. Each of the other users still receives 25% of the total cycles. Figure 6.3 illustrates the resource allocations for these four users.

If a new user E starts a process on the system, the scheduler will reapportion the available CPU cycles so that each user gets 20% of the whole (100% / 5 = 20%). The way we schedule our workloads to execute in our cluster in figure 6.3 is called *fair-share scheduling*. It is a scheduling algorithm for computer operating systems in which the

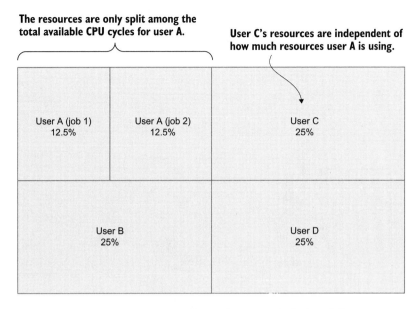

The resources are only split among the total available CPU cycles for user A.

User C's resources are independent of how much resources user A is using.

Figure 6.3 The resource allocations for the four users (A, B, C, and D)

CPU usage is equally distributed among system users or groups, as opposed to equal distribution among processes.

So far, we have only discussed partitioning resources among the users. When multiple teams are using the system to train their machine learning models and each team has multiple members, we can partition users into different groups and then apply the fair-share scheduling algorithm to both the users and the groups. Specifically, we first divide the available CPU cycles among the groups and then divide further among the users within each group. For example, if three groups contain three, two, and four users, respectively, each group will be able to use 33.3% (100% / 3) of the total available CPU cycles. We can then calculate the available CPU cycles for each user in each group as follows:

- *Group 1*—33.3% / 3 users = 11.1% per user
- *Group 2*—33.3% / 2 users = 16.7% per user
- *Group 3*—33.3% / 4 users = 8.3% per user

Figure 6.4 summarizes the resource allocation we calculated for each individual user in the three groups.

Fair-share scheduling would help us resolve the problem of multiple users running distributed training jobs concurrently. We can apply this scheduling strategy at each level of abstraction, such as processes, users, groups, etc. All users have their own pool of available resources without interfering with each other.

However, in some situations, certain jobs should be executed earlier. For example, a cluster administrator would like to submit jobs for cluster maintenance, such as

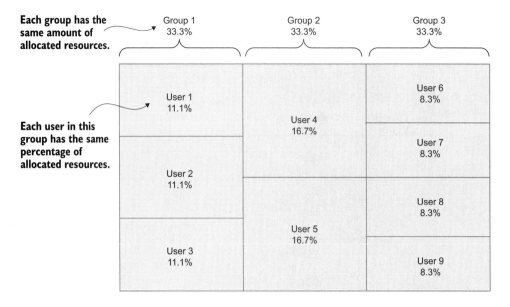

Figure 6.4   A summary of the resource allocation for each user in three groups

deleting jobs that have been stuck and taking up resources for a long time. Executing these cluster maintenance jobs earlier would help make more computational resources available and thus unblock others from submitting new jobs.

Let's assume the cluster administrator is user 1 in group 1. Two other nonadmin users are also in group 1, as in the previous example. User 2 is running job 1, which is using all of the 11.1% of the CPU cycles allocated to them based on the fair-share scheduling algorithm.

Even though user 2 has enough computational power to perform job 1, the job depends on the success of job 2 from user 3. For example, job 2 from user 3 produces a table in the database that job 1 needs to perform a distributed model training task. Figure 6.5 summarizes the resource allocations and usages for each user in the first group.

Unfortunately, job 2 is stuck due to an unstable database connection and keeps trying to reconnect to produce the data that job 1 needs. To fix the problem, the administrator needs to submit job 3 that kills and then restarts the stuck job 2.

Now assume that the admin user 1 is already using 11.1% of the total CPU cycles available. As a result, since maintenance job 3 is submitted later than all previous jobs, it is added to the job queue and waits to be executed when resources are released, based on the first-come, first-served nature of our fair-share scheduling algorithm. As a result, we encounter a *deadlock* where no job can proceed, as illustrated in figure 6.6.

To fix this problem, we can allow users to assign *priorities* to each of the jobs so that jobs with higher priority are executed earlier, in contrast to the first-come, first-served nature of the fair-share scheduling algorithm. In addition, the jobs that are already

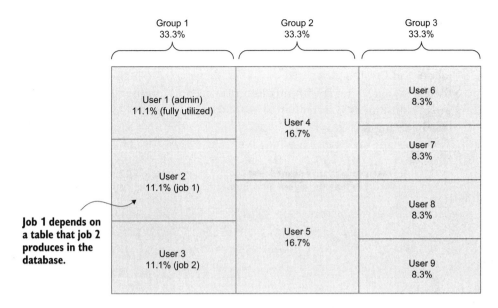

Figure 6.5   A summary of resource allocations and usages for each user in the first group

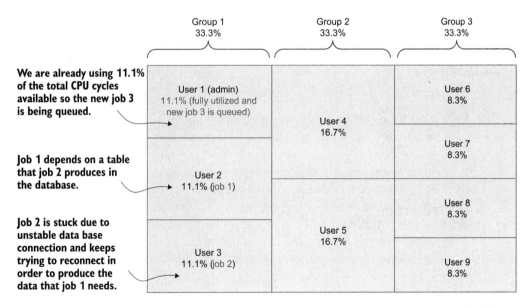

Figure 6.6   The admin user (user 1) in group 1 is trying to schedule a job to restart the stuck job (job 3) but encounters a deadlock where no job can proceed.

running can be *preempted* or *evicted* to make room for jobs with higher priorities if not enough computational resources are available. This way of scheduling jobs based on priorities is called *priority scheduling*.

Say, for example, four jobs (A, B, C, and D) have been submitted concurrently. Each job has been marked with priorities by the users. Jobs A and C are high priority, whereas job B is low priority, and job D is medium priority. With priority scheduling, jobs A and C will be executed first since they have the highest priorities, followed by the execution of job D with medium priority and, eventually low-priority job B. Figure 6.7 illustrates the order of execution for the four jobs (A, B, C, and D) when priority scheduling is used.

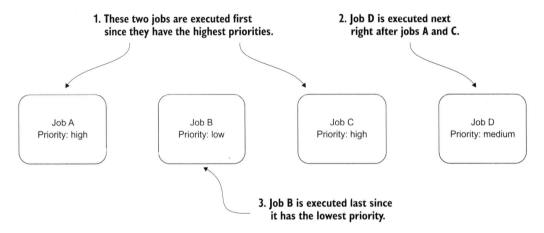

Figure 6.7   The order of execution for the four concurrently submitted jobs (A, B, C, and D) when priority scheduling is used

Let's consider another example. Assume three jobs (B, C, and D) with different priorities are submitted concurrently and are executed based on their priorities, similar to the previous example. If another job (job A) with high priority is submitted after job B, which is low priority, has already started running, job B will be preempted, and then job A will start. The computational resources previously allocated to job B will be released and taken over by job A. Figure 6.8 summarizes the order of execution for the four jobs (A, B, C, and D) where the low-priority job B already running is preempted by a new job (job A) with higher priority.

With priority scheduling, we can effectively eliminate the problem we previously encountered, where jobs can only be executed sequentially on a first-come, first-served basis. Jobs can now be preempted in favor of tasks with high priorities.

However, for distributed machine learning tasks—specifically, model training tasks—we want to ensure that all workers are ready before starting distributed training. Otherwise, the ones that are ready would be waiting for the remaining workers before the training can proceed, which wastes resources.

For example, in figure 6.9, three worker processes in the same process group are performing an allreduce operation. However, two workers are not ready because the

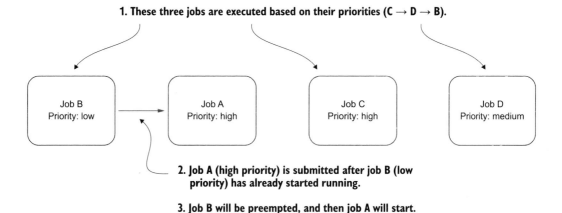

1. These three jobs are executed based on their priorities (C → D → B).

| Job B
Priority: low | Job A
Priority: high | Job C
Priority: high | Job D
Priority: medium |

2. Job A (high priority) is submitted after job B (low priority) has already started running.

3. Job B will be preempted, and then job A will start.

Figure 6.8   The order of execution for the four jobs (A, B, C, and D) where the running low-priority job is preempted by a new job with higher priority

underlying distributed cluster is experiencing an unstable network. As a result, two of the processes (processes 1 and 3) that depend on those affected communications would not receive some of the calculated gradient values (v0 and v2) on time (denoted by question marks in figure 6.9), and the entire allreduce operation is stuck until everything is received.

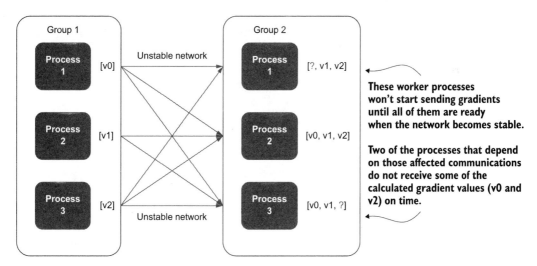

Figure 6.9   An example of the allreduce process with an unstable network between the worker processes that blocks the entire model training process

Gang scheduling is usually used to run distributed model training tasks. It ensures that if two or more workers communicate with each other, they will be ready to do so at the same time. In other words, gang scheduling only schedules workers when enough workers are available and ready to communicate.

If they are not gang scheduled, one worker may wait to send or receive a message while the other worker is sleeping, and vice versa. When the workers are waiting for other workers to be ready for communication, we are wasting allocated resources on the workers that are ready, and the entire distributed model training task is stuck.

For example, for collective communication–based distributed model training tasks, all workers must be ready to communicate the calculated gradients and update the models on each worker to complete an allreduce operation. I assume that the machine learning framework does not support elastic scheduling yet, which we will discuss in the next section. As shown in figure 6.10, the gradients are all denoted by question marks since they have not yet arrived in any of those worker processes in the second worker group. All worker processes have not yet started sending the gradients, and they won't until they all move to the ready state after the network stabilizes.

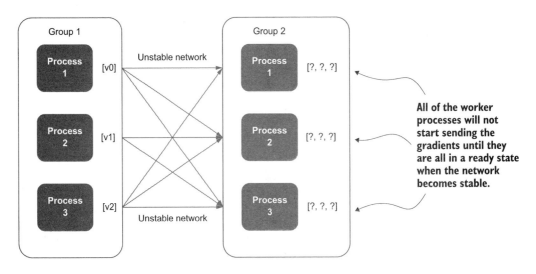

Figure 6.10 With gang scheduling, the worker processes will not start sending the gradients until they are all in the ready state after the network becomes stable.

With gang scheduling, we can make sure not to start any of the worker processes until all workers are ready, so none of them will be waiting for the remaining worker processes. As a result, we can avoid wasting computational resources. Once the network becomes stable, all of the gradients (v0, v1, and v2) arrive on each worker process after a successful allreduce operation, as shown in figure 6.11.

NOTE The details of different types of gang scheduling and their algorithms are out of the scope of this book and will not be discussed here. However, we will be using an existing open source framework to integrate gang scheduling into distributed training in the last part of the book.

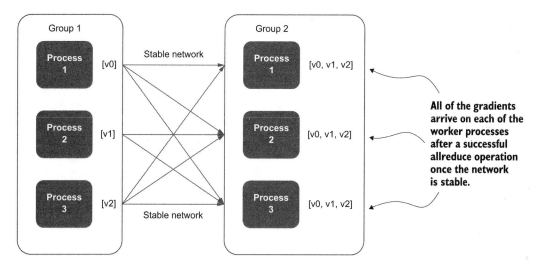

Figure 6.11   **All of the gradients arrive on each of the worker processes after a successful allreduce operation once the network is stable.**

By incorporating different scheduling patterns, we are able to address various problems that arise when multiple users are using the infrastructure to schedule different types of jobs. Although we looked at a few specific use cases for these scheduling patterns, the patterns can be found in many systems that require careful management of computational resources, especially when resources are scarce. Many scheduling techniques are applied to even lower-level operating systems to make sure the applications run efficiently and reasonably share resources.

6.2.3 Discussion

We've seen how fair-share scheduling can help us solve the problem of multiple users running distributed training jobs concurrently. Fair-share scheduling allows us to apply a scheduling strategy at each level of abstraction, such as processes, users, groups, etc. We also discussed priority scheduling, which can be used to effectively eliminate the problem we encounter when jobs can only be executed sequentially on a first-come, first-served basis. Priority scheduling allows jobs to be executed based on their priority levels, preempting low-priority jobs to make room for high-priority jobs.

With priority scheduling, if a cluster is used by a large number of users, a malicious user could create jobs at the highest possible priority, causing other jobs to be evicted or not get scheduled at all. To deal with this potential problem, administrators of real-world clusters usually enforce certain rules and limits to prevent users from creating a huge number of jobs at high priorities.

We also discussed gang scheduling, which ensures if two or more workers communicate with each other, they will all be ready to communicate at the same time. Gang scheduling is especially helpful for collective communication–based distributed model training jobs where all workers need to be ready to communicate the calculated gradients to avoid wasting computational resources.

Some machine learning frameworks support elastic scheduling (see chapter 3), which allows distributed model training jobs to start with any number of workers available without waiting for all the requested workers to be ready. In this case, gang scheduling is not suitable because we would need to wait for all workers to be ready. Instead, we can begin making significant progress toward model training with elastic scheduling.

Because the number of workers may change during model training, the batch size (sum of the size of mini-batches on each worker) will affect the model training accuracy. In that case, additional modifications to the model training strategy are needed. For example, we can support a customized learning rate scheduler that will account for epoch or batch or adjust the batch size dynamically based on the number of workers. Together with these algorithmic improvements, we can allocate and utilize existing computational resources more wisely and improve the user experience.

In practice, distributed model training jobs greatly benefit from scheduling patterns like gang scheduling. As a result, we can avoid wasting computational resources. However, one problem we might be neglecting is that any of these worker processes scheduled by gang scheduling may fail, leading to unexpected consequences. Often it's hard to debug these types of failures. In the next section, I'll introduce a pattern that will make debugging and handling failures easier.

6.2.4   *Exercises*

1   Can we only apply fair-share scheduling at the user level?
2   Is gang scheduling suitable for all distributed model training jobs?

6.3   *Metadata pattern: Handle failures appropriately to minimize the negative effect on users*

When building the most basic machine learning workflow that includes only data ingestion, model training, and model serving, where each component only appears once as an individual step in the workflow, everything seems pretty straightforward. Each step runs sequentially to reach completion. If any of these steps fail, we pick up where it's left off. For example, imagine the model training step has failed to take the ingested data (e.g., lost the connection to the database where the ingested data is stored). We can retry the failed step and easily continue model training without rerunning the entire data ingestion process, as shown in figure 6.12.

However, when the workflow gets more complicated, any failures are not trivial to handle. For example, consider the workflow from chapter 5. This workflow trains models via three model training steps that arrive at different accuracies when tagging entities. Then, a model selection step picks the top two models with at least 90% accuracy trained from the first two model training steps, which will be used in

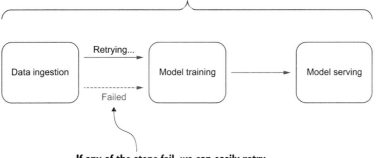

Baseline workflow that includes only data ingestion, model training, and model serving where each of these components only appears once as individual steps in the workflow

If any of the steps fail, we can easily retry the failed step and pick up from what's left.

Figure 6.12 A baseline workflow where the model training step has failed to take the ingested data. We retry the failed step and pick up from the failed step to continue model training without rerunning the entire data ingestion process.

the following two separate model serving steps. The results from the two model serving steps are then aggregated via a result aggregation step to present to users.

Now let's consider the case where the second and the third model training steps have both failed during execution (e.g., some of the workers allocated for model training are preempted). These two model training steps would have provided both the most and the least accurate model if they had finished successfully, as shown in figure 6.13.

At this point, one might think that we should rerun both steps to proceed to the model selection and model serving steps. However, in practice, since we already wasted some time training part of the models, we may not want to start everything from scratch. It would be much longer before our users can see the aggregated results from our best models. Is there a better way to handle such kinds of failures?

6.3.1 The problem

For complicated machine learning workflows, such as the one we discussed in chapter 5, where we want to train multiple models and then select the top-performing models for model serving, the decision on which strategy to use to handle failures of certain steps due to real-world requirements is not always trivial. For example, when two out of three model training steps fail due to preempted workers, we don't want to start training those models from scratch, which greatly increases the time needed to complete the workflow. How do we handle these failures appropriately so the negative effect on users can be minimized?

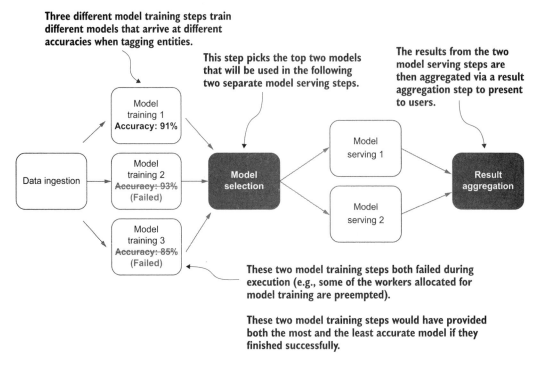

Figure 6.13   A machine learning workflow that trains models with different accuracies when tagging entities. The model selection step identifies the top two models with at least 90% accuracy to be used for model serving. The accuracies are crossed out in these two steps because the steps failed without arriving at the expected accuracies. The results from the two model serving steps are then aggregated to present to users.

6.3.2   *The solution*

Whenever we encounter a failure in a machine learning workflow, we should first understand the root cause (e.g., loss of network connections, lack of computational resources, etc). Knowing the root cause is important because we need to understand the nature of the failure to predict whether retrying the failed steps would help. If the failures are due to some long-lasting shortages that could very likely lead to repetitive failures when retrying, we could better utilize the computational resources to run some other tasks. Figure 6.14 illustrates the difference in the effectiveness of retrying for permanent and temporary failures. When we retry the model training step when encountering permanent failures, the retries are ineffective and lead to repetitive failures.

For example, in our case, we should first check whether the dependencies of a model training step are met, such as whether the ingested data from the previous step is still available. If the data has been persisted to a local disk to a database, we can proceed to model training. However, if the data was located in memory and lost when the model training step failed, we cannot start model training without ingesting the data again. Figure 6.15 shows the process of restarting the data ingestion step when there's a permanent failure during model training.

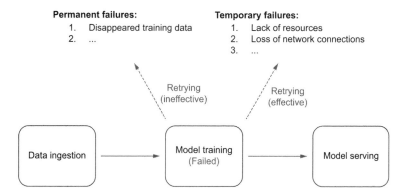

Figure 6.14 **The difference in the effectiveness of retrying for permanent and temporary failures**

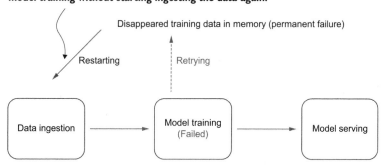

Figure 6.15 **The process of restarting the data ingestion step when a permanent failure occurs during model training**

Similarly, if the model training step fails due to preempted training workers or out-of-memory problems, we need to make sure we still have sufficient computational resources allocated to rerun the model training step.

However, we won't know what information to analyze to determine the root cause unless we intentionally record it as metadata during the runtime of each step in the entire machine learning workflow. For example, for each model training step, we can record metadata on the availability of the ingested data and whether different computational resources, such as memory and CPU usage, exceeded the limit before the step failed.

Figure 6.16 is a workflow where the model training step failed. Metadata is collected every 5 minutes on memory usage (in megabytes) and the availability of the training data (yes/no) during the runtime of this step. We can notice a sudden huge memory spike from 23 MB to 200 MB after 30 minutes. In this case, we can retry this step with an increase in requested memory, and it would then successfully produce a trained model that will be used for the next model serving step.

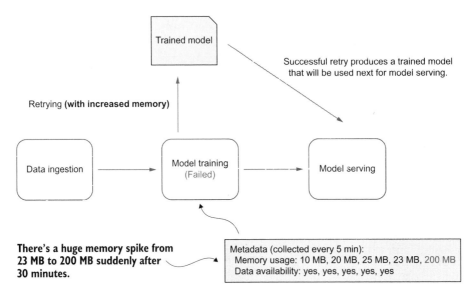

Figure 6.16   An example workflow where the model training step failed, with the metadata collected showing an unexpected memory spike during runtime

In practice, for complex workflows like in figure 6.13, even when we know all the dependencies of model training steps are met (e.g., we have enough computational resources and a good database connection to access the data source), we should also think about whether we want to handle the failures and how we'd like to handle them. We've spent a lot of time on the training steps already, but now, the steps have suddenly failed, and we've lost all the progress. In other words, we don't want to start re-training all the models from scratch, which may add considerable time before we can deliver the aggregated results from our best models to users. Is there a better way to handle this without a huge effect on our user experience?

In addition to the metadata we've recorded for each of the model training steps, we could save more useful metadata that can be used to figure out whether it's worth rerunning all the model training steps. For example, the model accuracy over time indicates whether the model is being trained effectively.

Model accuracy that remains steady or even decreases (from 30% to 27%, as shown in figure 6.17) may indicate that the model already converges and continuing training would no longer improve model accuracy. In this example, even though two model training steps fail, it's not necessary to retry the third model training step from scratch since it would lead to a model that converges fast but with low accuracy. Another example of metadata that can be potentially useful is the percentage of completed model training (e.g., if we've iterated through all the requested number of batches and epochs, the completion is 100%).

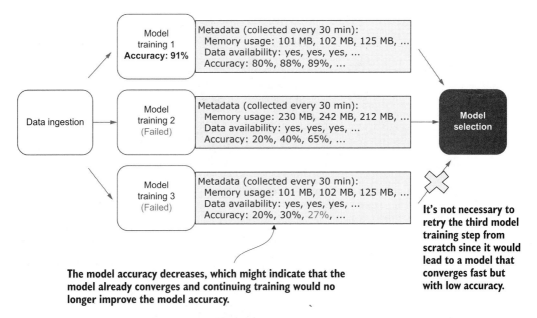

The model accuracy decreases, which might indicate that the model already converges and continuing training would no longer improve the model accuracy.

It's not necessary to retry the third model training step from scratch since it would lead to a model that converges fast but with low accuracy.

Figure 6.17   An example workflow where two model training steps fail and one has decreasing model accuracy

Once we have this additional metadata about model training steps, we can tell how well each started model training step progresses. For example, for the workflow in figure 6.18, we could potentially conclude ahead of time that the third model training step was progressing very slowly (only 1% of completion every 30 minutes) due to a smaller amount of allocated computational resources or more complex model architecture. We know that it's highly likely that, given the limited time, we end up with a model with low accuracy. As a result, we can disregard this model training step in favor of allocating more computational resources to the other model training steps with more potential, which leads to more accurate models faster.

Recording these metadata may help us derive more insights specific to each of the failed steps in the end-to-end machine learning workflow. We can then decide on a strategy to handle the failed steps appropriately to avoid wasting computational resources and minimize the effect on existing users. The metadata patterns provide great visibility into our machine learning pipelines. They can also be used to search, filter, and analyze the artifacts produced in each step in the future if we run a lot of pipelines on a regular basis. For example, we might want to know which models are

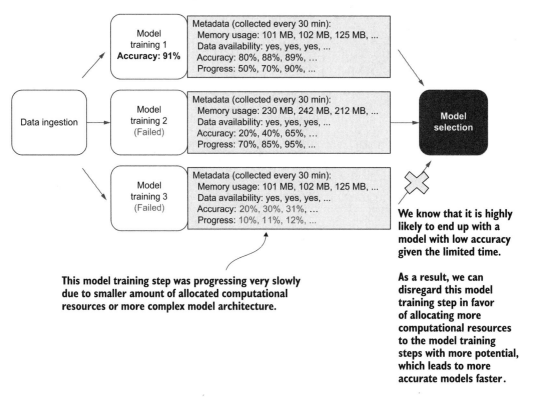

Figure 6.18   An example workflow where two model training steps fail. One is disregarded because it is progressing very slowly, and the model will likely have low accuracy given the limited time.

performant or which datasets contribute the most to those models based on the historical training metrics.

6.3.3   *Discussion*

With the help of the metadata pattern, we can gain additional insights into the individual steps in machine learning workflows. Then, if any fail, we can respond based on what's beneficial to our users and thus reduce any negative effect due to the step failures.

One common type of metadata is the various network performance (http://mng .bz/D4lR) metrics while the model is being trained (e.g., bandwidth, throughput, latency). This type of information is very useful for detecting when certain workers experience poor network performance that blocks the entire training process. We can take down slow workers and start new workers to continue training, assuming the underlying machine learning frameworks support elastic scheduling and fault-tolerance (see chapter 3). For example, in figure 6.19, based on the metadata, the worker on the right-hand side has extremely high latency (10 times the latency of the other workers), which slows down the entire model training process. Ideally, this worker would be taken down and restarted.

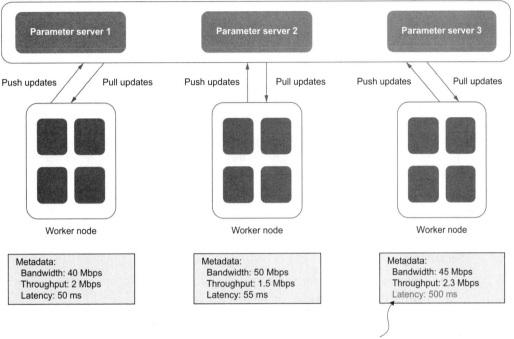

This worker node has extremely high latency (10 times the latency of the other workers) that slows down the entire model training process.

Figure 6.19   An example parameter server–based model training where the worker on the right-hand side has extremely high latency (10 times the latency of the other workers), which slows down the entire model training process

One additional benefit of introducing the metadata pattern to our machine learning workflows is to use the metadata recorded to establish relationships between the individual steps or across different workflows. For example, modern model management tools can use the recorded metadata to help users build the lineage of the trained models and visualize what individual steps/factors contributed to the model artifacts.

6.3.4   Exercises

1 If the training step failed due to the loss of training data source, what should we do?

2 What type of metadata can be collected if we look at individual workers or parameter servers?

6.4   Answers to exercises

Section 6.2

1 No, we can apply this scheduling strategy at each level of abstraction, such as processes, users, groups, etc.

2 No, some machine learning frameworks support elastic scheduling, which allows distributed model training jobs to start with any number of workers available without waiting for all the requested workers to be ready for communication. In this case, gang scheduling is not suitable.

Section 6.3

1 We should rerun data ingestion before retrying the model training step since this failure is permanent, and simply retrying would lead to repetitive failures.

2 Various network performance metrics while the model is being trained (e.g., bandwidth, throughput, and latency). This type of information is very useful when we want to detect when workers experience poor network performance that blocks the entire training process.

Summary

- There are different areas of improvement related to operations in machine learning systems, such as job scheduling and metadata.
- Various scheduling patterns, such as fair-share scheduling, priority scheduling, and gang scheduling, can be used to prevent resource starvation and avoid deadlocks.
- We can collect metadata to gain insights from machine learning workflows and handle failures more appropriately to reduce any negative effects on users.

Part 3

Building a distributed machine learning workflow

If you've survived the training up to this point, congratulations! You've just learned many common patterns that can be used in real-world machine learning systems, as well as understanding the tradeoffs when deciding which patterns to apply to your system.

In the last part of the book, we will build an end-to-end machine learning system to apply what we learned previously. We will gain hands-on experience implementing many patterns previously learned in this project. We'll learn how to solve problems at a larger scale and take what's developed on our laptops to large distributed clusters.

In chapter 7, we'll go through the project background and system components. Then, we'll go through the challenges in each of these components and share the patterns that we will apply to address them. Chapter 8 covers the basic concepts of the four technologies (TensorFlow, Kubernetes, Kubeflow, and Argo Workflows) and provides an opportunity to gain hands-on experience in each one of them to prepare our implementation of the final project.

In the last chapter of the book, we'll implement the end-to-end machine learning system with the architecture we designed in chapter 7. Our complete implementation of each of the components will incorporate the previously discussed patterns. We'll use the technologies we learned in chapter 8 to build different components of a distributed machine learning workflow.

Project overview
and system architecture

This chapter covers

- Providing a high-level overall design of our system
- Optimizing the data ingestion component for multiple epochs of the dataset
- Deciding which distributed model training strategy best minimizes overhead
- Adding model server replicas for high-performance model serving
- Accelerating the end-to-end workflow of our machine learning system

In the previous chapters, we learned to choose and apply the correct patterns for building and deploying distributed machine learning systems to gain practical experience managing and automating machine learning tasks. In chapter 2, I introduced a couple of practical patterns that can be incorporated into data ingestion, usually the first process of a distributed machine learning system and responsible for monitoring incoming data and performing necessary preprocessing steps to prepare for model training.

In chapter 3, we explored some challenges dealing with the distributed training component, and I introduced a couple of practical patterns that can be incorporated into the component. The distributed training component is the most critical part of a distributed machine learning system and is what makes the system unique from general distributed systems. In chapter 4, we covered the challenges involved in distributed model serving systems, and I introduced a few commonly used patterns. You can use replicated services to achieve horizontal scaling and the sharded services pattern to process large model serving requests. You also learned how to assess model serving systems and determine whether the event-driven design is beneficial in real-world scenarios.

In chapter 5, we discussed machine learning workflows, one of the most essential components in machine learning systems, as it connects all other components in a machine learning system. Finally, in chapter 6, we discussed some operational efforts and patterns that can greatly accelerate the end-to-end workflow and reduce maintenance and communication efforts when engineering teams collaborate with teams of data scientists or machine learning practitioners before the systems become production ready.

For the remaining chapters of the book, we will build an end-to-end machine learning system to apply what we learned previously. You will gain hands-on experience implementing many patterns we've previously discussed. You'll learn how to solve problems at a larger scale and take what you've developed on your laptop to large distributed clusters. In this chapter, we'll go through the project background and system components. Then we'll go through the challenges related to the components and discuss the patterns we can apply to address them.

Note that although we won't dive into the implementation details in this chapter, in the remaining chapters, we'll use several popular frameworks and cutting-edge technologies—particularly TensorFlow, Kubernetes, Kubeflow, Docker, and Argo Workflows—to build the components of a distributed machine learning workflow.

7.1 Project overview

For this project, we will build an image classification system that takes raw images downloaded from the data source, performs necessary data cleaning steps, builds a machine learning model in a distributed Kubernetes cluster, and then deploys the trained model to the model serving system for users to use. We also want to establish an end-to-end workflow that is efficient and reusable. Next, I will introduce the project background and the overall system architecture and components.

7.1.1 Project background

We will build an end-to-end machine learning system to apply what we learned previously. We'll build a data ingestion component that downloads the Fashion-MNIST dataset and a model training component to train and optimize the image classification model. Once the final model is trained, we'll build a high-performance model serving system to start making predictions using the trained model.

As previously mentioned, we will use several frameworks and technologies to build distributed machine learning workflow components. For example, we'll use Tensor-Flow with Python to build the classification model on the Fashion-MNIST dataset and make predictions. We'll use Kubeflow to run distributed machine learning model training on a Kubernetes cluster. Furthermore, we'll use Argo Workflows to build a machine learning pipeline that consists of many important components of a distributed machine learning system. The basics of these technologies will be introduced in the next chapter, and you'll gain hands-on experience with them before diving into the actual implementation of the project in chapter 9. In the next section, we'll examine the project's system components.

7.1.2   System components

Figure 7.1 is the architecture diagram of the system we will be building. First, we will build the data ingestion component responsible for ingesting data and storing the dataset in the cache using some of the patterns discussed in chapter 2. Next, we will build three different model training steps that train different models and incorporate the collective communication pattern addressed in chapter 3. Once we finish the model training steps, we will build the model selection step that picks the top model. The selected optimal model will be used for model serving in the following two steps. At the end of the model serving steps, we aggregate the predictions and present the result to users. Finally, we want to ensure all these steps are part of a reproducible workflow that can be executed at any time in any environment.

We'll build the system based on the architecture diagram in Figure 7.1 and dive into the details of the individual components. We'll also discuss the patterns we can use to address the challenges in building those components.

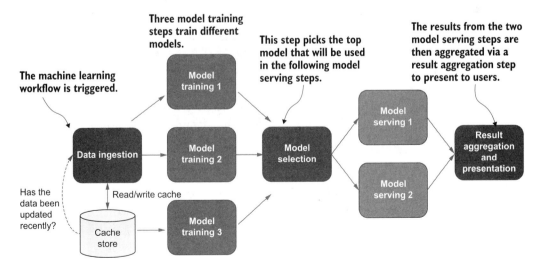

Figure 7.1   The architecture diagram of the end-to-end machine learning system we will be building

7.2   *Data ingestion*

For this project, we will use the Fashion-MNIST dataset, introduced in section 2.2, to build the data ingestion component, as shown in figure 7.2. This dataset consists of a training set of 60,000 examples and a test set of 10,000 examples. Each example is a 28 × 28 grayscale image that represents one Zalando's article image associated with a label from 10 classes. Recall that the Fashion-MNIST dataset is designed to serve as a direct drop-in replacement for the original MNIST dataset for benchmarking machine learning algorithms. It shares the same image size and structure of training and testing splits.

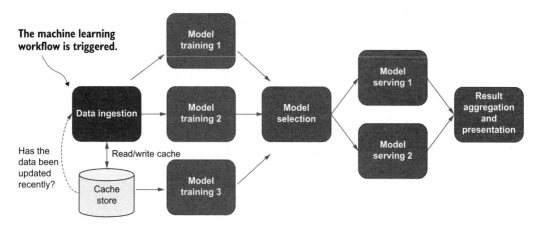

Figure 7.2   The data ingestion component (dark box) in the end-to-end machine learning system

As a recap, figure 7.3 is a screenshot of the collection of images for all 10 classes (T-shirt/top, trouser, pullover, dress, coat, sandal, shirt, sneaker, bag, and ankle boot) from Fashion-MNIST, where each class takes three rows in the screenshot.

Figure 7.4 is a closer look at the first few example images in the training set together with their corresponding text labels.

The downloaded Fashion-MNIST dataset should only take 30 MBs on disk if compressed. It's easy to load the entire downloaded dataset into memory at once.

7.2.1   *The problem*

Although the Fashion-MNIST data is not large, we may want to perform additional computations before feeding the dataset into the model, which is common for tasks that require additional transformations and cleaning. We may want to resize, normalize, or convert the images to grayscale. We also may want to perform complex mathematical operations such as convolution operations, which can require large additional memory space allocations. Our available computational resources may or

Every three rows represent
example images that represent a
class. For example, the top three
rows are images of T-shirts.

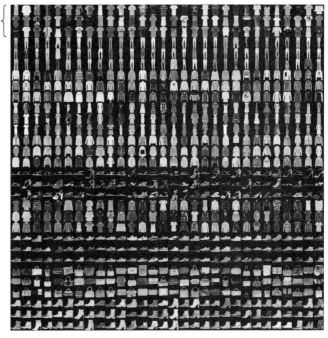

Figure 7.3 A screenshot of the collection of images from the Fashion-MNIST dataset for all 10 classes
(T-shirt/top, trouser, pullover, dress, coat, sandal, shirt, sneaker, bag, and ankle boot)

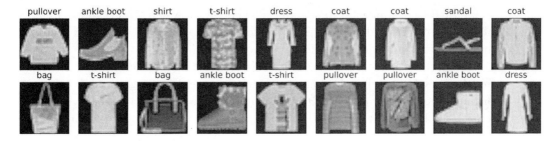

Figure 7.4 A closer look at the first few example images in the training set with their corresponding labels in text

may not be sufficient after we load the entire dataset in memory, depending on the distributed cluster size.

In addition, the machine learning model we are training from this dataset requires multiple epochs on the training dataset. Suppose training one epoch on the entire training dataset takes 3 hours. If we want to train two epochs, the time needed for model training would double, as shown in figure 7.5.

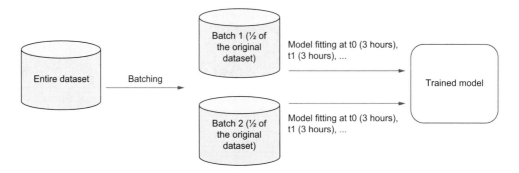

Figure 7.5   A diagram of model training for multiple epochs at time t0, t1, etc. where we spent 3 hours for each epoch

In real-world machine learning systems, a larger number of epochs is often needed, and training each epoch sequentially is inefficient. In the next section, we will discuss how we can tackle that inefficiency.

7.2.2   *The solution*

Let's take a look at the first challenge we have: the mathematical operations in the machine learning algorithms may require a lot of additional memory space allocations while computational resources may or may not be sufficient. Given that we don't have too much free memory, we should not load the entire Fashion-MNIST dataset into memory directly. Let's assume that the mathematical operations that we want to perform on the dataset can be performed on subsets of the entire dataset. Then, we could use the batching pattern introduced in chapter 2, which would group a number of data records from the entire dataset into batches, which will be used to train the machine learning model sequentially on each batch.

To apply the batching pattern, we first divide the dataset into smaller subsets or mini-batches, load each individual mini-batch of example images, perform expensive mathematical operations on each batch, and then use only one mini-batch of images in each model training iteration. For example, we can perform convolution or other heavy mathematical operations on the first mini-batch, which consists of only 20 images, and then send the transformed images to the machine learning model for model training. We then repeat the same process for the remaining mini-batches while continuing to perform model training.

Since we've divided the dataset into many small subsets (mini-batches), we can avoid any potential problems with running out of memory when performing various heavy mathematical operations on the entire dataset necessary for achieving an accurate classification model on the Fashion-MNIST dataset. We can then handle even larger datasets using this approach by reducing the size of the mini-batches.

With the help of the batching pattern, we are no longer concerned about potential out-of-memory problems when ingesting the dataset for model training. We don't have to load the entire dataset into memory at once, and instead, we are consuming the dataset batch by batch sequentially. For example, if we have a dataset with 1,000 records, we can first take 500 of the 1,000 records to form a batch and then train the model using this batch of records. Subsequently, we can repeat this batching and model training process for the remaining records. Figure 7.6 illustrates this process, where the original dataset gets divided into two batches and processed sequentially. The first batch gets consumed to train the model at time t0, and the second batch gets consumed at time t1.

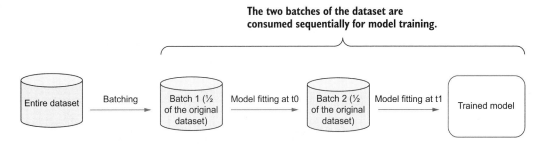

Figure 7.6   The dataset is divided into two batches and processed sequentially. The first batch is consumed to train the model at time t0, and the second batch is consumed at time t1.

Now, let's tackle the second challenge mentioned in section 7.2.1: we want to avoid wasting time if we need to train a machine learning model that involves iterating on multiple epochs of the original dataset. Recall that, in chapter 2, we talked about the caching pattern, which would solve this type of problem. With the help of the caching pattern, we can greatly speed up the re-access to the dataset for the model training process that involves training on the same dataset for multiple epochs.

We can't do anything special to the first epoch since it's the first time the machine learning model has seen the entire training dataset. We can store the cache of the training examples in memory, making it much faster to re-access when needed for the second and subsequent epochs.

Let's assume that the single laptop we use to train the model has sufficient computational resources such as memory and disk space. As soon as the machine learning model consumes each training example from the entire dataset, we can hold off recycling and instead keep the consumed training examples in memory. For example, in figure 7.7, after we have finished fitting the model for the first epoch, we can store a cache for both batches used for the first epoch of model training.

Then, we can start training the model for the second epoch by feeding the stored in-memory cache to the model directly without repeatedly reading from the data source for future epochs. Next, we will discuss the model training component we will build in our project.

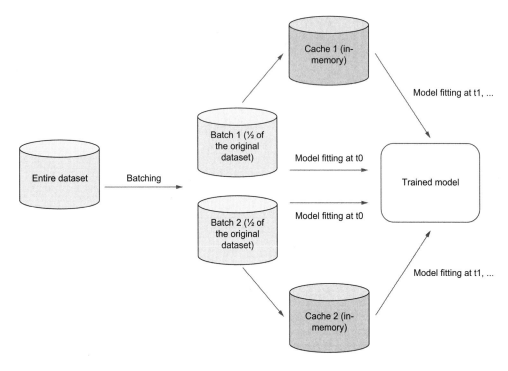

Figure 7.7   A diagram of model training for multiple epochs at time t0, t1, etc. using cache, making reading from the data source repeatedly unnecessary

7.2.3   Exercises

1   Where do we store the cache?
2   Can we use the batching pattern when the Fashion-MNIST dataset gets large?

7.3   Model training

In the previous section, we've talked about the data ingestion component of the system we are building and how we can use the caching and batching pattern to handle large datasets and make the system more efficient. Next, let's discuss the model training component we are building. Figure 7.8 is a diagram of the model training component in the overall architecture.

In the diagram, three different model training steps are followed by a model selection step. These model training steps can train three different models competing with each other for better statistical performance. The dedicated model selection step then picks the top model, which will be used in the subsequent components in the end-to-end machine learning workflow.

In the next section, we will look more closely at the model training component in figure 7.8 and discuss potential problems when implementing this component.

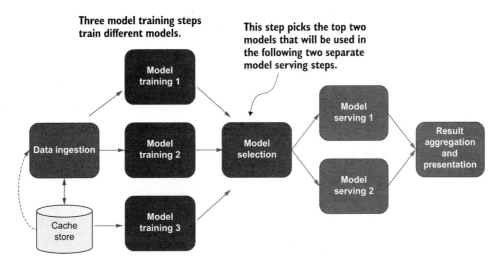

Figure 7.8 The model training component (dark boxes) in the end-to-end machine learning system

7.3.1 *The problem*

In chapter 3, I introduced the parameter server and the collective communication patterns. The parameter server pattern is handy when the model is too large to fit in a single machine, such as the one for tagging entities in the 8 million YouTube videos (section 3.2). The collective communication pattern is useful to speed up the training process for medium-sized models when the communication overhead is significant. Which pattern should we select for our model training component?

7.3.2 *The solution*

With the help of parameter servers, we can effectively resolve the challenge of building an extremely large machine learning model that may not fit a single machine. Even when the model is too large to fit in a single machine, we can still successfully train the model efficiently with parameter servers. For example, figure 7.9 is an architecture diagram of the parameter server pattern using multiple parameter servers. Each worker node takes a subset of the dataset, performs calculations required in each neural network layer, and sends the calculated gradients to update one model partition stored in one of the parameter servers.

Because all workers perform calculations in an asynchronous fashion, the model partitions each worker node uses to calculate the gradients may not be up to date. For instance, two workers can block each other when sending gradients to the same parameter server, which makes it hard to gather the calculated gradients on time and requires a strategy to resolve the blocking problem. Unfortunately, in real-world distributed training systems where parameter servers are incorporated, multiple workers may send the gradients at the same time, and thus many blocking communications must be resolved.

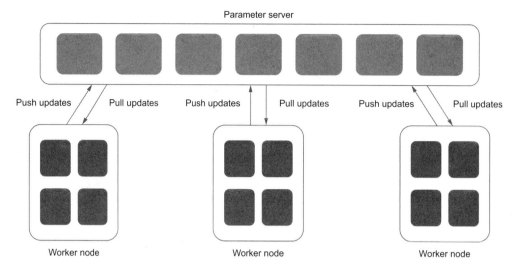

Figure 7.9   A machine learning training component with multiple parameter servers

Another challenge comes when deciding the optimal ratio between the number of workers and the number of parameter servers. For example, many workers are sending gradients to the same parameter server at the same time; the problem gets even worse, and eventually, the blocking communications between different workers or parameter servers become a bottleneck.

Now, let's return to our original application, the Fashion-MNIST classification model. The model we are building is not as large as large recommendation system models; it can easily fit in a single machine if we give the machine sufficient computational resources. It's only 30 MBs in compressed form. Thus, the collective communication model is perfect for the system we are building.

Now, without parameter servers, each worker node stores a copy of the entire set of model parameters, as shown in figure 7.10. I previously mentioned that every worker consumes some portion of data and calculates the gradients needed to update the model parameters stored locally on this worker node (see chapter 3). We want to aggregate all the gradients as soon as all worker nodes have successfully completed their calculation of gradients. We also want to make sure every worker's entire set of model parameters is updated based on the aggregated gradients. In other words, each worker should store a copy of the exact same updated model.

Going back to the architecture diagram in figure 7.8, each model training step uses the collective communication pattern, taking advantage of the underlying network infrastructure to perform allreduce operations to communicate gradients between multiple workers. The collective communication pattern also allows us to train multiple medium-sized machine learning models in a distributed setting. Once the model is trained, we can start a separate process to pick the top model to be used for model serving. This step is pretty intuitive, and I'll defer the implementation

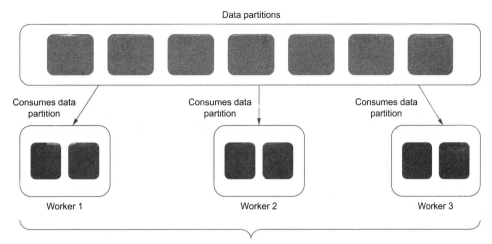

Data partitions

Consumes data partition Consumes data partition Consumes data partition

Worker 1 Worker 2 Worker 3

Each of these workers contains a copy of the entire set of model parameters and consumes partitions of data to calculate the gradients.

Figure 7.10 Distributed model training component with only worker nodes, where every worker stores a copy of the entire set of model parameters and consumes partitions of data to calculate the gradients

details to chapter 9. In the next section, we will discuss the model serving component of our system.

7.3.3 Exercises

1 Why isn't the parameter server pattern a good fit for our model?
2 Does each worker store different parts of the model when using the collective communication pattern?

7.4 Model serving

We've talked about both the data ingestion and model training components of the system we are building. Next, let's discuss the model server component, which is essential to the end-user experience. Figure 7.11 shows the serving training component in the overall architecture.

Next, let's take a look at a potential problem and its solution we will encounter when we begin building this component.

7.4.1 The problem

The model serving system needs to take raw images uploaded by users and send the requests to the model server to make inferences using the trained model. These model serving requests are being queued and waiting to be processed by the model server.

If the model serving system is a single-node server, it can only serve a limited number of model serving requests on a first-come, first-served basis. As the number of requests grows in the real world, the user experience suffers when users must wait a long time to receive the model serving result. In other words, all requests are waiting

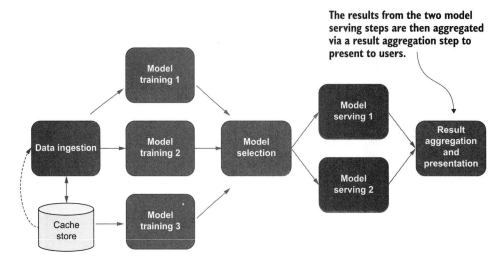

The results from the two model
serving steps are then aggregated
via a result aggregation step to
present to users.

Figure 7.11   The model serving component (dark boxes) in the end-to-end machine learning system

to be processed by the model serving system, but the computational resources are limited to this single node. How do we build a more efficient model serving system?

7.4.2   *The solution*

The previous section lays a perfect use case for the replicated services pattern discussed in chapter 4. Our model serving system takes the images uploaded by users and sends requests to the model server. In addition, unlike the simple single-server design, the system has multiple model server replicas to process the model serving requests asynchronously. Each model server replica takes a single request, retrieves the previously trained classification model from the model training component, and classifies the images that don't existed in the Fashion-MNIST dataset.

With the help of the replicated services pattern, we can easily scale up our model server by adding model server replicas to the single-server model serving system. The new architecture is shown in figure 7.12. The model server replicas can handle many requests at a time since each replica can process individual model serving requests independently.

Multiple model serving requests from users are sent to the model server replicas at the same time after we've introduced them. We also need to define a clear mapping relationship between the requests and the model server replicas, which determines which requests are processed by which of the model server replicas.

To distribute the model server requests among the replicas, we need to add an additional load balancer layer. For example, the load balancer takes multiple model serving requests from our users. It then distributes the requests evenly among the model server replicas, which are responsible for processing individual requests, including model retrieval and inference on the new data in the request. Figure 7.13 illustrates this process.

**Users upload images and then submit
requests to the model serving system
for classification.**

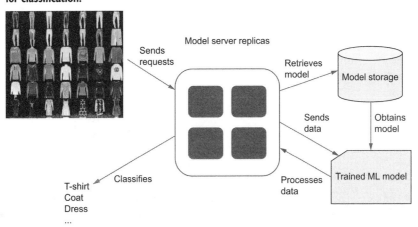

Figure 7.12   **The system architecture of the replicated model serving services**

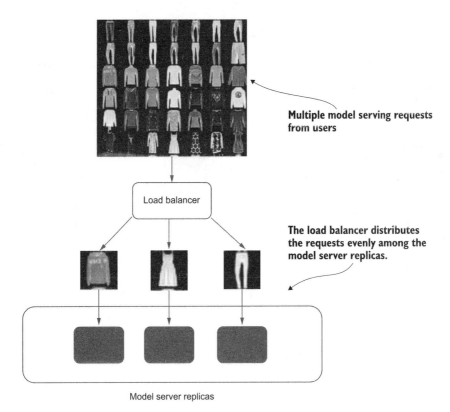

Figure 7.13   **A diagram showing how a loader balancer distributes requests evenly across
the model server replicas**

The load balancer uses different algorithms to determine which request goes to which particular model server replica. Example algorithms for load balancing include round robin, least-connection method, and hashing.

Note that from our original architecture diagram in figure 7.11, there are two individual steps for model serving, each using different models. Each model serving step consists of a model serving service with multiple replicas to handle model serving traffic for different models.

7.4.3   Exercises

1   What happens when we don't have a load balancer as part of the model serving system?

7.5   End-to-end workflow

Now that we've looked at the individual components, let's see how to compose an end-to-end workflow that consists of all those components in a scalable and efficient way. We will also incorporate a few patterns from chapter 5 into the workflow. Figure 7.14 is a diagram of the end-to-end workflow we are building.

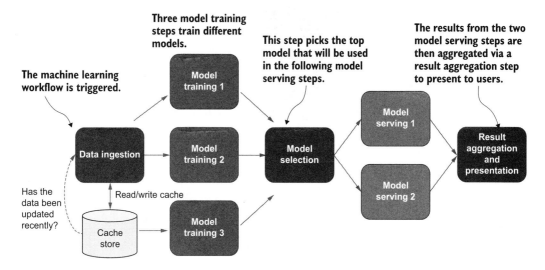

Figure 7.14   The architecture diagram of the end-to-end machine learning system we will build

Instead of paying attention to individual components, we will look at the entire machine learning system, which chains all the components together in an end-to-end workflow.

7.5.1   The problems

First, the Fashion-MNIST dataset is static and does not change over time. However, to design a more realistic system, let's assume we'll manually update the Fashion-MNIST dataset regularly. Whenever the updates happen, we may want to rerun the entire machine learning workflow to train a fresh machine learning model that includes the new data. In other words, we need to execute the data ingestion step every time when changes happen. In the meantime, when the dataset is not updated, we want to experiment with new machine learning models. Thus, we still need to execute the entire workflow, including the data ingestion step. The data ingestion step is usually very time consuming, especially for large datasets. Is there a way to make this workflow more efficient?

Second, we want to build a machine learning workflow that can train different models and then select the top model, which will be used in model serving to generate predictions using the knowledge from both models. Due to the variance of completion time for each of the model training steps in the existing machine learning workflow, the start of each following step, such as model selection and model serving, depends on the completion of the previous steps. However, this sequential execution of steps in the workflow is quite time-consuming and blocks the rest of the steps. For example, say one model training step takes much longer to complete than the rest of the steps. The model selection step that follows can only start to execute after this long-running model training step has completed. As a result, the entire workflow is delayed by this particular step. Is there a way to accelerate this workflow so it will not be affected by the duration of individual steps?

7.5.2   The solutions

For the first problem, we can use the step memoization pattern from chapter 5. Recall that step memoization can help the system decide whether a step should be executed or skipped. With the help of step memoization, a workflow can identify steps with redundant workloads that can be skipped without being re-executed and thus greatly accelerate the execution of the end-to-end workflow.

For instance, figure 7.15 contains a simple workflow that only executes the data ingestion step when we know the dataset has been updated. In other words, we don't want to re-ingest the data that's already collected if the new data has not been updated.

Many strategies can be used to determine whether the dataset has been updated. With a predefined strategy, we can conditionally reconstruct the machine learning workflow and control whether we would like to include a data ingestion step to be re-executed, as shown in figure 7.16.

Cache is one way to identify whether a dataset has been updated. Since we suppose our Fashion-MNIST dataset is being updated regularly on a fixed schedule (e.g., once a month), we can create a time-based *cache* that stores the location of the ingested and cleaned dataset (assuming the dataset is located in a remote database) and the time-stamp of its last updated time.

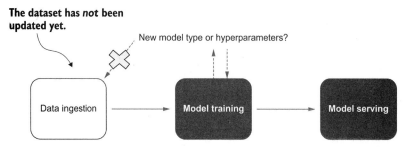

Figure 7.15   A diagram of skipping the data ingestion step when the dataset has not been updated

As in figure 7.16, the data ingestion step in the workflow will then be constructed and executed dynamically based on whether the last updated timestamp is within a particular window. For example, if the time window is set to two weeks, we consider the ingested data as fresh if it has been updated within the past two weeks. The data ingestion step will be skipped, and the following model training steps will use the already ingested dataset from the location in the cache. The time window can be used to control how old a cache can be before we consider the dataset fresh enough to be used directly for model training instead of re-ingesting the data from scratch.

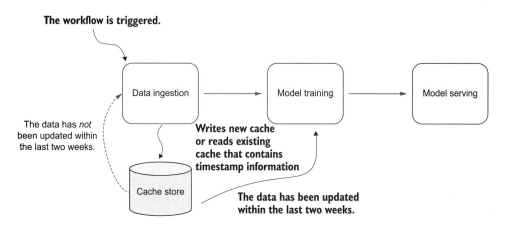

Figure 7.16   The workflow has been triggered. We check whether the data has been updated within the last two weeks by accessing the cache. If the data is fresh, we can skip the unnecessary data ingestion step and execute the model training step directly.

Now, let's take a look at the second problem: sequential execution of the steps blocks the subsequent steps in the workflow and is inefficient. The synchronous and asynchronous patterns introduced in chapter 5 can help.

When a short-running model training step finishes—for example, model training step 2 in figure 7.17—we successfully obtain a trained machine learning model. In fact, we can use this already-trained model directly in our model serving system without waiting for the rest of the model training steps to complete. As a result, users will be able to see the results of image classification from their model serving requests that contain videos as soon as we have trained one model from one of the steps in the workflow. After a second model training step (figure 7.17, model training step 3) finishes, the two trained models are sent to model serving. Now, users benefit from the aggregated results obtained from both models.

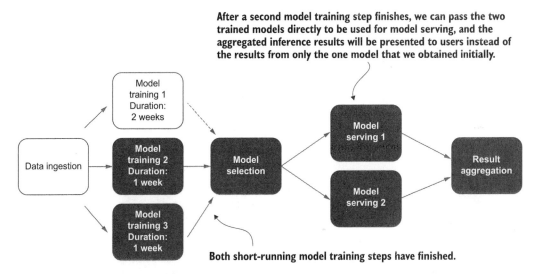

Figure 7.17   After a second model training step finishes, we can pass the two trained models directly to model serving. The aggregated inference results will be presented to users instead of only the results from the first model.

As a result, we can continue to use the trained models for model selection and model serving; in the meantime, the long-running model training steps are still running. In other words, they execute asynchronously without depending on each other's completion. The workflow can proceed and execute the next step before the previous one finishes. The long-running model training step will no longer block the entire workflow. Instead, it can continue to use the already-trained models from the short-running model training steps in the model serving system. Thus, it can start handling users' model serving requests.

7.5.3 *Exercises*

1 Which component can benefit the most from step memoization?
2 How do we tell whether a step's execution can be skipped if its workflow has been triggered to run again?

7.6   *Answers to exercises*

Section 7.2

1 In memory
2 Yes

Section 7.3

1 There are blocking communications between workers and parameter servers.
2 No, each worker stores exactly the same copy of the model.

Section 7.4

1 We cannot balance or distribute the model serving requests among the replicas.

Section 7.5

1 The data ingestion component
2 Using the metadata in the step cache

Summary

- The data ingestion component uses the caching pattern to speed up the processing of multiple epochs of the dataset.
- The model training component uses the collective communication pattern to avoid the potential communication overhead between workers and parameter servers.
- We can use model server replicas, which are capable of handling many requests at one time since each replica processes individual model serving requests independently.
- We can chain all our components into a workflow and use caching to effectively skip time-consuming components such as data ingestion.

Overview of relevant technologies

This chapter covers

- Getting familiar with model building using TensorFlow
- Understanding key terminologies on Kubernetes
- Running distributed machine learning workloads with Kubeflow
- Deploying container-native workflows using Argo Workflows

In the previous chapter, we went through the project background and system components to understand our strategies for implementing each component. We also discussed the challenges related to each component and discussed the patterns we will apply to address them. As previously mentioned, we will dive into the project's implementation details in chapter 9, the book's last chapter. However, since we will use different technologies in the project and it's not easy to cover all the basics on the fly, in this chapter, you will learn the basic concepts of the four technologies (Tensor-Flow, Kubernetes, Kubeflow, and Argo Workflows) and gain hands-on experience.

Each of these four technologies has a different purpose, but all will be used to implement the final project in chapter 9. TensorFlow will be used for data processing, model building, and evaluation. We will use Kubernetes as our core distributed infrastructure. On top of that, Kubeflow will be used for submitting distributed model training jobs to the Kubernetes cluster, and Argo Workflows will be used to construct and submit the end-to-end machine learning workflows.

8.1 *TensorFlow: The machine learning framework*

TensorFlow is an end-to-end machine learning platform. It has been widely adopted in academia and industries for different applications and uses cases, such as image classification, recommendation systems, natural language processing, etc. TensorFlow is highly portable, deployable on different hardware, and has multilanguage support.

TensorFlow has a large ecosystem. The following are some highlighted projects in this ecosystem:

- TensorFlow.js is a library for machine learning in JavaScript. Users can use machine learning directly in the browser or in Node.js.
- TensorFlow Lite is a mobile library for deploying models on mobile, microcontrollers, and other edge devices.
- TFX is an end-to-end platform for deploying production machine learning pipelines.
- TensorFlow Serving is a flexible, high-performance serving system for machine learning models designed for production environments.
- TensorFlow Hub is a repository of trained machine learning models ready for fine-tuning and deployable anywhere. Reuse trained models like BERT and Faster R-CNN with just a few lines of code.

More can be found in the TensorFlow GitHub organization (https://github.com/tensorflow). We will use TensorFlow Serving in our model serving component. In the next section, we'll walk through some basic examples in TensorFlow to train a machine learning model locally using the MNIST dataset.

8.1.1 *The basics*

Let's first install Anaconda for Python 3 for the basic examples we will use. Anaconda (https://www.anaconda.com) is a distribution of the Python and R programming languages for scientific computing that aims to simplify package management and deployment. The distribution includes data-science packages suitable for Windows, Linux, and macOS. Once Anaconda is installed, use the following command in your console to install a Conda environment with Python 3.9.

Listing 8.1 Creating a Conda environment

```
> conda create --name dist-ml python=3.9 -y
```

Next, we can activate this environment with the following code.

Listing 8.2   Activating a Conda environment

```
> conda activate dist-ml
```

Then, we can install TensorFlow in this Python environment.

Listing 8.3   Installing TensorFlow

```
> pip install --upgrade pip
> pip install tensorflow==2.10.0
```

If you encounter any problems, please refer to the installation guide (https://www .tensorflow.org/install).

   In some cases, you may need to uninstall your existing NumPy and reinstall it.

Listing 8.4   Installing NumPy

```
> pip install numpy --ignore-installed
```

If you are on Mac, check out the Metal plugin for acceleration (https://developer .apple.com/metal/tensorflow-plugin/).

   Once we've successfully installed TensorFlow, we can start with a basic image classification example! Let's first load and preprocess our simple MNIST dataset. Recall that the MNIST dataset contains images for handwritten digits from 0 to 9. Each row represents images for a particular handwritten digit, as shown in figure 8.1.

Each row represents images for a particular handwritten digit. For example, the first row represents images of the digit 0.

Figure 8.1   Some example images for handwritten digits from 0 to 9 where each row represents images for a particular handwritten digit

Keras API (`tf.keras`) is a high-level API for model training in TensorFlow, and we will use it for both loading the built-in datasets and model training and evaluation.

Listing 8.5   Loading the MNIST dataset

```
> import tensorflow as tf
> (x_train, y_train), (x_test, y_test) = tf.keras.datasets.mnist.load_data()
```

The function `load_data()` uses a default path to save the MNIST dataset if we don't specify a path. This function will return NumPy arrays for training and testing images and labels. We split the dataset into training and testing so we can run both model training and evaluation in our example.

A NumPy array is a common data type in Python's scientific computing ecosystem. It describes multidimensional arrays and has three properties: data, shape, and dtype. Let's use our training images as an example.

Listing 8.6   Inspecting the dataset

```
> x_train.data
<memory at 0x16a392310>
> x_train.shape
(60000, 28, 28)
> x_train.dtype
dtype('uint8')
> x_train.min()
0
> x_train.max()
255
```

`x_train` is a $60,000 \times 28 \times 28$ three-dimensional array. The data type is `uint8` from `0` to `255`. In other words, this object contains 60,000 grayscale images with a resolution of 28×28.

Next, we can perform some feature preprocessing on our raw images. Since many algorithms and models are sensitive to the scale of the features, we often center and scale features into a range such as `[0, 1]` or `[-1, 1]`. In our case, we can do this easily by dividing the images by 255.

Listing 8.7   The preprocessing function

```
def preprocess(ds):
    return ds / 255.0

x_train = preprocess(x_train)
x_test = preprocess(x_test)

> x_train.dtype
dtype('float64')

> x_train.min()
0.0

> x_train.max()
1.0
```

After preprocessing the images in the training and testing set, we can instantiate a simple multilayer neural network model. We use `tf.keras` to define the model architecture. First, we use Flatten to expand the two-dimensional images into a one-dimensional array by specifying the input shape as 28×28. The second layer is densely connected and uses the `'relu'` activation function to introduce some non-linearity. The third layer is a dropout layer to reduce overfitting and make the model more generalizable. Since the handwritten digits consist of 10 different digits from 0 to 9, our last layer is densely connected for 10-class classification with soft-max activation.

Listing 8.8   The sequential model definition

```
model = tf.keras.models.Sequential([
  tf.keras.layers.Flatten(input_shape=(28, 28)),
  tf.keras.layers.Dense(128, activation='relu'),
  tf.keras.layers.Dropout(0.2),
  tf.keras.layers.Dense(10, activation='softmax')
])
```

After we've defined the model architecture, we need to specify three different components: the evaluation metric, loss function, and optimizer.

Listing 8.9   Model compilation with optimizer, loss function, and optimizer

```
model.compile(optimizer='adam',
    loss='sparse_categorical_crossentropy',
    metrics=['accuracy'])
```

We can then start our model training with five epochs as well as evaluation via the following.

Listing 8.10   Model training using the training data

```
model.fit(x_train, y_train, epochs=5)
model.evaluate(x_test, y_test)
```

We should see training progress in the log:

```
Epoch 1/5
1875/1875 [======] - 11s 4ms/step - loss: 0.2949 - accuracy: 0.9150
Epoch 2/5
1875/1875 [======] - 9s 5ms/step - loss: 0.1389 - accuracy: 0.9581
Epoch 3/5
1875/1875 [======] - 9s 5ms/step - loss: 0.1038 - accuracy: 0.9682
Epoch 4/5
1875/1875 [======] - 8s 4ms/step - loss: 0.0841 - accuracy: 0.9740
Epoch 5/5
1875/1875 [======] - 8s 4ms/step - loss: 0.0707 - accuracy: 0.9779
10000/10000 [======] - 0s - loss: 0.0726 - accuracy: 0.9788
```

And the log from the model evaluation should look like the following:

```
313/313 [======] - 1s 4ms/step - loss: 0.0789 - accuracy: 0.9763
[0.07886667549610138, 0.976300060749054]
```

We should observe that as the loss decreases during training, the accuracy increases to 97.8% on training data. The final trained model has an accuracy of 97.6% on the testing data. Your result might be slightly different due to the randomness in the modeling process.

After we've trained the model and are happy with its performance, we can save it using the following code so that we don't have to retrain it from scratch next time.

Listing 8.11 Saving the trained model

```
model.save('my_model.h5')
```

This code saves the model as file `my_model.h5` in the current working directory. When we start a new Python session, we can import TensorFlow and load the model object from the `my_model.h5` file.

Listing 8.12 Loading the saved model

```
import tensorflow as tf
model = tf.keras.models.load_model('my_model.h5')
```

We've learned how to train a model using TensorFlow's Keras API for a single set of hyperparameters. These hyperparameters remain constant over the training process and directly affect the performance of your machine learning program. Let's learn how to tune hyperparameters for your TensorFlow program with Keras Tuner (https://keras.io/keras_tuner/). First, install the Keras Tuner library.

Listing 8.13 Installing the Keras Tuner package

```
pip install -q -U keras-tuner
```

Once it's installed, you should be able to import all the required libraries.

Listing 8.14 Importing necessary packages

```
import tensorflow as tf
from tensorflow import keras
import keras_tuner as kt
```

We will use the same MNIST dataset and the preprocessing functions for our hyperparameter tuning example. We then wrap our model definition into a Python function.

Listing 8.15 The model building function using TensorFlow and Keras Tuner

```
def model_builder(hp):
  model = keras.Sequential()
  model.add(keras.layers.Flatten(input_shape=(28, 28)))
  hp_units = hp.Int('units', min_value=32, max_value=512, step=32)
  model.add(keras.layers.Dense(units=hp_units, activation='relu'))
  model.add(keras.layers.Dense(10))
  hp_learning_rate = hp.Choice('learning_rate', values=[1e-2, 1e-3, 1e-4])
  model.compile(optimizer=keras.optimizers.Adam(learning_rate=hp_learning_rate),
              loss=keras.losses.SparseCategoricalCrossentropy(from_logits=True),
              metrics=['accuracy'])
  return model
```

This code is essentially the same as what we used previously for training a model with a single set of hyperparameters, except that we also defined `hp_units` and `hp_learning_rate` objects that are used in our dense layer and optimizer.

The `hp_units` object instantiates an integer that will be tuned between 32 and 512 and used as the number of units in the first densely connected layer. The `hp_learning_rate` object will tune the learning rate for the `adam` optimizer that will be chosen among these values: 0.01, 0.001, or 0.0001.

Once the model builder is defined, we can then instantiate our tuner. There are several tuning algorithms we can use (e.g., random search, Bayesian optimization, Hyperband). Here we use the hyperband tuning algorithm. It uses adaptive resource allocation and early stopping to converge faster on a high-performing model.

Listing 8.16 The Hyperband model tuner

```
tuner = kt.Hyperband(model_builder,
                   objective='val_accuracy',
                   max_epochs=10,
                   factor=3,
                   directory='my_dir',
                   project_name='intro_to_kt')
```

We use the validation accuracy as the objective, and the maximum number of epochs is 10 during model tuning.

To reduce overfitting, we can create an `EarlyStopping` callback to stop training as soon as the model reaches a threshold for the validation loss. Make sure to reload the dataset into memory if you've started a new Python session.

Listing 8.17 The `EarlyStopping` callback

```
early_stop = tf.keras.callbacks.EarlyStopping(
    monitor='val_loss', patience=4)
```

Now we can start our hyperparameter search via `tuner.search()`.

Listing 8.18   The Hyperparameter search with early-stopping

```
tuner.search(x_train, y_train,
    epochs=30, validation_split=0.2,
    callbacks=[early_stop])
```

Once the search is complete, we can identify the optimal hyperparameters and train the model on the data for 30 epochs.

Listing 8.19   Obtaining the best hyperparameters and training the model

```
best_hps = tuner.get_best_hyperparameters(num_trials=1)[0]
model = tuner.hypermodel.build(best_hps)
model.fit(x_train, y_train, epochs=50, validation_split=0.2)
```

When we evaluate the model on our test data, we should see it's more performant than our baseline model without hyperparameter tuning.

Listing 8.20   Model evaluation on the test data

```
model.evaluate(x_test, y_test)
```

You've learned how to run TensorFlow locally on a single machine. To take the most advantage of TensorFlow, the model training process should be run in a distributed cluster, which is where Kubernetes comes into play. In the next section, I will introduce Kubernetes and provide hands-on examples of the fundamentals.

8.1.2   Exercises

1   Can you use the previously saved model directly for model evaluation?
2   Instead of using the Hyperband tuning algorithm, could you try the random search algorithm?

8.2   Kubernetes: The distributed container orchestration system

Kubernetes (also known as K8s) is an open source system for automating the deployment, scaling, and management of containerized applications. It abstracts away complex container management and provides declarative configurations to orchestrate containers in different computing environments.

Containers are grouped into logical units for a particular application for easy management and discovery. Kubernetes builds upon more than 16 years of experience running production workloads at Google, combined with best-in-class ideas and practices from the community. Its main design goal is to make it easy to deploy and manage complex distributed systems, while still benefiting from the improved utilization that containers enable. It's open source, which gives the community the freedom to take advantage of on-premises, hybrid, or public cloud infrastructure and lets you effortlessly move workloads to where it matters.

Kubernetes is designed to scale without increasing your operations team. Figure 8.2 is an architecture diagram of Kubernetes and its components. However, we won't be discussing those components because they are not the focus of this book. We will, however, use `kubectl` (on the left-hand side of the diagram), a command-line interface of Kubernetes, to interact with the Kubernetes cluster and obtain information that we are interested in.

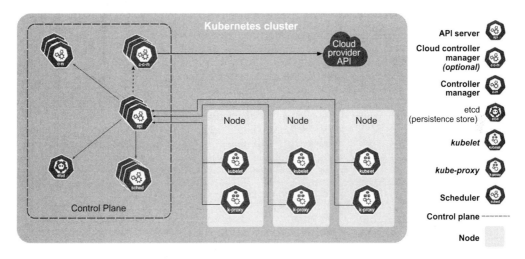

Figure 8.2 An architecture diagram of Kubernetes

We will go through some basic concepts and examples to build our knowledge and prepare the following sections on Kubeflow and Argo Workflows.

8.2.1 The basics

First, let's set up a local Kubernetes cluster. We'll use k3d (https://k3d.io) to bootstrap the local cluster. k3d is a lightweight wrapper to run k3s (a minimal Kubernetes distribution provided by Rancher Lab) in Docker. k3d makes it very easy to create either single-node or multinode k3s clusters in Docker for local development that requires a Kubernetes cluster. Let's create a Kubernetes cluster called `distml` via k3s.

Listing 8.21 Creating a local Kubernetes cluster

```
> k3d cluster create distml --image rancher/k3s:v1.25.3-rc3-k3s1
```

We can get the list of nodes for the cluster we created via the following listing.

Listing 8.22   Obtaining the list of nodes in the cluster

```
> kubectl get nodes

NAME                   STATUS   ROLES                 AGE   VERSION
K3d-distml-server-0    Ready    control-plane,master  1m    v1.25.3+k3s1
```

In this case, the node was created 1 minute ago, and we are running the `v1.25.3+k3s1` version of the k3s distribution. The status is ready so that we can proceed to the next steps.

We can also look at the node's details via `kubectl describe node k3d-distml-server-0`. For example, the labels and system info contain information on the operating system and its architecture, whether this node is a master node, etc.:

```
Labels:                    beta.kubernetes.io/arch=arm64
                           beta.kubernetes.io/instance-type=k3s
                           beta.kubernetes.io/os=linux
                           kubernetes.io/arch=arm64
                           kubernetes.io/hostname=k3d-distml-server-0
                           kubernetes.io/os=linux
                           node-role.kubernetes.io/control-plane=true
                           node-role.kubernetes.io/master=true
                           node.kubernetes.io/instance-type=k3s

System Info:
  Machine ID:
  System UUID:
  Boot ID:                 73db7620-c61d-432c-a1ab-343b28ab8563
  Kernel Version:          5.10.104-linuxkit
  OS Image:                K3s dev
  Operating System:        linux
  Architecture:            arm64
  Container Runtime Version: containerd://1.5.9-k3s1
  Kubelet Version:         v1.22.7+k3s1
  Kube-Proxy Version:      v1.22.7+k3s1

The node's addresses are shown as part of it:

Addresses:
  InternalIP:  172.18.0.3
  Hostname:    k3d-distml-server-0

The capacity of the node is also available,
indicating how much computational resources are there:

Capacity:
  cpu:                 4
  ephemeral-storage:   61255492Ki
  hugepages-1Gi:       0
  hugepages-2Mi:       0
  hugepages-32Mi:      0
  hugepages-64Ki:      0
  memory:              8142116Ki
  pods:                110
```

Then we'll create a *namespace* called `basics` in this cluster for our project. Namespaces in Kubernetes provide a mechanism for isolating groups of resources within a single cluster (see http://mng.bz/BmN1). Names of resources need to be unique within a namespace but not across namespaces. The following examples will be in this single namespace.

Listing 8.23 Creating a new namespace

```
> kubectl create ns basics
```

Once the cluster and namespace are set up, we'll use a convenient tool called `kubectx` to help us inspect and navigate between namespaces and clusters (https://github .com/ahmetb/kubectx). Note that this tool is not required for day-to-day work with Kubernetes, but it should make Kubernetes much easier to work with for developers. For example, we can obtain a list of clusters and namespaces that we can connect to via the following listing.

Listing 8.24 Switching contexts and namespaces

```
> kubectx
d3d-k3s-default
k3d-distml

> kubens
default
kube-system
kube-public
kube-node-lease
basics
```

For example, we can switch to the `distml` cluster via the `k3d-distml` context and the `basics` namespace that we just created using the following listing.

Listing 8.25 Activate context

```
> kubectx k3d-distml
Switched to context "k3d-distml".

> kubens basics
Active namespace is "basics".
```

Switching contexts and namespaces is often needed when working with multiple clusters and namespaces. We are using the basics namespace to run the examples in this chapter, but we will switch to another namespace dedicated to our project in the next chapter.

Next, we will create a Kubernetes *Pod*. Pods are the smallest deployable units of computing that you can create and manage in Kubernetes. A Pod may consist of one or more containers with shared storage and network resources and a specification for how to run the containers. A Pod's contents are always co-located and co-scheduled and run in a shared context. The concept of the Pod models an application-specific "logical host," meaning that it contains one or more application containers that are relatively tightly coupled. In noncloud contexts, applications executed on the same physical or virtual machine are analogous to cloud applications executed on the same logical host. In other words, a Pod is similar to a set of containers with shared namespaces and shared filesystem volumes.

The following listing provides an example of a Pod that consists of a container running the image whalesay to print out a "hello world" message. We save the following Pod spec in a file named hello-world.yaml.

Listing 8.26 An example Pod

```
apiVersion: v1
kind: Pod
metadata:
  name: whalesay
spec:
  containers:
  - name: whalesay
    image: docker/whalesay:latest
    command: [cowsay]
    args: ["hello world"]
```

To create the Pod, run the following command.

Listing 8.27 Creating the example Pod in the cluster

```
> kubectl create -f basics/hello-world.yaml

pod/whalesay created
```

We can then check whether the Pod has been created by retrieving the list of Pods. Note that pods is plural so we can get the full list of created Pods. We will use the singular form to get the details of this particular Pod later.

Listing 8.28 Getting the list of Pods in the cluster

```
> kubectl get pods

NAME        READY    STATUS      RESTARTS      AGE
whalesay    0/1      Completed   2 (20s ago)   37s
```

The Pod status is Completed so we can look at what's being printed out in the whalesay container like in the following listing.

Listing 8.29   Checking the Pod logs

```
> kubectl logs whalesay

 _____
< hello world >
 -------------
        \
         \
          \
                          ##         .
                    ## ## ##        ==
                    ## ## ## ##     ===
                /"""""""""""""""""___/ ===
           ~~~ {~~ ~~~~ ~~~ ~~~~ ~~ ~ /  ===- ~~~
                _____ o          __/
                 \    \        __/
                  _____/
```

We can also retrieve the raw YAML of the Pod via `kubectl`. Note that we use `-o yaml` here to get the plain YAML, but other formats, such as JSON, are also supported. We use the singular `pod` to get the details of this particular Pod instead of the full list of existing Pods, as mentioned earlier.

Listing 8.30   Getting the raw Pod YAML

```
> kubectl get pod whalesay -o yaml

apiVersion: v1
kind: Pod
metadata:
  creationTimestamp: "2022-10-22T14:30:19Z"
  name: whalesay
  namespace: basics
  resourceVersion: "830"
  uid: 8e5e13f9-cd58-45e8-8070-c6bbb2dddb6e
spec:
  containers:
  - args:
    - hello world
    command:
    - cowsay
    image: docker/whalesay:latest
    imagePullPolicy: Always
    name: whalesay
    resources: {} '
    terminationMessagePath: /dev/termination-log
    terminationMessagePolicy: File
    volumeMounts:
    - mountPath: /var/run/secrets/kubernetes.io/serviceaccount
    name: kube-api-access-x826t
    readOnly: true
```

```
    dnsPolicy: ClusterFirst
    enableServiceLinks: true
    nodeName: k3d-distml-server-

<...truncated...>

    volumes:
  - name: kube-api-access-x826t
    projected:
    defaultMode: 420
    sources:
    - serviceAccountToken:
          expirationSeconds: 3607
          path: token
    - configMap:
          items:
          - key: ca.crt
          path: ca.crt
          name: kube-root-ca.crt
    - downwardAPI:
          items:
            - fieldRef:
            apiVersion: v1
            fieldPath: metadata.namespace
            path: namespace
status:
  conditions:
  - lastProbeTime: null
    lastTransitionTime: "2022-10-22T14:30:19Z"
    status: "True"
    type: Initialized
  - lastProbeTime: null
    lastTransitionTime: "2022-10-22T14:30:19Z"
    message: 'containers with unready status: [whalesay]'
    reason: ContainersNotReady
    status: "False"
    type: Ready
```

You may be surprised how much additional content, such as status and conditions, has been added to the original YAML we used to create the Pod. The additional information is appended and updated via the Kubernetes server so that client-side applications know the current status of the Pod. Even though we didn't specify the namespace explicitly, the Pod was created in the basics namespace since we have used the kubens command to set the current namespace.

That's it for the basics of Kubernetes! In the next section, we will study how to use Kubeflow to run distributed model training jobs in the local Kubernetes cluster we just set up.

8.2.2   *Exercises*

1 How do you get the Pod information in JSON format?
2 Can a Pod contain multiplier containers?

8.3 Kubeflow: Machine learning workloads on Kubernetes

The Kubeflow project is dedicated to making deployments of machine learning workflows on Kubernetes simple, portable, and scalable. The goal of Kubeflow is not to re-create other services but to provide a straightforward way to deploy best-in-class open source systems for machine learning to diverse infrastructures. Anywhere you run Kubernetes, you should be able to run Kubeflow. We will use Kubeflow to submit distributed machine learning model training jobs to a Kubernetes cluster.

Let's first take a look at what components Kubeflow provides. Figure 8.3 is a diagram that consists of the main components.

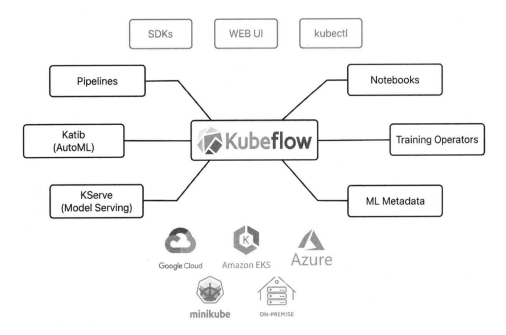

Figure 8.3   Main components of Kubeflow

Kubeflow Pipelines (KFP; https://github.com/kubeflow/pipelines) provides Python SDK to make machine learning pipelines easier. It is a platform for building and deploying portable and scalable machine learning workflows using Docker containers. The primary objectives of KFP are to enable the following:

- End-to-end orchestration of ML workflows
- Pipeline composability through reusable components and pipelines
- Easy management, tracking, and visualization of pipeline definitions, runs, experiments, and machine learning artifacts
- Efficient use of computing resources by eliminating redundant executions through caching

- Cross-platform pipeline portability through a platform-neutral IR YAML pipeline definition

KFP uses Argo Workflows as the backend workflow engine, which I will introduce in the next section, and we'll use Argo Workflows directly instead of using a higher-level wrapper like KFP. The ML metadata project has been merged into KFP and serves as the backend for logging metadata produced in machine learning workflows written in KFP.

Next is Katib (https://github.com/kubeflow/katib). Katib is a Kubernetes-native project for automated machine learning. Katib supports hyperparameter tuning, early stopping, and neural architecture search. Katib is agnostic to machine learning frameworks. It can tune hyperparameters of applications written in any language of the users' choice and natively supports many machine learning frameworks, such as TensorFlow, Apache MXNet, PyTorch, XGBoost, and others. Katib can perform training jobs using any Kubernetes custom resource with out-of-the-box support for Kubeflow Training Operator, Argo Workflows, Tekton Pipelines, and many more. Figure 8.4 is a screenshot of the Katib UI that performs experiment tracking.

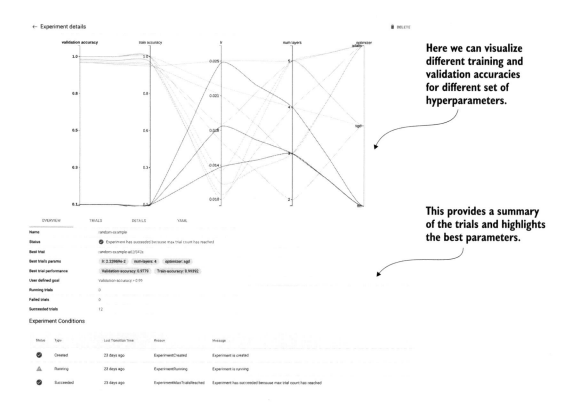

Figure 8.4 A screenshot of the Katib UI that performs experiment tracking

KServe (https://github.com/kserve/kserve) was born as part of the Kubeflow project and was previously known as KFServing. KServe provides a Kubernetes custom resource definition (CRD) for serving machine learning models on arbitrary frameworks. It aims to solve production model serving use cases by providing performant, high-abstraction interfaces for common ML frameworks. It encapsulates the complexity of autoscaling, networking, health checking, and server configuration to bring cutting-edge serving features like GPU autoscaling, scale to zero, and canary rollouts to your machine learning deployments. Figure 8.5 is a diagram that illustrates the position of KServe in the ecosystem.

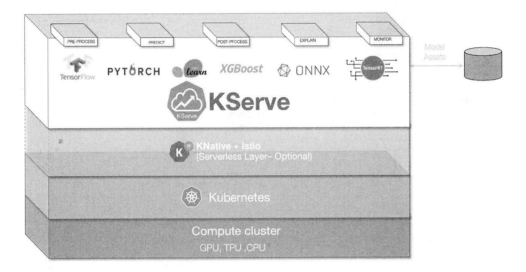

Figure 8.5   KServe positioning in the ecosystem

Kubeflow provides web UI. Figure 8.6 provides a screenshot of the UI. Users can access the models, pipelines, experiments, artifacts, etc. to facilitate the iterative process of the end-to-end model machine life cycle in each tab on the left side.

The web UI is integrated with Jupyter Notebooks to be easily accessible. There are also SDKs in different languages to help users integrate with any internal systems. In addition, users can interact with all the Kubeflow components via `kubectl` since they are all native Kubernetes custom resources and controllers. The training operator (https://github.com/kubeflow/training-operator) provides Kubernetes custom resources that make it easy to run distributed or nondistributed TensorFlow, PyTorch, Apache MXNet, XGBoost, or MPI jobs on Kubernetes.

The Kubeflow project has accumulated more than 500 contributors and 20,000 GitHub stars. It's heavily adopted in various companies and has more than 10 vendors, including Amazon AWS, Azure, Google Cloud, IBM, etc. Seven working groups maintain different subprojects independently. We will use the training operator to submit

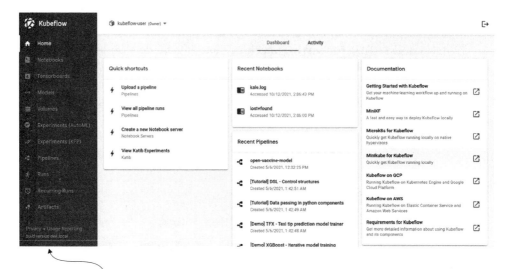

Users can access the models, pipelines, experiments, artifacts, etc., to facilitate the iterative process of the end-to-end model machine life cycle.

Figure 8.6   A screenshot of the Kubeflow UI

distributed model training jobs and KServe to build our model serving component. Once you complete the next chapter, I recommend trying out the other subprojects in the Kubeflow ecosystem on your own when needed. For example, if you'd like to tune the performance of the model, you can use Katib's automated machine learning and hyperparameter tuning functionalities.

8.3.1   The basics

Next, we'll take a closer look at the distributed training operator of Kubeflow and submit a distributed model training job that runs locally in the Kubernetes local cluster we created in the previous section. Let's first create and activate a dedicated `kubeflow` namespace for our examples and reuse the existing cluster we created earlier.

Listing 8.31   Creating and switching to a new namespace

```
> kubectl create ns kubeflow
> kns kubeflow
```

Then, we must go back to our project folder and apply all the manifests to install all the tools we need.

Listing 8.32   Applying all manifests and installing all the tools

```
> cd code/project
> kubectl kustomize manifests | k apply -f -
```

Note that we've bundled all the necessary tools in this manifests folder:

- Kubeflow Training Operator, which we will use in this chapter for distributed model training.
- Argo Workflows (https://github.com/argoproj/argo-workflows), which we address in chapter 9 when we discuss workflow orchestration and chain all the components together in a machine learning pipeline. We can ignore Argo Workflows for now.

As introduced earlier, the Kubeflow Training Operator provides Kubernetes custom resources that make it easy to run distributed or nondistributed jobs on Kubernetes, including TensorFlow, PyTorch, Apache MXNet, XGBoost, MPI jobs, etc.

Before we dive into Kubeflow, we need to understand what *custom resources* are. A custom resource is an extension of the Kubernetes API not necessarily available in a default Kubernetes installation. It is a customization of a particular Kubernetes installation. However, many core Kubernetes functions are now built using custom resources, making Kubernetes more modular (http://mng.bz/lWw2).

Custom resources can appear and disappear in a running cluster through dynamic registration, and cluster admins can update custom resources independently of the cluster. Once a custom resource is installed, users can create and access its objects using `kubectl`, just as they do for built-in resources like Pods. For example, the following listing defines the `TFJob` custom resource that allows us to instantiate and submit a distributed TensorFlow training job to the Kubernetes cluster.

Listing 8.33 `TFJob` CRD

```
apiVersion: apiextensions.k8s.io/v1
kind: CustomResourceDefinition
metadata:
  annotations:
    controller-gen.kubebuilder.io/version: v0.4.1
  name: tfjobs.kubeflow.org
spec:
  group: kubeflow.org
  names:
    kind: TFJob
    listKind: TFJobList
    plural: tfjobs
    singular: tfjob
```

All instantiated `TFJob` custom resource objects (`tfjobs`) will be handled by the training operator. The following listing provides the definition of the deployment of the training operator that runs a stateful controller to continuously monitor and process any submitted `tfjobs`.

Listing 8.34 Training operator deployment

```
apiVersion: apps/v1
kind: Deployment
```

```
metadata:
  name: training-operator
  labels:
    control-plane: kubeflow-training-operator
spec:
  selector:
    matchLabels:
      control-plane: kubeflow-training-operator
  replicas: 1
  template:
    metadata:
      labels:
        control-plane: kubeflow-training-operator
      annotations:
        sidecar.istio.io/inject: "false"
    spec:
      containers:
        - command:
            - /manager
          image: kubeflow/training-operator
          name: training-operator
          env:
            - name: MY_POD_NAMESPACE
              valueFrom:
                fieldRef:
                  fieldPath: metadata.namespace
            - name: MY_POD_NAME
              valueFrom:
                fieldRef:
                  fieldPath: metadata.name
          securityContext:
            allowPrivilegeEscalation: false
          livenessProbe:
            httpGet:
              path: /healthz
              port: 8081
            initialDelaySeconds: 15
            periodSeconds: 20
          readinessProbe:
            httpGet:
              path: /readyz
              port: 8081
            initialDelaySeconds: 5
            periodSeconds: 10
          resources:
            limits:
              cpu: 100m
              memory: 30Mi
            requests:
              cpu: 100m
              memory: 20Mi
      serviceAccountName: training-operator
      terminationGracePeriodSeconds: 10
```

With this abstraction, data science teams can focus on writing the Python code in TensorFlow that will be used as part of a `TFJob` specification and don't have to manage the infrastructure themselves. For now, we can skip the low-level details and use `TFJob` to implement our distributed model training. Next, let's define our `TFJob` in a file named tfjob.yaml.

Listing 8.35   An example `TFJob` definition

```
apiVersion: kubeflow.org/v1
kind: TFJob
metadata:
  namespace: kubeflow
  generateName: distributed-tfjob-
spec:
  tfReplicaSpecs:
    Worker:
      replicas: 2
      restartPolicy: OnFailure
      template:
        spec:
          containers:
            - name: tensorflow
              image: gcr.io/kubeflow-ci/tf-mnist-with-summaries:1.0
              command:
                - "python"
                - "/var/tf_mnist/mnist_with_summaries.py"
                - "--log_dir=/train/metrics"
                - "--learning_rate=0.01"
                - "--batch_size=100"
```

In this spec, we are asking the controller to submit a distributed TensorFlow model training model with two worker replicas where each worker replica follows the same container definition, running the MNIST image classification example.

Once it's defined, we can submit it to our local Kubernetes cluster via the following listing.

Listing 8.36   Submitting `TFJob`

```
> kubectl create -f basics/tfjob.yaml
tfjob.kubeflow.org/distributed-tfjob-qc8fh created
```

We can see whether the `TFJob` has been submitted successfully by getting the `TFJob` list.

Listing 8.37   Getting the `TFJob` list

```
> kubectl get tfjob

NAME                        AGE
Distributed-tfjob-qc8fh     1s
```

When we get the list of Pods, we can see two worker Pods, `distributed-tfjob-qc8fh-worker-1` and `distributed-tfjob-qc8fh-worker-0`, have been created and started running. The other Pods can be ignored since they are the Pods that are running the Kubeflow and Argo Workflow operators.

Listing 8.38   Getting the list of Pods

```
> kubectl get pods

NAME                                    READY   STATUS    RESTARTS   AGE
workflow-controller-594494ffbd-2dpkj    1/1     Running   0          21m
training-operator-575698dc89-mzvwb      1/1     Running   0          21m
argo-server-68c46c5c47-vfh82            1/1     Running   0          21m
distributed-tfjob-qc8fh-worker-1        1/1     Running   0          10s
distributed-tfjob-qc8fh-worker-0        1/1     Running   0          12s
```

A machine learning system consists of many different components. We only used Kubeflow to submit distributed model training jobs, but it's not connected to other components yet. In the next section, we'll explore the basic functionalities of Argo Workflows to connect different steps in a single workflow so that they can be executed in a particular order.

8.3.2   Exercises

1   If your model training requires parameter servers, can you express that in a `TFJob`?

8.4   *Argo Workflows: Container-native workflow engine*

The Argo Project is a suite of open-source tools for deploying and running applications and workloads on Kubernetes. It extends the Kubernetes APIs and unlocks new and powerful capabilities in application deployment, container orchestration, event automation, progressive delivery, and more. It consists of four core projects: Argo CD, Argo Rollouts, Argo Events, and Argo Workflows. Besides these core projects, many other ecosystem projects are based on, extend, or work well with Argo. A complete list of resources related to Argo can be found at https://github.com/terrytangyuan/awesome-argo.

Argo CD is a declarative, GitOps application delivery tool for Kubernetes. It manages application definitions, configurations, and environments declaratively in Git. Argo CD user experience makes Kubernetes application deployment and life-cycle management automated, auditable, and easy to grasp. It comes with a UI so engineers can see what's happening in their clusters and watch for applications deployments, etc. Figure 8.7 is a screenshot of the resource tree in the Argo CD UI.

Argo Rollouts is a Kubernetes controller and set of CRDs that provides progressive deployment capabilities. It introduces blue–green and canary deployments, canary analysis, experimentation, and progressive delivery features to your Kubernetes cluster.

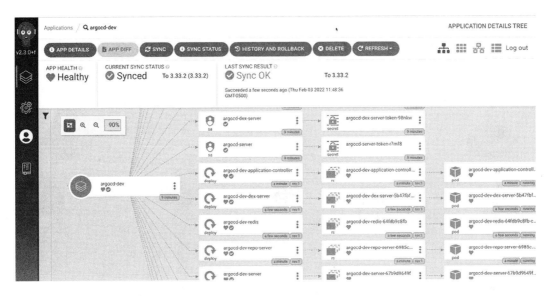

Figure 8.7   A screenshot of the resources tree in Argo CD UI

Next is Argo Events. It's an event-based dependency manager for Kubernetes. It can define multiple dependencies from various event sources like webhooks, Amazon S3, schedules, and streams and trigger Kubernetes objects after successful event dependencies resolution. A complete list of available event sources can be found in figure 8.8.

Finally, Argo Workflows is a container-native workflow engine for orchestrating parallel jobs, implemented as Kubernetes CRD. Users can define workflows where each step is a separate container, model multistep workflows as a sequence of tasks or capture the dependencies between tasks using a graph, and run compute-intensive jobs for machine learning or data processing. Users often use Argo Workflows together with Argo Events to trigger event-based workflows. The main use cases for Argo Workflows are machine learning pipelines, data processing, ETL (extract, transform, load), infrastructure automation, continuous delivery, and integration.

Argo Workflows also provides interfaces such as a command-line interface (CLI), server, UI, and SDKs for different languages. The CLI is useful for managing workflows and performing operations such as submitting, suspending, and deleting workflows through the command line. The server is used for integrating with other services. There are both REST and gRPC service interfaces. The UI is useful for managing and visualizing workflows and any artifacts/logs created by the workflows, as well as other useful information, such as resource usage analytics. We will walk through some examples of Argo Workflows to prepare for our project.

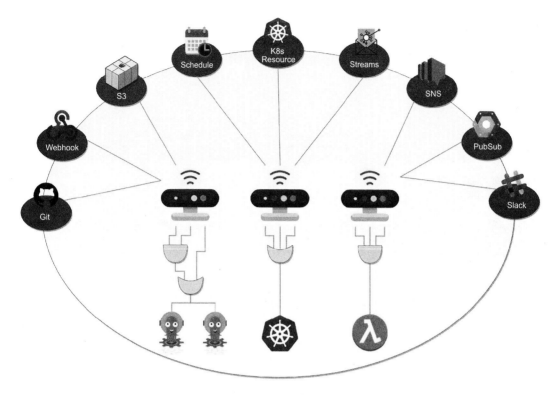

Figure 8.8   Available event sources in Argo Events

8.4.1   *The basics*

Before we look at some examples, let's make sure we have the Argo Workflows UI at hand. It's optional since you can still be successful in these examples in the command line to interact directly with Kubernetes via `kubectl`, but it's nice to see the directed-acyclic graph (DAG) visualizations in the UI as well as access additional functionalities. By default, the Argo Workflows UI service is not exposed to an external IP. To access the UI, use the method in the following listing.

Listing 8.39   Port-forwarding the Argo server

```
> kubectl port-forward svc/argo-server 2746:2746
```

Next, visit the following URL to access the UI: https://localhost:2746. Alternatively, you can expose a load balancer to get an external IP to access the Argo Workflows UI in your local cluster. Check out the official documentation for more details: https://argoproj.github.io/argo-workflows/argo-server/. Figure 8.9 is a screenshot of what the Argo Workflows UI looks like for a map-reduce–style workflow.

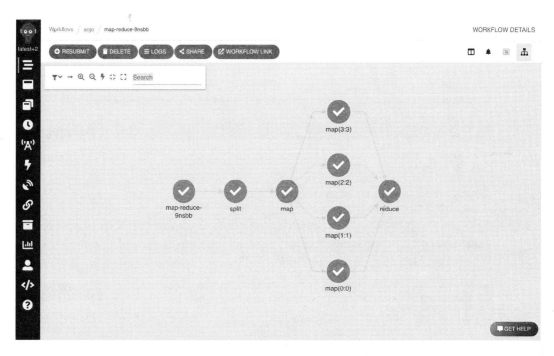

Figure 8.9   Argo Workflows UI illustrating a map-reduce–style workflow

The following listing is a basic "hello world" example of Argo Workflows. We can specify the container image and the command to run for this workflow and print out a "hello world" message.

Listing 8.40   "Hello world" example

```
apiVersion: argoproj.io/v1alpha1
kind: Workflow
metadata:
  generateName: hello-world-
spec:
  entrypoint: whalesay
  serviceAccountName: argo
  templates:
  - name: whalesay
    container:
      image: docker/whalesay
      command: [cowsay]
      args: ["hello world"]
```

Let's go ahead and submit the workflow to our cluster.

Listing 8.41   Submitting the workflow

```
> kubectl create -f basics/argo-hello-world.yaml
workflow.argoproj.io/hello-world-zns4g created
```

We can then check whether it was submitted successfully and has started running.

Listing 8.42   Getting the list of workflows

```
> kubectl get wf

NAME               STATUS    AGE
hello-world-zns4g  Running   2s
```

Once the workflow status has changed to `Succeeded`, we can check the statuses of the Pods created by the workflow. First, let's find all the Pods associated with the workflow. We can use a label selector to get the list of Pods.

Listing 8.43   Getting the list of Pods belonging to this workflow

```
> kubectl get pods -l workflows.argoproj.io/workflow=hello-world-zns4g

NAME               READY   STATUS      RESTARTS   AGE
hello-world-zns4g  0/2     Completed   0          8m57s
```

Once we know the Pod name, we can get the logs of that Pod.

Listing 8.44   Checking the Pod logs

```
> kubectl logs hello-world-zns4g -c main

 _____
< hello world >
 -------------
    \
     \
      \
                    ##        .
              ## ## ##       ==
           ## ## ## ##      ===
       /""""""""""""""""___/ ===
  ~~~ {~~ ~~~~ ~~~ ~~~~ ~~ ~ /  ===- ~~~
       _____ o          __/
        \    \        __/
          _____/
```

As expected, we get the same logs as the ones we had with the simple Kubernetes Pod in the previous sections since this workflow only runs one "hello world" step.

The next example uses a resource template where you can specify a Kubernetes custom resource that will be submitted by the workflow to the Kubernetes cluster.

Here we create a Kubernetes config map named `cm-example` with a simple key-value pair. The config map is a Kubernetes-native object to store key-value pairs.

Listing 8.45 Resource template

```
apiVersion: argoproj.io/v1alpha1
kind: Workflow
metadata:
  generateName: k8s-resource-
spec:
  entrypoint: k8s-resource
  serviceAccountName: argo
  templates:
  - name: k8s-resource
    resource:
      action: create
      manifest: |
        apiVersion: v1
        kind: ConfigMap
        metadata:
          name: cm-example
        data:
          some: value
```

This example is perhaps most useful to Python users. You can write a Python script as part of the template definition. We can generate some random numbers using the built-in random Python module. Alternatively, you can specify the execution logic of the script inside a container template without writing inline Python code, as seen in the "hello world" example.

Listing 8.46 Script template

```
apiVersion: argoproj.io/v1alpha1
kind: Workflow
metadata:
  generateName: script-tmpl-
spec:
  entrypoint: gen-random-int
  serviceAccountName: argo
  templates:
  - name: gen-random-int
    script:
      image: python:alpine3.6
      command: [python]
      source: |
        import random
        i = random.randint(1, 100)
        print(i)
```

Let's submit it.

Listing 8.47   Submitting the script template workflow

```
> kubectl create -f basics/argo-script-template.yaml
workflow.argoproj.io/script-tmpl-c5lhb created
```

Now, let's check its logs to see whether a random number was generated.

Listing 8.48   Check the Pod logs

```
> kubectl logs script-tmpl-c5lhb
25
```

So far, we've only seen examples of single-step workflows. Argo Workflow also allows users to define the workflow as a DAG by specifying the dependencies of each task. The DAG can be simpler to maintain for complex workflows and allows maximum parallelism when running tasks.

Let's look at an example of a diamond-shaped DAG created by Argo Workflows. This DAG consists of four steps (A, B, C, and D), and each has its own dependencies. For example, step C depends on step A, and step D depends on steps B and C.

Listing 8.49   A diamond example using DAG

```
apiVersion: argoproj.io/v1alpha1
kind: Workflow
metadata:
  generateName: dag-diamond-
spec:
  serviceAccountName: argo
  entrypoint: diamond
  templates:
  - name: echo
    inputs:
      parameters:
        - name: message
    container:
      image: alpine:3.7
      command: [echo, "{{inputs.parameters.message}}"]
  - name: diamond
    dag:
      tasks:
          - name: A
    template: echo
    arguments:
            parameters: [{name: message, value: A}]
          - name: B
            dependencies: [A]
            template: echo
            arguments:
              parameters: [{name: message, value: B}]
          - name: C
            dependencies: [A]
            template: echo
```

```
arguments:
            parameters: [{name: message, value: C}]
        - name: D
dependencies: [B, C]
template: echo
arguments:
            parameters: [{name: message, value: D}]
```

Let's submit it.

Listing 8.50   Submitting the DAG workflow

```
> kubectl create -f basics/argo-dag-diamond.yaml
workflow.argoproj.io/dag-diamond-6swfg created
```

When the workflow is completed, we will see four Pods for each of the steps where each step prints out its step name—A, B, C, and D.

Listing 8.51   Getting the list of Pods belonging to this workflow

```
> kubectl get pods -l workflows.argoproj.io/workflow=dag-diamond-6swfg
```

NAME	READY	STATUS	RESTARTS	AGE
dag-diamond-6swfg-echo-4189448097	0/2	Completed	0	76s
dag-diamond-6swfg-echo-4155892859	0/2	Completed	0	66s
dag-diamond-6swfg-echo-4139115240	0/2	Completed	0	66s
dag-diamond-6swfg-echo-4239780954	0/2	Completed	0	56s

The visualization of the DAG is available in the Argo Workflows UI. It's usually more intuitive to see how the workflow is executed in a diamond-shaped flow in the UI, as seen in figure 8.10.

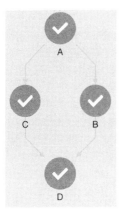

Figure 8.10   A screenshot of a diamond-shaped workflow in the UI

Next, we will look at a simple coin-flip example to showcase the conditional syntax provided by Argo Workflows. We can specify a condition to indicate whether we want to run the next step. For example, we run the `flip-coin` step first, which is the Python script we saw earlier, and if the result returns heads, we run the template called `heads`, which prints another log saying it was heads. Otherwise, we print that it was tails. So we can specify these conditionals inside the `when` clause in the different steps.

Listing 8.52   Coin-flip example

```
apiVersion: argoproj.io/v1alpha1
kind: Workflow
metadata:
  generateName: coinflip-
spec:
  serviceAccountName: argo
  entrypoint: coinflip
  templates:
  - name: coinflip
    steps:
    - - name: flip-coin
        template: flip-coin
    - - name: heads
        template: heads
        when: "{{steps.flip-coin.outputs.result}} == heads"
      - name: tails
        template: tails
        when: "{{steps.flip-coin.outputs.result}} == tails"

  - name: flip-coin
    script:
      image: python:alpine3.6
      command: [python]
      source: |
        import random
        result = "heads" if random.randint(0,1) == 0 else "tails"
        print(result)

  - name: heads
    container:
      image: alpine:3.6
      command: [sh, -c]
      args: ["echo \"it was heads\""]

  - name: tails
    container:
      image: alpine:3.6
      command: [sh, -c]
      args: ["echo \"it was tails\""]
```

Let's submit the workflow.

Listing 8.53   Submitting the coin-flip example

```
> kubectl create -f basics/argo-coinflip.yaml
workflow.argoproj.io/coinflip-p87ff created
```

Figure 8.11 is a screenshot of what this `flip-coin` workflow looks like in the UI.

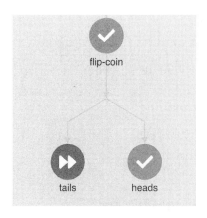

Figure 8.11 Screenshot of the `flip-coin` workflow in the UI

When we get the list of workflows, we find only two Pods.

Listing 8.54   Getting the list of Pods belonging to this workflow

```
> kubectl get pods -l workflows.argoproj.io/workflow=coinflip-p87ff

coinflip-p87ff-flip-coin-1071502578    0/2  Completed    0    23s
coinflip-p87ff-tails-2208102039        0/2  Completed    0    13s
```

We can check the logs of the `flip-coin` step to see whether it prints out `tails` since the next step executed is the `tails` step:

```
> kubectl logs coinflip-p87ff-flip-coin-1071502578
tails
```

That's a wrap! We've just learned the basic syntax of Argo Workflows, which should cover all the prerequisites for the next chapter! In the next chapter, we will use Argo Workflows to implement the end-to-end machine learning workflow that consists of the actual system components introduced in chapter 7.

8.4.2 Exercises

1 Besides accessing the output of each step like `{{steps.flip-coin.outputs.result}}`, what are other available variables?
2 Can you trigger workflows automatically by Git commits or other events?

8.5 Answers to exercises

Section 8.1

1 Yes, via `model = tf.keras.models.load_model('my_model.h5'); modele.evaluate(x_test, y_test)`

2 You should be able to do it easily by changing the tuner to `kt.RandomSearch` `(model_builder)`.

Section 8.2

1 `kubectl get pod <pod-name> -o json`
2 Yes, you can define additional containers in the `pod.spec.containers` in addition to the existing single container.

Section 8.3

1 Similar to worker replicas, define `parameterServer` replicas in your `TFJob` spec to specify the number of parameter servers.

Section 8.4

1 The complete list is available here: http://mng.bz/d1Do.
2 Yes, you can use Argo Events to watch Git events and trigger workflows.

Summary

- We used TensorFlow to train a machine learning model for the MNIST dataset in a single machine.
- We learned the basic concepts in Kubernetes and gained hands-on experience by implementing them in a local Kubernetes cluster.
- We submitted distributed model training jobs to Kubernetes via Kubeflow.
- We learned about different types of templates and how to define either DAGs or sequential steps using Argo Workflows.

A complete implementation

This chapter covers

- Implementing data ingestion component with TensorFlow
- Defining the machine learning model and submitting distributed model training jobs
- Implementing a single-instance model server as well as replicated model servers
- Building an efficient end-to-end workflow of our machine learning system

In the previous chapter of the book, we learned the basics of the four core technologies that we will use in our project: TensorFlow, Kubernetes, Kubeflow, and Argo Workflows. We learned that TensorFlow performs data processing, model building, and model evaluation. We also learned the basic concepts of Kubernetes and started our local Kubernetes cluster, which we will use as our core distributed infrastructure. In addition, we successfully submitted distributed model training jobs to the local Kubernetes cluster using Kubeflow. At the end of the last chapter, we learned how to use Argo Workflows to construct and submit a basic "hello world" workflow and a complex DAG-structured workflow.

In this chapter, we'll implement the end-to-end machine learning system with the architecture we designed in chapter 7. We will completely implement each component, which will incorporate the previously discussed patterns. We'll use several popular frameworks and cutting-edge technologies, particularly TensorFlow, Kubernetes, Kubeflow, Docker, and Argo Workflows, which we introduced in chapter 8 to build different components of a distributed machine learning workflow in this chapter.

9.1   Data ingestion

The first component in our end-to-end workflow is data ingestion. We'll be using the Fashion-MNIST dataset introduced in section 2.2 to build the data ingestion component. Figure 9.1 shows this component in the dark box on the left of the end-to-end workflow.

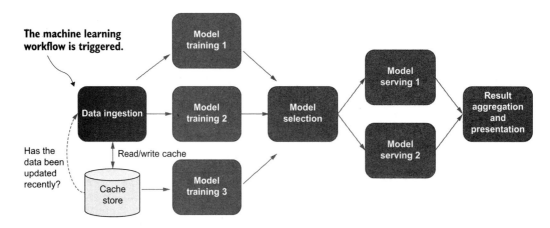

Figure 9.1   The data ingestion component (dark box) in the end-to-end machine learning system

Recall that this dataset consists of a training set of 60,000 examples and a test set of 10,000 examples. Each example is a 28 × 28 grayscale image representing one Zalando's article image and associated with a label from 10 classes. In addition, the Fashion-MNIST dataset is designed to serve as a direct drop-in replacement for the original MNIST dataset for benchmarking machine learning algorithms. It shares the same image size and structure of training and testing splits. Figure 9.2 is a screenshot of the collection of images for all 10 classes (T-shirt/top, trouser, pullover, dress, coat, sandal, shirt, sneaker, bag, and ankle boot) from Fashion-MNIST, where each class takes three rows in the screenshot.

Figure 9.3 is a closer look at the first few example images in the training set together with their corresponding labels in text above each of the images.

In section 9.1.1, we'll go through the implementation of a single-node data pipeline that ingests the Fashion-MNIST dataset. Furthermore, section 9.1.2 will cover the

Every three rows represent example images that represent a class. For example, the top three rows are images of T-shirts.

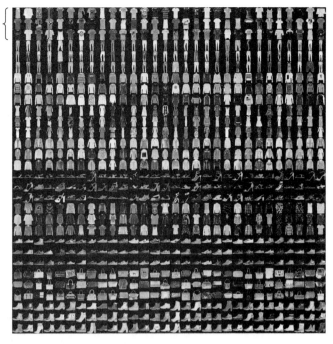

Figure 9.2 A screenshot of the collection of images from the Fashion-MNIST dataset for all 10 classes (T-shirt/top, trouser, pullover, dress, coat, sandal, shirt, sneaker, bag, and ankle boot)

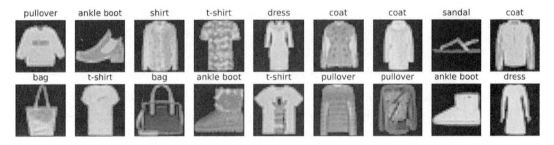

Figure 9.3 A closer look at the first few example images in the training set with their corresponding labels in text

implementation of the distributed data pipeline to prepare the data for our distributed model training in section 9.2.

9.1.1 Single-node data pipeline

Let's first take a look at how to build a single-node data pipeline that works locally on your laptop without using a local Kubernetes cluster. The best way for a machine learning program written in TensorFlow to consume data is through methods in `tf.data` module. The `tf.data` API allows users to build complex input pipelines easily. For example, the pipeline for an image model might aggregate data from files in various file systems, apply random transformations to each image, and create batches from the images for model training.

The `tf.data` API enables it to handle large amounts of data, read from different data formats, and perform complex transformations. It contains a `tf.data.Dataset` abstraction that represents a sequence of elements, in which each element consists of one or more components. Let's use the image pipeline to illustrate this. An element in an image input pipeline might be a single training example, with a pair of tensor components representing the image and its label.

The following listing provides the code snippet to load the Fashion-MNIST dataset into a `tf.data.Dataset` object and performs some necessary preprocessing steps to prepare for our model training:

1 Scale the dataset from the range (0, 255] to (0., 1.].

2 Cast the image multidimensional arrays into float32 type that our model can accept.

3 Select the training data, cache it in memory to speed up training, and shuffle it with a buffer size of 10,000.

Listing 9.1 Loading the Fashion-MNIST dataset

```
import tensorflow_datasets as tfds
import tensorflow as tf
def make_datasets_unbatched():
  def scale(image, label):
    image = tf.cast(image, tf.float32)
    image /= 255
    return image, label
  datasets, _ = tfds.load(name='fashion_mnist',
    with_info=True, as_supervised=True)
  return datasets['train'].map(scale).cache().shuffle(10000)
```

Note that we imported `tensorflow_datasets` module. The TensorFlow Datasets, which consists of a collection of datasets for various tasks such as image classification, object detection, document summarization, etc., can be used with TensorFlow and other Python machine learning frameworks.

The `tf.data.Dataset` object is a shuffled dataset where each element consists of the images and their labels with the shape and data type information as in the following listing.

Listing 9.2 Inspecting the `tf.data` object

```
>>> ds = make_datasets_unbatched()
>>> ds
<ShuffleDataset element_spec=(
  TensorSpec(shape=(28, 28, 1),
  dtype=tf.float32, name=None),
TensorSpec(shape=(), dtype=tf.int64, name=None))>
```

9.1.2 *Distributed data pipeline*

Now let's look at how we can consume our dataset in a distributed fashion. We'll be using `tf.distribute.MultiWorkerMirroredStrategy` for distributed training in the next section. Let's assume we have instantiated a strategy object. We will instantiate our dataset inside the strategy's scope via Python's `with` syntax using the same function we previously defined for the single-node use case.

We will need to tweak a few configurations to build our distributed input pipeline. First, we create repeated batches of data where the total batch size equals the batch size per replica times the number of replicas over which gradients are aggregated. This ensures that we will have enough records to train each batch in each of the model training workers. In other words, the number of replicas in sync equals the number of devices taking part in the gradient allreduce operation during model training. For instance, when a user or the training code calls `next()` on the distributed data iterator, a per replica batch size of data is returned on each replica. The rebatched dataset cardinality will always be a multiple of the number of replicas.

In addition, we want to configure `tf.data` to enable automatic data sharding. Since the dataset is in the distributed scope, the input dataset will be sharded automatically in multiworker training mode. More specifically, each dataset will be created on the CPU device of the worker, and each set of workers will train the model on a subset of the entire dataset when `tf.data.experimental.AutoShardPolicy` is set to `AutoShardPolicy.DATA`. One benefit is that during each model training step, a global batch size of non-overlapping dataset elements will be processed by each worker. Each worker will process the whole dataset and discard the portion that is not for itself. Note that for this mode to partition the dataset elements correctly, the dataset needs to produce elements in a deterministic order, which should already be guaranteed by the TensorFlow Datasets library we use.

Listing 9.3 Configuring distributed data pipeline

```
BATCH_SIZE_PER_REPLICA = 64
BATCH_SIZE = BATCH_SIZE_PER_REPLICA * strategy.num_replicas_in_sync
with strategy.scope():
  ds_train = make_datasets_unbatched().batch(BATCH_SIZE).repeat()
  options = tf.data.Options()
  options.experimental_distribute.auto_shard_policy = \
    tf.data.experimental.AutoShardPolicy.DATA
  ds_train = ds_train.with_options(options)
  model = build_and_compile_model()
model.fit(ds_train, epochs=1, steps_per_epoch=70)
```

9.2 *Model training*

We went through the implementation of the data ingestion component for both local-node and distributed data pipelines and discussed how we can shard the dataset properly across different workers so that it would work with distributed model training. In this section, let's dive into the implementation details for our model training component. An architecture diagram of the model training component can be found in figure 9.4.

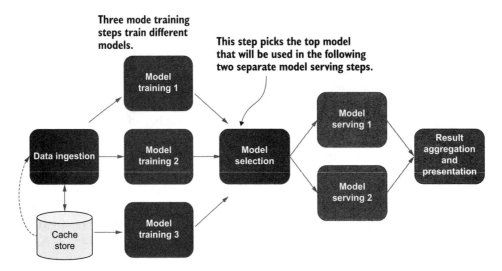

Figure 9.4   A diagram of the model training component in the overall architecture. Three different model training steps are followed by a model selection step. These model training steps would train three different models—namely, CNN, CNN with dropout, and CNN with batch normalization—competing with each other for better statistical performance.

We will learn how to define those three models with TensorFlow in section 9.2.1 and execute the distributed model training jobs with Kubeflow in section 9.2.2. In section 9.2.3, we will implement the model selection step that picks the top model that will be used in the model serving component in our end-to-end machine learning workflow.

9.2.1   *Model definition and single-node training*

Next, we'll look at the TensorFlow code to define and initialize the first model, a convolutional neural network (CNN) model we introduced in previous chapters with three convolutional layers. We initialize the model with `Sequential()`, meaning we'll add the layers sequentially. The first layer is the input layer, where we specify the shape of the input pipeline that we defined previously. Note that we also explicitly give a name to the input layer so we can pass the correct key in our inference inputs, which we will discuss in more depth in section 9.3.

After adding the input layer, three convolutional layers, followed by max-pooling layers and dense layers, are added to the sequential model. We'll then print out a summary of the model architecture and compile the model with Adam as its optimizer, accuracy as the metric we use to evaluate the model, and sparse categorical cross-entropy as the loss function.

Listing 9.4 Defining the basic CNN model

```
def build_and_compile_cnn_model():
  print("Training CNN model")
  model = models.Sequential()
  model.add(layers.Input(shape=(28, 28, 1), name='image_bytes'))
  model.add(
          layers.Conv2D(32, (3, 3), activation='relu'))
  model.add(layers.MaxPooling2D((2, 2)))
  model.add(layers.Conv2D(64, (3, 3), activation='relu'))
  model.add(layers.MaxPooling2D((2, 2)))
  model.add(layers.Conv2D(64, (3, 3), activation='relu'))
  model.add(layers.Flatten())
  model.add(layers.Dense(64, activation='relu'))
  model.add(layers.Dense(10, activation='softmax'))
  model.summary()
  model.compile(optimizer='adam',
          loss='sparse_categorical_crossentropy',
          metrics=['accuracy'])
  return model
```

We've successfully defined our basic CNN model. Next, we define two models based on the CNN model. One adds a batch normalization layer to force the pre-activations to have zero mean and unit standard deviation for every neuron (activation) in a particular layer. The other model has an additional dropout layer where half of the hidden units will be dropped randomly to reduce the complexity of the model and speed up computation. The rest of the code is the same as the basic CNN model.

Listing 9.5 Defining the variations of the basic CNN model

```
def build_and_compile_cnn_model_with_batch_norm():
  print("Training CNN model with batch normalization")
  model = models.Sequential()
  model.add(layers.Input(shape=(28, 28, 1), name='image_bytes'))
  model.add(
          layers.Conv2D(32, (3, 3), activation='relu'))
  model.add(layers.BatchNormalization())
  model.add(layers.Activation('sigmoid'))
  model.add(layers.MaxPooling2D((2, 2)))
  model.add(layers.Conv2D(64, (3, 3), activation='relu'))
  model.add(layers.BatchNormalization())
  model.add(layers.Activation('sigmoid'))
  model.add(layers.MaxPooling2D((2, 2)))
  model.add(layers.Conv2D(64, (3, 3), activation='relu'))
  model.add(layers.Flatten())
  model.add(layers.Dense(64, activation='relu'))
  model.add(layers.Dense(10, activation='softmax'))

  model.summary()

  model.compile(optimizer='adam',
            loss='sparse_categorical_crossentropy',
```

```
                metrics=['accuracy'])
    return model

def build_and_compile_cnn_model_with_dropout():
    print("Training CNN model with dropout")
    model = models.Sequential()
    model.add(layers.Input(shape=(28, 28, 1), name='image_bytes'))
    model.add(
            layers.Conv2D(32, (3, 3), activation='relu'))
    model.add(layers.MaxPooling2D((2, 2)))
    model.add(layers.Conv2D(64, (3, 3), activation='relu'))
    model.add(layers.MaxPooling2D((2, 2)))
    model.add(layers.Dropout(0.5))
    model.add(layers.Conv2D(64, (3, 3), activation='relu'))
    model.add(layers.Flatten())
    model.add(layers.Dense(64, activation='relu'))
    model.add(layers.Dense(10, activation='softmax'))

    model.summary()

    model.compile(optimizer='adam',
            loss='sparse_categorical_crossentropy',
            metrics=['accuracy'])
    return model
```

Once the models are defined, we can train them locally on our laptops. Let's use the basic CNN model as an example. We will create four callbacks that will be executed during model training:

1 `PrintLR`—Callback to print the learning rate at the end of each epoch
2 `TensorBoard`—Callback to start the interactive TensorBoard visualization to monitor the training progress and model architecture
3 `ModelCheckpoint`—Callback to save model weights for model inference later
4 `LearningRateScheduler`—Callback to decay the learning rate at the end of each epoch

Once these callbacks are defined, we'll pass it to the `fit()` method for training. The `fit()` method trains the model with a specified number of epochs and steps per epoch. Note that the numbers here are for demonstration purposes only to speed up our local experiments and may not sufficiently produce a model with good quality in real-world applications.

Listing 9.6   Modeling training with callbacks

```
single_worker_model = build_and_compile_cnn_model()
checkpoint_prefix = os.path.join(args.checkpoint_dir, "ckpt_{epoch}")

class PrintLR(tf.keras.callbacks.Callback):
    def on_epoch_end(self, epoch, logs=None):
        print('\nLearning rate for epoch {} is {}'.format(
            epoch + 1, multi_worker_model.optimizer.lr.numpy()))
```

```
callbacks = [
        tf.keras.callbacks.TensorBoard(log_dir='./logs'),
        tf.keras.callbacks.ModelCheckpoint(filepath=checkpoint_prefix,
                                save_weights_only=True),
        tf.keras.callbacks.LearningRateScheduler(decay),
        PrintLR()
]

single_worker_model.fit(ds_train,
                    epochs=1,
                    steps_per_epoch=70,
                    callbacks=callbacks)
```

We'll see the model training progress like the following in the logs:

```
Learning rate for epoch 1 is 0.0010000000474974513
70/70 [========] - 16s 136ms/step - loss: 1.2853
- accuracy: 0.5382 - lr: 0.0010
```

Here's the summary of the model architecture in the logs:
Model: "sequential"

Layer (type)	Output Shape	Param #
conv2d (Conv2D)	(None, 26, 26, 32)	320
max_pooling2d (MaxPooling2D)	(None, 13, 13, 32)	0
conv2d_1 (Conv2D)	(None, 11, 11, 64)	18496
max_pooling2d_1	(MaxPooling2D) (None, 5, 5, 64)	0
conv2d_2 (Conv2D)	(None, 3, 3, 64)	36928
flatten (Flatten)	(None, 576)	0
dense (Dense)	(None, 64)	36928
dense_1 (Dense)	(None, 10)	650

```
Total params: 93,322
Trainable params: 93,322
Non-trainable params: 0
```

Based on this summary, 93,000 parameters will be trained during the process. The shape and the number of parameters in each layer can also be found in the summary.

9.2.2 *Distributed model training*

Now that we've defined our models and can train them locally in a single machine, the next step is to insert the distributed training logic in the code so that we can run model training with multiple workers using the collective communication pattern that we introduced in the book. We'll use the tf.distribute module that contains Multi-WorkerMirroredStrategy. It's a distribution strategy for synchronous training on multiple workers. It creates copies of all variables in the model's layers on each device across all workers. This strategy uses a distributed collective implementation (e.g., all-reduce), so multiple workers can work together to speed up training. If you don't have appropriate GPUs, you can replace communication_options with other implementations. Since we want to ensure the distributed training can run on different machines that might not have GPUs, we'll replace it with `CollectiveCommunication.AUTO` so that it will pick any available hardware automatically.

Once we define our distributed training strategy, we'll initiate our distributed input data pipeline (as mentioned previously in section 9.1.2) and the model inside the strategy scope. Note that defining the model inside the strategy scope is required since TensorFlow knows how to copy the variables in the model's layers to each worker adequately based on the strategy. Here we define different model types (basic CNN, CNN with dropout, and CNN with batch normalization) based on the command-line arguments we pass to this Python script.

We'll get to the rest of the flags soon. Once the data pipeline and the model are defined inside the scope, we can use `fit()` to train the model outside the distribution strategy scope.

Listing 9.7   Distributed model training logic

```
strategy = tf.distribute.MultiWorkerMirroredStrategy(
    communication_options=tf.distribute.experimental.CommunicationOptions(
    implementation=tf.distribute.experimental.CollectiveCommunication.AUTO))

BATCH_SIZE_PER_REPLICA = 64
BATCH_SIZE = BATCH_SIZE_PER_REPLICA * strategy.num_replicas_in_sync

with strategy.scope():
    ds_train = make_datasets_unbatched().batch(BATCH_SIZE).repeat()
    options = tf.data.Options()
    options.experimental_distribute.auto_shard_policy = \
            tf.data.experimental.AutoShardPolicy.DATA
    ds_train = ds_train.with_options(options)
    if args.model_type == "cnn":
      multi_worker_model = build_and_compile_cnn_model()
    elif args.model_type == "dropout":
      multi_worker_model = build_and_compile_cnn_model_with_dropout()
    elif args.model_type == "batch_norm":
      multi_worker_model = build_and_compile_cnn_model_with_batch_norm()
    else:
      raise Exception("Unsupported model type: %s" % args.model_type)

multi_worker_model.fit(ds_train,
                       epochs=1,
                       steps_per_epoch=70)
```

Once the model training is finished via `fit()` function, we want to save the model. One common mistake that users can easily make is saving models on all the workers, which may not save the completed model correctly and wastes computational resources and storage. The correct way to fix this problem is to save only the model on the chief worker. We can inspect the environment variable `TF_CONFIG`, which contains the cluster information, such as the task type and index, to see whether the worker is chief. Also, we want to save the model to a unique path across workers to avoid unexpected errors.

Listing 9.8 Saving a model with a chief worker

```
def is_chief():
  return TASK_INDEX == 0

tf_config = json.loads(os.environ.get('TF_CONFIG') or '{}')
TASK_INDEX = tf_config['task']['index']

if is_chief():
  model_path = args.saved_model_dir
else:
  model_path = args.saved_model_dir + '/worker_tmp_' + str(TASK_INDEX)

multi_worker_model.save(model_path)
```

So far, we've seen two command-line flags already—namely, `saved_model_dir` and `model_type`. Listing 9.9 provides the rest of the `main` function that will parse those command-line arguments. In addition to those two arguments, there's another `checkpoint_dir` argument that we will use to save our model to the TensorFlow SavedModel format that can be easily consumed for our model serving component. We will discuss that in detail in section 9.3. We also disabled the progress bar for the TensorFlow Datasets module to reduce the logs we will see.

Listing 9.9 Entry point main function

```
if __name__ == '__main__':
  tfds.disable_progress_bar()

  parser = argparse.ArgumentParser()
  parser.add_argument('--saved_model_dir',
                      type=str,
                      required=True,
                      help='Tensorflow export directory.')

  parser.add_argument('--checkpoint_dir',
                      type=str,
                      required=True,
                      help='Tensorflow checkpoint directory.')

  parser.add_argument('--model_type',
                      type=str,
                      required=True,
                      help='Type of model to train.')

  parsed_args = parser.parse_args()
  main(parsed_args)
```

We've just finished writing our Python script that contains the distributed model training logic. Let's containerize it and build the image used to run distributed training in our local Kubernetes cluster. In our Dockerfile, we'll use the Python 3.9 base image, install TensorFlow and TensorFlow Datasets modules via pip, and copy our multi-worker distributed training Python script.

Listing 9.10 Containerization

```
FROM python:3.9
RUN pip install tensorflow==2.11.0 tensorflow_datasets==4.7.0
COPY multi-worker-distributed-training.py /
```

We then build the image from the Dockerfile we just defined. We also need to import the image to k3d cluster since our cluster does not have access to our local image registry. We then set the current namespace to be "kubeflow". Please read chapter 8 and follow the instructions to install the required components we need for this project.

Listing 9.11 Building and importing the docker image

```
> docker build -f Dockerfile -t kubeflow/multi-worker-strategy:v0.1 .
> k3d image import kubeflow/multi-worker-strategy:v0.1 --cluster distml
> kubectl config set-context --current --namespace=kubeflow
```

Once the worker Pods are completed, all files in the Pod will be recycled. Since we are running distributed model training across multiple workers in Kubernetes Pods, all the model checkpoints will be lost, and we don't have a trained model for model serving. To address this problem, we'll use PersistentVolume (PV) and PersistentVolumeClaim (PVC).

PV is a storage in the cluster that has been provisioned by an administrator or dynamically provisioned. It is a resource in the cluster, just like a node is a cluster resource. PVs are volume plugins like Volumes, but have a life cycle independent of any individual Pod that uses the PV. In other words, PVs will persist and live even after the Pods are completed or deleted.

A PVC is a request for storage by a user. It is similar to a Pod. Pods consume node resources, and PVCs consume PV resources. Pods can request specific levels of resources (CPU and memory). Claims can request specific size and access modes (e.g., they can be mounted `ReadWriteOnce`, `ReadOnlyMany`, or `ReadWriteMany`).

Let's create a PVC to submit a request for storage that will be used in our worker Pods to store the trained model. Here we only submit a request for 1 Gi storage with `ReadWriteOnce` access mode.

Listing 9.12 Persistent volume claim

```
kind: PersistentVolumeClaim
apiVersion: v1
metadata:
  name: strategy-volume
spec:
  accessModes: [ "ReadWriteOnce" ]
  resources:
    requests:
      storage: 1Gi
```

Next, we'll create the PVC.

Listing 9.13   Creating the PVC

```
> kubectl create -f multi-worker-pvc.yaml
```

Next, let's define the `TFJob` spec we introduced in chapter 7 with the image we just built that contains the distributed training script. We pass the necessary command arguments to the container to train the basic CNN model. The `volumes` field in the `Worker` spec specifies the name of the persistent volume claim that we just created, and the `volumeMounts` field in the `containers` spec specifies what folder to mount the files between the volume to the container. The model will be saved in the `/trained_model` folder inside the volume.

Listing 9.14   Distributed model training job definition

```
apiVersion: kubeflow.org/v1
kind: TFJob
metadata:
  name: multi-worker-training
spec:
  runPolicy:
    cleanPodPolicy: None
  tfReplicaSpecs:
    Worker:
      replicas: 2
      restartPolicy: Never
      template:
        spec:
          containers:
            - name: tensorflow
              image: kubeflow/multi-worker-strategy:v0.1
              imagePullPolicy: IfNotPresent
              command: ["python",
          "/multi-worker-distributed-training.py",
          "--saved_model_dir",
          "/trained_model/saved_model_versions/2/",
          "--checkpoint_dir",
          "/trained_model/checkpoint",
          "--model_type", "cnn"]
              volumeMounts:
                - mountPath: /trained_model
                  name: training
              resources:
                limits:
                  cpu: 500m
          volumes:
            - name: training
              persistentVolumeClaim:
                claimName: strategy-volume
```

Then we can submit this `TFJob` to our cluster to start our distributed model training.

Listing 9.15   Submitting `TFJob`

```
> kubectl create -f multi-worker-tfjob.yaml
```

Once the worker Pods are completed, we'll notice the following logs from the Pods that indicate we trained the model in a distributed fashion and the workers communicated with each other successfully:

```
Started server with target:
grpc://multi-worker-training-worker-0.kubeflow.svc:2222
/job:worker/replica:0/task:1 has connected to coordination service.
/job:worker/replica:0/task:0 has connected to coordination service.
Coordination agent has successfully connected.
```

9.2.3   *Model selection*

So far, we've implemented our distributed model training component. We'll eventually train three different models, as mentioned in section 9.2.1, and then pick the top model for model serving. Let's assume that we have trained those models successfully by submitting three different `TFJobs` with different model types.

Next, we write the Python code that loads the testing data and trained models and then evaluate their performance. We will load each trained model from different folders by `keras.models.load_model()` function and execute `model.evaluate()`, which returns the loss and accuracy. Once we find the model with the highest accuracy, we can copy the model to a new version in a different folder—namely, 4—which will be used by our model serving component.

Listing 9.16   Model evaluation

```
import numpy as np
import tensorflow as tf
from tensorflow import keras
import tensorflow_datasets as tfds
import shutil
import os

def scale(image, label):
    image = tf.cast(image, tf.float32)
    image /= 255
    return image, label

best_model_path = ""
best_accuracy = 0
for i in range(1, 4):
    model_path = "trained_model/saved_model_versions/" + str(i)
    model = keras.models.load_model(model_path)
```

```
  datasets, _ = tfds.load(
    name='fashion_mnist', with_info=True, as_supervised=True)
  ds = datasets['test'].map(scale).cache().shuffle(10000).batch(64)
  _, accuracy = model.evaluate(ds)
  if accuracy > best_accuracy:
    best_accuracy = accuracy
    best_model_path = model_path

destination = "trained_model/saved_model_versions/4"
if os.path.exists(destination):
  shutil.rmtree(destination)

shutil.copytree(best_model_path, destination)
print("Best model with accuracy %f is copied to %s" % (
  best_accuracy, destination))
```

Note that the latest version, 4, in the trained_model/saved_model_versions folder will be picked up by our serving component. We will talk about that in the next section.

We then add this Python script to our Dockerfile, rebuild the container image, and create a Pod that runs the model selection component. The following is the YAML file that configures the model selection Pod.

Listing 9.17   Model selection Pod definition

```
apiVersion: v1
kind: Pod
metadata:
  name: model-selection
spec:
  containers:
  - name: predict
    image: kubeflow/multi-worker-strategy:v0.1
    command: ["python", "/model-selection.py"]
    volumeMounts:
    - name: model
      mountPath: /trained_model
  volumes:
  - name: model
    persistentVolumeClaim:
      claimName: strategy-volume
```

When inspecting the logs, we see the third model has the highest accuracy, so we will copy it to a new version to be used for the model serving component:

```
157/157 [======] - 1s 5ms/step - loss: 0.7520 - accuracy: 0.7155
157/157 [======] - 1s 5ms/step - loss: 0.7568 - accuracy: 0.7267
157/157 [======] - 1s 5ms/step - loss: 0.7683 - accuracy: 0.7282
```

9.3   *Model serving*

Now that we have implemented our distributed model training as well as model selection among the trained models. The next component we will implement is the model serving component. The model serving component is essential to the end-user experience since the results will be shown to our users directly, and if it's not performant enough, our users will know immediately. Figure 9.5 shows the model training component in the overall architecture.

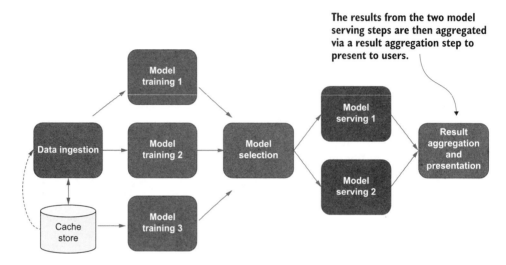

Figure 9.5   Model serving component (dark boxes) in the end-to-end machine learning system

In figure 9.5, the model serving components are shown as the two dark boxes between the model selection and result aggregation steps. Let's first implement our single-server model inference component in section 9.3.1 and then make it more scalable and performant in section 9.3.2.

9.3.1   *Single-server model inference*

The model inference Python code is very similar to the model evaluation code. The only difference is that we use the `model.predict()` method instead of `evaluate()` after we load the trained model. This is an excellent way to test whether the trained model can make predictions as expected.

Listing 9.18   Model prediction

```
import numpy as np
import tensorflow as tf
from tensorflow import keras
import tensorflow_datasets as tfds
model = keras.models.load_model("trained_model/saved_model_versions")
```

```
def scale(image, label):
  image = tf.cast(image, tf.float32)
  image /= 255
  return image, label
datasets, _ = tfds.load(
  name='fashion_mnist', with_info=True, as_supervised=True)
ds = datasets['test'].map(scale).cache().shuffle(10000).batch(64)
model.predict(ds)
```

Alternatively, you can start a TensorFlow Serving (https://github.com/tensorflow/serving) server locally like in the following listing once it's installed.

Listing 9.19   TensorFlow Serving command

```
tensorflow_model_server --model_name=flower-sample \
    --port=9000 \
    --rest_api_port=8080 \
    --model_base_path=trained_model/saved_model \
    --rest_api_timeout_in_ms=60000
```

This seems straightforward and works well if we are only experimenting locally. However, there are more performant ways to build our model serving component that will pave our path to running distributed model serving that incorporates the replicated model server pattern that we introduced in previous chapters.

Before we dive into a better solution, let's make sure our trained model can work with our prediction inputs, which will be a JSON-structured list of image bytes with the key "instances" and "image_bytes", like the following:

```
{
    "instances":[
        {
            "image_bytes":{
                "b64":"/9j/4AAQSkZJRgABAQAAAQABAAD
...
<truncated>
/hWY4+UVEhkoIYUx0psR+apm6VBRUZcUYFSuKZgUAf//Z"
            }
        }
    ]
}
```

Now is the time to modify our distributed model training code to make sure the model has the correct serving signature that's compatible with our supplied inputs. We define the preprocessing function that does the following:

1 Decodes the images from bytes
2 Resizes the image to 28×28 that's compatible with our model architecture
3 Casts the images to `tf.uint8`
4 Defines the input signature with string type and key as `image_bytes`

Once the preprocessing function is defined, we can define the serving signature via `tf.TensorSpec()` and then pass it to `tf.saved_model.save()` method to save the model that is compatible with our input format and preprocess it before TensorFlow Serving makes inference calls.

Listing 9.20 Model serving signature definitions

```python
def _preprocess(bytes_inputs):
    decoded = tf.io.decode_jpeg(bytes_inputs, channels=1)
    resized = tf.image.resize(decoded, size=(28, 28))
    return tf.cast(resized, dtype=tf.uint8)


def _get_serve_image_fn(model):
@tf.function(
  input_signature=[tf.TensorSpec([None],
    dtype=tf.string, name='image_bytes')])
    def serve_image_fn(bytes_inputs):
        decoded_images = tf.map_fn(_preprocess, bytes_inputs, dtype=tf.uint8)
        return model(decoded_images)
    return serve_image_fn
signatures = {
    "serving_default":
     _get_serve_image_fn(multi_worker_model).get_concrete_function(
        tf.TensorSpec(shape=[None], dtype=tf.string, name='image_bytes')
    )
    }

tf.saved_model.save(multi_worker_model, model_path, signatures=signatures)
```

Once the distributed model training script is modified, we can rebuild our container image and retrain our model from scratch, following the instructions in section 9.2.2.

Next, we will use KServe, as we mentioned in the technologies overview, to create an inference service. Listing 9.21 provides the YAML to define the KServe inference service. We need to specify the model format so that KServe knows what to use for serving the model (e.g., TensorFlow Serving). In addition, we need to supply the URI to the trained model. In this case, we can specify the PVC name and the path to the trained model, following the format `pvc://<pvc-name>/<model-path>`.

Listing 9.21 Inference service definition

```yaml
apiVersion: serving.kserve.io/v1beta1
kind: InferenceService
metadata:
  name: flower-sample
spec:
  predictor:
    model:
      modelFormat:
        name: tensorflow
      storageUri: "pvc://strategy-volume/saved_model_versions"
```

Let's install KServe and create our inference service!

Listing 9.22 Installing KServe and creating the inference service

```
> curl -s "https://raw.githubusercontent.com/
  kserve/kserve/v0.10.0-rc1/hack/quick_install.sh" | bash
> kubectl create -f inference-service.yaml
```

We can check its status to make sure it's ready for serving.

Listing 9.23 Getting the details of the inference service

```
> kubectl get isvc
NAME            URL                           READY      AGE
flower-sample   <truncated...example.com>     True       25s
```

Once the service is created, we port-forward it to local so that we can send requests to it locally.

Listing 9.24 Port-forwarding the inference service

```
> INGRESS_GATEWAY_SERVICE=$(kubectl get svc --namespace \
istio-system --selector="app=istio-ingressgateway" --output \
    jsonpath='{.items[0].metadata.name}')
> kubectl port-forward --namespace istio-system svc/${INGRESS_GATEWAY_SERVICE}
    8080:80
```

You should be able to see the following if the port-forwarding is successful:

```
Forwarding from 127.0.0.1:8080 -> 8080
Forwarding from [::1]:8080 -> 8080
```

Let's open another terminal and execute the following Python script to send a sample inference request to our model serving service and print out the response text.

Listing 9.25 Using Python to send an inference request

```
import requests
import json
input_path = "inference-input.json"

with open(input_path) as json_file:
    data = json.load(json_file)

r = requests.post(
 url="http://localhost:8080/v1/models/flower-sample:predict",
 data=json.dumps(data),
 headers={'Host': 'flower-sample.kubeflow.example.com'})
print(r.text)
```

The response from our KServe model serving service, which includes the predicted probabilities for each class in the Fashion-MNIST dataset, is as follows:

```
{
  "predictions": [[0.0, 0.0, 1.22209595e-11,
    0.0, 1.0, 0.0, 7.07406329e-32, 0.0, 0.0, 0.0]]
}
```

Alternatively, we can use curl to send requests.

Listing 9.26   Using curl to send an inference request

```
# Start another terminal
export INGRESS_HOST=localhost
export INGRESS_PORT=8080
MODEL_NAME=flower-sample
INPUT_PATH=@./inference-input.json
SERVICE_HOSTNAME=$(kubectl get inferenceservice \
${MODEL_NAME} -o jsonpath='{.status.url}' | \
cut -d "/" -f 3)
curl -v -H "Host: ${SERVICE_HOSTNAME}" "http://${INGRESS_HOST}:${INGRESS_PORT}/v1/
models/$MODEL_NAME:predict" -d $INPUT_PATH
```

The output probabilities should be the same as the ones we just saw:

```
*    Trying ::1:8080...
* Connected to localhost (::1) port 8080 (#0)
> POST /v1/models/flower-sample:predict HTTP/1.1
> Host: flower-sample.kubeflow.example.com
> User-Agent: curl/7.77.0
> Accept: */*
> Content-Length: 16178
> Content-Type: application/x-www-form-urlencoded
>
* Mark bundle as not supporting multiuse
< HTTP/1.1 200 OK
< content-length: 102
< content-type: application/json
< date: Thu, 05 Jan 2023 21:11:36 GMT
< x-envoy-upstream-service-time: 78
< server: istio-envoy
<
{
    "predictions": [[0.0, 0.0, 1.22209595e-11, 0.0,
  1.0, 0.0, 7.07406329e-32, 0.0, 0.0, 0.0]
    ]
* Connection #0 to host localhost left intact
}
```

As mentioned previously, even though we specified the entire directory that contains the trained model in the KServe `InferenceService` spec, the model serving service that utilizes TensorFlow Serving will pick the latest version 4 from that particular folder, which is our best model we selected in section 9.2.3. We can observe that from the logs of the serving Pod.

Listing 9.27 Inspecting the model server logs

```
> kubectl logs flower-sample-predictor-default
-00001-deployment-f67767f6c2fntx  -c kserve-container
```

Here's the logs:

```
Building single TensorFlow model file config:
model_name: flower-sample model_base_path: /mnt/models
Adding/updating models.
...
<truncated>
Successfully loaded servable version
  {name: flower-sample version: 4}
```

9.3.2 Replicated model servers

In the previous section, we successfully deployed our model serving service in our local Kubernetes cluster. This might be sufficient for running local serving experiments, but it's far from ideal if it's deployed to production systems that serve real-world model serving traffic. The current model serving service is a single Kubernetes Pod, where the allocated computational resources are limited and requested in advance. When the number of model serving requests increases, the single-instance model server can no longer support the workloads and may run out of computational resources.

To address the problem, we need to have multiple instances of model servers to handle a larger amount of dynamic model serving requests. Fortunately, KServe can autoscale based on the average number of in-flight requests per Pod, which uses the Knative Serving autoscaler.

The following listing provides the inference service spec with autoscaling enabled. The scaleTarget field specifies the integer target value of the metric type the autoscaler watches for. In addition, the scaleMetric field defines the scaling metric type watched by autoscaler. The possible metrics are concurrency, RPS, CPU, and memory. Here we only allow one concurrent request to be processed by each inference service instance. In other words, when there are more requests, we will start a new inference service Pod to handle each additional request.

Listing 9.28 Replicated model inference services

```
apiVersion: serving.kserve.io/v1beta1
kind: InferenceService
metadata:
  name: flower-sample
```

```
spec:
  predictor:
    scaleTarget: 1
    scaleMetric: concurrency
    model:
      modelFormat:
        name: tensorflow
        storageUri: "pvc://strategy-volume/saved_model_versions"
```

Let's assume there's no request, and we should only see one inference service Pod that's up and running. Next, let's send traffic in 30-second spurts, maintaining five in-flight requests. We use the same service hostname and ingress address, as well as the same inference input and trained model. Note that we are using the tool hey, a tiny program that sends some load to a web application. Follow the instructions at https:// github.com/rakyll/hey to install it before executing the following command.

> ## Listing 9.29   Sending traffic to test the load

```
> hey -z 30s -c 5 -m POST \
 -host ${SERVICE_HOSTNAME} \
 -D inference-input.json "http://${INGRESS_HOST}:${INGRESS_PORT}
/v1/models/$MODEL_NAME:predict"
```

The following is the expected output from the command, which includes a summary of how the inference service handled the requests. For example, the service has processed 230,160 bytes of inference inputs and 95.7483 requests per second. You can also find a nice response-time histogram and a latency distribution that might be useful:

```
Summary:
  Total:        30.0475 secs
  Slowest:      0.2797 secs
  Fastest:      0.0043 secs
  Average:      0.0522 secs
  Requests/sec: 95.7483
  Total data:   230160 bytes
  Size/request: 80 bytes
Response time histogram:
  0.004 [1]     |
  0.032 [1437]  |■■■■■■■■■■■■■■■■■■■■■■■■■■■■■■■■■■■■■■■■■■■■■■
  0.059 [3]     |
  0.087 [823]   |■■■■■■■■■■■■■■■■■■■■■■■■■■■
  0.114 [527]   |■■■■■■■■■■■■■■■■
  0.142 [22]    |■
  0.170 [5]     |
  0.197 [51]    |■
  0.225 [7]     |
  0.252 [0]     |
  0.280 [1]     |

Latency distribution:
  10% in 0.0089 secs
  25% in 0.0123 secs
```

```
  50% in 0.0337 secs
  75% in 0.0848 secs
  90% in 0.0966 secs
  95% in 0.1053 secs
  99% in 0.1835 secs
Details (average, fastest, slowest):
  DNS+dialup:     0.0000 secs, 0.0043 secs, 0.2797 secs
  DNS-lookup:     0.0000 secs, 0.0000 secs, 0.0009 secs
  req write:      0.0000 secs, 0.0000 secs, 0.0002 secs
  resp wait:      0.0521 secs, 0.0042 secs, 0.2796 secs
  resp read:      0.0000 secs, 0.0000 secs, 0.0005 secs
Status code distribution:
  [200]   2877 responses
```

As expected, we see five running inference service Pods processing the requests concurrently, where each Pod handles only one request.

Listing 9.30 Getting the list of model server Pods

```
> kubectl get pods
NAME                            READY   STATUS    RESTARTS   AGE
flower-<truncated>-sr5wd        3/3     Running   0          12s
flower--<truncated>-swnk5       3/3     Running   0          22s
flower--<truncated>-t2njf       3/3     Running   0          22s
flower--<truncated>-vdlp9       3/3     Running   0          22s
flower--<truncated>-vm58d       3/3     Running   0          42s
```

Once the hey command is completed, we will only see one running Pod.

Listing 9.31 Getting the list of model server Pods again

```
> kubectl get pods
NAME                            READY   STATUS    RESTARTS   AGE
flower-<truncated>-sr5wd        3/3     Running   0          62s
```

9.4 *The end-to-end workflow*

We have just implemented all the components in the previous sections. Now it's time to put things together! In this section, we'll define an end-to-end workflow using Argo Workflows that includes the components we just implemented. Please go back to previous sections if you are still unfamiliar with all the components and refresh your knowledge of basic Argo Workflows from chapter 8.

Here's a recap of what the end-to-end workflow we will implement looks like. Figure 9.6 is a diagram of the end-to-end workflow that we are building. The diagram includes two model serving steps for illustration purposes, but we will only implement one step in our Argo workflow. It will autoscale to more instances based on requests traffic, as mentioned in section 9.3.2.

In the next sections, we will define the entire workflow by connecting the steps sequentially with Argo and then optimize the workflow for future executions by implementing step memoization.

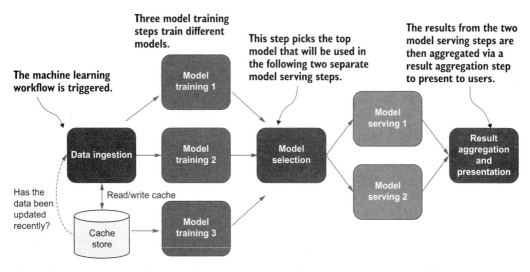

Figure 9.6 An architecture diagram of the end-to-end machine learning system we are building

9.4.1 *Sequential steps*

First, let's look at the entry point templates and the main steps involved in the workflow. The entry point template name is `tfjob-wf`, which consists of the following steps (for simplicity, each step uses a template with the same name):

1. `data-ingestion-step` contains the data ingestion step, which we will use to download and preprocess the dataset before model training.

2. `distributed-tf-training-steps` is a step group that consists of multiple substeps, where each substep represents a distributed model training step for a specific model type.

3. `model-selection-step` is a step that selects the top model from among the different models we have trained in previous steps.

4. `create-model-serving-service` creates the model serving serve via KServe.

Listing 9.32 Workflow entry point templates

```
apiVersion: argoproj.io/v1alpha1
kind: Workflow
metadata:
  generateName: tfjob-wf-
  namespace: kubeflow
spec:
  entrypoint: tfjob-wf
  podGC:
    strategy: OnPodSuccess
  volumes:
  - name: model
    persistentVolumeClaim:
      claimName: strategy-volume
```

```
  templates:
- name: tfjob-wf
    steps:
    - - name: data-ingestion-step
        template: data-ingestion-step
    - - name: distributed-tf-training-steps
        template: distributed-tf-training-steps
    - - name: model-selection-step
        template: model-selection-step
    - - name: create-model-serving-service
        template: create-model-serving-service
```

Note that we specify the `podGC` strategy to be `OnPodSuccess` since we'll be creating a lot of Pods for different steps within our local k3s cluster with limited computational resources, so deleting the Pods right after they are successful can free up computational resources for the subsequent steps. The `OnPodCompletion` strategy is also available; it deletes Pods on completion regardless of whether they failed or succeeded. We won't use that since we want to keep failed Pods to debug what went wrong.

In addition, we also specify our volumes and PVC to ensure we can persist any files that will be used in the steps. We can save the downloaded dataset into the persistent volume for model training and then persist the trained model for the subsequent model serving step.

The first step, the data ingestion step, is very straightforward. It only specifies the container image and the data ingestion Python script to execute. The Python script is a one-line code with `tfds.load(name='fashion_mnist')` to download the dataset to the container's local storage, which will be mounted to our persistent volume.

> **Listing 9.33 Data ingestion step**

```
- name: data-ingestion-step
    serviceAccountName: argo
    container:
      image: kubeflow/multi-worker-strategy:v0.1
      imagePullPolicy: IfNotPresent
      command: ["python", "/data-ingestion.py"]
```

The next step is a step group that consists of multiple substeps, where each substep represents a distributed model training step for a specific model type (e.g., basic CNN, CNN with dropout, and CNN with batch norm). The following listing provides the template that defines all the substeps. Distributed training steps for multiple models dictate that these will be executed in parallel.

> **Listing 9.34 Distributed training step groups**

```
- name: distributed-tf-training-steps
    steps:
    - - name: cnn-model
        template: cnn-model
      - name: cnn-model-with-dropout
```

```
      template: cnn-model-with-dropout
   - name: cnn-model-with-batch-norm
      template: cnn-model-with-batch-norm
```

Let's use the first substep, which runs a distributed model training for the basic CNN model, as an example. The main content of this step template is the `resource` field, which includes the following:

- The custom resource definition (CRD) or manifest to take action upon. In our case, we create a `TFJob` as part of this step.
- The conditions that indicate whether the CRD is created successfully. In our case, we ask Argo to watch the field `status.replicaStatuses.Worker.succeeded` and `status.replicaStatuses.Worker.failed`.

Inside the `container` spec in the `TFJob` definition, we specify the model type and save the trained model to a different folder so it's easy to pick and save the best model for model serving in subsequent steps. We also want to make sure to attach the persistent volumes so the trained model can be persisted.

Listing 9.35   CNN model training step

```
- name: cnn-model
   serviceAccountName: training-operator
   resource:
     action: create
     setOwnerReference: true
     successCondition: status.replicaStatuses.Worker.succeeded = 2
     failureCondition: status.replicaStatuses.Worker.failed > 0
     manifest: |
       apiVersion: kubeflow.org/v1
       kind: TFJob
       metadata:
         generateName: multi-worker-training-
       spec:
         runPolicy:
           cleanPodPolicy: None
         tfReplicaSpecs:
           Worker:
             replicas: 2
             restartPolicy: Never
             template:
               spec:
                 containers:
                   - name: tensorflow
                     image: kubeflow/multi-worker-strategy:v0.1
                     imagePullPolicy: IfNotPresent
                     command: ["python",
"/multi-worker-distributed-training.py",
"--saved_model_dir",
"/trained_model/saved_model_versions/1/",
"--checkpoint_dir",
"/trained_model/checkpoint",
"--model_type", "cnn"]
```

```
            volumeMounts:
              - mountPath: /trained_model
                name: training
            resources:
              limits:
                cpu: 500m
        volumes:
          - name: training
            persistentVolumeClaim:
              claimName: strategy-volume
```

For the rest of the substeps in `distributed-tf-training-steps`, the spec is very similar, except the saved model directory and model type arguments are different. The next step is model selection, for which we will supply the same container image but execute the model selection Python script we implemented earlier.

Listing 9.36   Model selection step Caption here

```
- name: model-selection-step
  serviceAccountName: argo
  container:
    image: kubeflow/multi-worker-strategy:v0.1
    imagePullPolicy: IfNotPresent
    command: ["python", "/model-selection.py"]
    volumeMounts:
    - name: model
      mountPath: /trained_model
```

Make sure these additional scripts are included in your Dockerfile and that you have rebuilt the image and re-imported it to your local Kubernetes cluster.

Once the model selection step is implemented, the last step in the workflow is the model serving step that starts a KServe model inference service. It's a resource template similar to the model training steps but with KServe's `InferenceService` CRD and a success condition that applies to this specific CRD.

Listing 9.37   The model serving step

```
- name: create-model-serving-service
  serviceAccountName: training-operator
  successCondition: status.modelStatus.states.transitionStatus = UpToDate
  resource:
    action: create
    setOwnerReference: true
    manifest: |
      apiVersion: serving.kserve.io/v1beta1
      kind: InferenceService
      metadata:
        name: flower-sample
      spec:
        predictor:
          model:
```

```
modelFormat:
  name: tensorflow
image: "emacski/tensorflow-serving:2.6.0"
storageUri: "pvc://strategy-volume/saved_model_versions"
```

Let's submit this workflow now!

Listing 9.38   Submitting the end-to-end workflow

```
> kubectl create -f workflow.yaml
```

Once the data ingestion step is completed, the associated Pod will be deleted. When we list the Pods again while it's executing the distributed model training steps, we'll see the Pods with names prefixed by `tfjob-wf-f4bql-cnn-model-`, which are the Pods responsible for monitoring the status of distributed model training for different model types. In addition, each model training for each model type contains two workers with the name matching the pattern `multi-worker-training-*-worker-*`.

Listing 9.39   Getting the list of Pods

```
> kubectl get pods
NAME                              READY   STATUS    RESTARTS   AGE
multi-<truncated>-worker-0        1/1     Running   0          50s
multi-<truncated -worker-1        1/1     Running   0          49s
multi-<truncated -worker-0        1/1     Running   0          47s
multi-<truncated -worker-1        1/1     Running   0          47s
multi-<truncated -worker-0        1/1     Running   0          54s
multi-<truncated -worker-1        1/1     Running   0          53s
<truncated>-cnn-model             1/1     Running   0          56s
<truncated>-batch-norm            1/1     Running   0          56s
<truncated>-dropout               1/1     Running   0          56s
```

Once the remaining steps are completed, and the model serving has started successfully, the workflow should have a `Succeeded` status. We've just finished the execution of the end-to-end workflow.

9.4.2   *Step memoization*

To speed up future executions of workflows, we can utilize cache and skip certain steps that have recently run. In our case, the data ingestion step can be skipped since we don't have to download the same dataset again and again.

Let's first take a look at the logs from our data ingestion step:

```
Downloading and preparing dataset 29.45 MiB
(download: 29.45 MiB, generated: 36.42 MiB,
total: 65.87 MiB) to
/root/tensorflow_datasets/fashion_mnist/3.0.1...
Dataset fashion_mnist downloaded and prepared to
     /root/tensorflow_datasets/fashion_mnist/3.0.1.
Subsequent calls will reuse this data.
```

The dataset has been downloaded to a path in the container. If the path is mounted to our persistent volume, it will be available for any future workflow runs. Let's use the step memoization feature provided by Argo Workflows to optimize our workflow.

Inside the step template, we supply the `memoize` field with the cache key and age of the cache. When a step is completed, a cache will be saved. When this step runs again in a new workflow, it will check whether the cache is created within the past hour. If so, this step will be skipped, and the workflow will proceed to execute subsequent steps. For our application, our dataset does not change so, theoretically, the cache should always be used, and we specify 1 hour here for demonstration purposes only. In real-world applications, you may want to adjust that according to how frequently the data is updated.

Listing 9.40 Memoization for the data ingestion step

```
- name: data-ingestion-step
    serviceAccountName: argo
    memoize:
      key: "step-cache"
      maxAge: "1h"
      cache:
        configMap:
          name: my-config
          key: step-cache
    container:
      image: kubeflow/multi-worker-strategy:v0.1
      imagePullPolicy: IfNotPresent
      command: ["python", "/data-ingestion.py"]
```

Let's run the workflow for the first time and pay attention to the `Memoization Status` field in the workflow's node status. The cache is not hit because this is the first time the step is run.

Listing 9.41 Checking the node statuses of the workflow

```
> kubectl get wf tfjob-wf-kjj2q -o yaml
The following is the section for node statuses:
Status:
  Nodes:
    tfjob-wf-crfhx-2213815408:
      Boundary ID:   tfjob-wf-crfhx
      Children:
        tfjob-wf-crfhx-579056679
      Display Name:   data-ingestion-step
      Finished At:    2023-01-04T20:57:44Z
      Host Node Name: distml-control-plane
      Id:             tfjob-wf-crfhx-2213815408
      Memoization Status:
        Cache Name:  my-config
        Hit:         false
        Key:         step-cache
      Name:          tfjob-wf-crfhx[0].data-ingestion-step
```

If we run the same workflow again within one hour, we will notice that the step is skipped (indicated by `hit: true` in the `Memoization Status` field):

```
Status:
  Nodes:
    tfjob-wf-kjj2q-1381200071:
      Boundary ID:  tfjob-wf-kjj2q
      Children:
        tfjob-wf-kjj2q-2031651288
      Display Name:  data-ingestion-step
      Finished At:   2023-01-04T20:58:31Z
      Id:            tfjob-wf-kjj2q-1381200071
      Memoization Status:
        Cache Name:  my-config
        Hit:         true
        Key:         step-cache
      Name:          tfjob-wf-kjj2q[0].data-ingestion-step
      Outputs:
        Exit Code:   0
      Phase:         Succeeded
      Progress:      1/1
      Started At:    2023-01-04T20:58:31Z
      Template Name:  data-ingestion-step
      Template Scope: local/tfjob-wf-kjj2q
      Type:          Pod
```

In addition, note that the `Finished At` and `Started At` timestamps are the same. That is, this step is completed instantly without having to re-execute from scratch.

All the cache in Argo Workflows is saved in a Kubernetes `ConfigMap` object. The cache contains the node ID, step outputs, and cache creation timestamp, as well as the timestamp when this cache is last hit.

Listing 9.42 Checking the details of the configmap

```
> kubectl get configmap -o yaml my-config
apiVersion: v1
data:
  step-cache: '{"nodeID":"tfjob-wf-dmtn4-
3886957114","outputs":{"exitCode":"0"},
"creationTimestamp":"2023-01-04T20:44:55Z",
"lastHitTimestamp":"2023-01-04T20:57:44Z"}'
kind: ConfigMap
metadata:
  creationTimestamp: "2023-01-04T20:44:55Z"
  labels:
    workflows.argoproj.io/configmap-type: Cache
  name: my-config
  namespace: kubeflow
  resourceVersion: "806155"
  uid: 0810a68b-44f8-469f-b02c-7f62504145ba
```

Summary

- The data ingestion component implements a distributed input pipeline for the Fashion-MNIST dataset with TensorFlow that makes it easy to integrate with distributed model training.

- Machine learning models and distributed model training logic can be defined in TensorFlow and then executed in a distributed fashion in the Kubernetes cluster with the help of Kubeflow.

- Both the single-instance model server and the replicated model servers can be implemented via KServe. The autoscaling functionality of KServe can automatically create additional model serving Pods to handle the increasing number of model serving requests.

- We implemented our end-to-end workflow that includes all the components of our system in Argo Workflows and used step memoization to avoid time-consuming and redundant data ingestion step.

index

RELATED MANNING TITLES

Deep Learning with Python, Second Edition
by François Chollet

ISBN 9781617296864
504 pages, $59.99
October 2021

API Design Patterns
by JJ Geewax
Foreword by Jon Skeet

ISBN 9781617295850
480 pages, $59.99
June 2021

Microservices Patterns
by Chris Richardson

ISBN 9781617294549
520 pages, $49.99
October 2018

Designing Deep Learning Systems
by Chi Wang and Donald Szeto
Foreword by Silvio Savarese and Caiming Xiong

ISBN 9781633439863
360 pages, $59.99
June 2023

For ordering information, go to www.manning.com